# THESES and DISSERTATIONS

second edition

# THESES and DISSERTATIONS

second edition

## A Guide to PLANNING, RESEARCH, AND WRITING

R. Murray Thomas • Dale L. Brubaker

*For information:*

Corwin Press
A Sage Publications Company
2455 Teller Road
Thousand Oaks, California 91320
www.corwinpress.com

Sage Publications Ltd.
1 Oliver's Yard
55 City Road
London EC1Y 1SP
United Kingdom

Sage Publications India Pvt. Ltd.
B 1/I 1 Mohan Cooperative
Industrial Area
Mathura Road, New Delhi 110 044
India

Sage Publications Asia-Pacific Pte. Ltd.
33 Pekin Street #02–01
Far East Square
Singapore 048763

Printed in the United States of America.

*Library of Congress Cataloging-in-Publication Data*

Thomas, R. Murray (Robert Murray), 1921-
Theses and dissertations: a guide to planning, research, and writing/R. Murray Thomas, Dale L. Brubaker. —2nd ed.
p. cm.
Includes bibliographical references and index.
ISBN 978-1-4129-5115-9 (cloth)
ISBN 978-1-4129-5116-6 (pbk.)
1. Dissertations, Academic—Handbooks, manuals, etc. 2. Report writing—Handbooks, manuals, etc. I. Brubaker, Dale L. II. Title.

LB2369.T458 2008
808′.02—dc22 2007008778

This book is printed on acid-free paper.

12 13 14 15 16 10 9 8 7 6 5 4 3 2

*Acquisitions Editors:* Rachel Livsey and Debra Stollenwerk
*Editorial Assistants:* Phyllis Cappello and Jordan Barbakow
*Production Editor:* Jenn Reese
*Typesetter:* C&M Digitals (P) Ltd.
*Proofreader:* Andrea Martin
*Cover Designer:* Scott Van Atta

# CONTENTS

# PREFACE

This book is designed for graduate students who are preparing master's degree theses or doctoral dissertations. As the table of contents indicates, the book is organized according to stages of the research-and-writing process. Although those stages are applicable in all academic disciplines, the book's examples of topics and data-gathering methods are more directly associated with the social and behavioral sciences than they are with the physical sciences and the arts. Thus, students in the social and behavioral sciences—and in such allied fields as education, social work, and business—are likely the ones for whom this volume will be most useful. The writing style throughout is intentionally conversational, as if we were talking directly with students.

We expect that readers may wonder from what sorts of experiences the authors of this book have derived the suggestions they offer about how to create respectable theses and dissertations. Here is the answer:

R. Murray Thomas, during a 40-year career of directing graduate students' work, served as an advisor and committee member for scores of theses and dissertations in three universities in the United States (San Francisco State, the State University of New York at Brockport, and the University of California at Santa Barbara) as well as at Pajajaran University in Bandung, Indonesia. He also has been an external examiner of doctoral dissertations for five universities in Australia, four in India, two in Malaysia, one in Hong Kong, and one in Fiji.

Dale L. Brubaker, in a 34-year career of guiding graduate students, has functioned as an advisor and committee member for over 50 theses and dissertations at the University of California (Santa Barbara), the University of Wisconsin (Milwaukee), and the University of North Carolina (Greensboro).

Readers acquainted with the first edition of *Theses and Dissertations* may be interested in learning how this revised edition differs from the first version. The following are the most significant changes:

- References and resources have been updated.
- A section on searching the World Wide Web and another on plagiarism have been added to Chapter 3.
- The introductory section of Chapter 11 is new.
- The discussion of narrative summaries in Chapter 12 has been expanded, and proposed uses of maps from the Internet have been added.
- Chapter 15 includes an extended description of Internet publishing options.

Finally, we wish to express our appreciation to Rachel Livsey, Phyllis Cappello, and Jennifer Reese at Corwin Press for their efficient and good-natured guidance in bringing this second edition of *Theses and Dissertations* to the public.

## ACKNOWLEDGMENTS

Corwin Press gratefully acknowledges the contributions of the following individuals:

Betty J. Alford
Department Chair and Doctoral Program Coordinator
Department of Secondary Education and Educational Leadership
Stephen F. Austin State University
Nacogdoches, TX

Karen Hayes
Associate Professor
Department of Educational Administration & Supervision
University of Omaha
Omaha, NE

Susan Doran Quandt
Director
Continuing Education Advising
Academic Achievement Center
Westfield State College
Westfield, MA

Mark H. Rossman
Professor Emeritus
Capella University
Minneapolis, MN

Kim Shahabudin
University Study Advisor
Study Support & Learning Development
University of Reading
Reading, United Kingdom

# ABOUT THE AUTHORS

**R. Murray Thomas** is Professor Emeritus at the University of California, Santa Barbara. He holds a PhD degree in educational psychology from Stanford University. His professional publications exceed 380, including 52 books for which he served as author, coauthor, or editor.

**Dale L. Brubaker** is Professor Emeritus of Educational Leadership and Cultural Studies at the University of North Carolina in Greensboro. He also served on the faculties of the University of California, Santa Barbara, and the University of Wisconsin, Milwaukee. He received his PhD from Michigan State University. He is the author of numerous books on education and educational leadership, the most recent of which are *Creative Curriculum Leadership: Inspiring and Empowering Your School Community* (Corwin Press, 1994, 2004) and *The Charismatic Leader: The Presentation of Self and the Creation of Educational Settings* (Corwin Press, 2006).

*To the grandchildren—*
*Courtney, Devon, and Kaitlin*
*Ellie, Mitch, Amy, Matthew, and Kaylee*

ONE

# THE NATURE OF THESES AND DISSERTATIONS

*"It's never been clear to me why I'm expected to do a thesis in order to earn my degree."*

The threefold purpose of this chapter is to set the foundation for subsequent chapters by identifying functions that theses and dissertations can serve, by considering relationships among academic disciplines, and by describing the structure of the rest of the book.

(To avoid the tedium occasioned by our endlessly repeating the phrase *thesis and dissertation* throughout the book, we adopt the following alternatives as equivalents of that phrase—*project, study, enterprise, investigation, research,* and *work.*)

## FUNCTIONS OF THESES AND DISSERTATIONS

Traditionally in academia, the two main purposes of master's degree and doctoral projects are (a) to provide graduate students guided practice in conducting and presenting research and (b) to make a contribution to the world's fund of knowledge or to improve the conduct of some activity.

The *practice* aspect goes well beyond the demands of a typical term paper or individual-study assignment, since the aim is to equip students to do research and writing of respectable, publishable quality in the future.

The contribution-to-knowledge aspect is intended to make the student's study more than just a learning exercise by using this opportunity to produce valued information or to introduce a point of view not available before. This aspect is what usually distinguishes a master's thesis from a doctoral dissertation, in that the contribution of the dissertation is expected to be of greater magnitude than that of the thesis. Several things may add to the import of a contribution—the difficulty of the problem that the study addresses, the number of people to be affected by a solution, the amount of controversy the problem has engendered in the past, the extent to which the study offers an innovative point of view, and more.

At the outset of your project, you can profit from recognizing the type of knowledge that your work might provide. Four familiar types are substantive, theoretical, methodological, and practical.

*Substantive* refers to new *facts, information,* or *data.* Here are titles of studies offering substantive contributions.

*Sea Shell Exchange Systems in the Foi and Taude Cultures of Papua New Guinea*
*Parents' Reactions to Preschoolers' "Toilet Talk"*
*The Role of the School Principal as Viewed by North Carolina State Legislators*
*Power Struggles in a City Council: Strategies, Tactics, and Outcomes*
*Social Stratification in an Urban Medical School*

*Theoretical* refers to ways of explaining phenomena. Theoretical contributions typically consist of new ways to view and interpret familiar events. A theory usually identifies (a) which facts or variables are important for understanding the issue at hand and (b) how those variables interact to produce some outcome of interest. (Chapter 4 includes a description of roles theories can play in research projects, and Chapter 5 describes ways of creating or adapting theories as components of theses and dissertations.) The following are titles of studies intended to advance the understanding of theories in representative academic fields.

*Contrasting Conceptions of Dream Interpretation*
*An Inquiry Into the Problematics and Possibilities of a Pedagogy of Compassion*

*Folk Theories of the Learning Process in Four Isolated Cultures*
*The Suitability of Functional Theory for Analyzing Politics in a Frontier Town*
*Testing Gilligan's Feminist Model of Morality*

The term *methodological* refers to ways of collecting, classifying, and interpreting knowledge, as implied by these titles:

*Narrative History and the Objectivity Question*
*A Taxonomy of Social Services*
*Alternative Field-Note Techniques*
*A Validation Study of the Cross-Cultural Self-Perception Scale*
*Modes of Hermeneutic Analysis*
*Interviewing Teacher-Education Candidates—Two Alternatives*

The word *practical* in the present context refers to studies whose purpose is to improve the conduct of some activity. The author's aim is to help people do a job more efficiently. The job can be of various sorts—teaching children, furnishing social services to the needy, directing a political campaign, guiding individuals' vocational choices, planning a company's financial future, establishing a health-enhancement routine, searching the World Wide Web, and thousands more.

In summary, then, your investigation is expected to furnish you guided practice in conducting serious research and in presenting the results in a manner that offers at least a modest contribution to knowledge or to the practical conduct of some activity.

## ACADEMIC DISCIPLINES

It is useful to recognize that the traditional categories of academic disciplines were not defined by some divine power but have been created by academics themselves—past and present. It is also useful to note that the borders of the disciplines are indistinct and permeable. The domain of anthropology merges into the domains of psychology, sociology, economics, and literature. Political science spills into the arts, astronomy, paleontology, and linguistics. Such spillages are often reflected in hybrid disciplines—social psychology, sociobiology, biochemistry, astrophysics, and the like.

However, it's also true that specialists in each discipline have identified certain core concerns, viewpoints, and investigative methods they regard as unique to their field. And the resulting ways they define their field help explain the perspective they bring to their work.

> **Anthropology** is the scholarly discipline that focuses on the study of human beings, especially the study of their physical characteristics, cultural characteristics, evolutionary history, racial classification, geographic distribution, and group relationships. Thus, anthropology involves the naturalistic description and interpretation of the diverse peoples of the world.
>
> **Economics** is the science that seeks to analyze and describe the production, distribution, and consumption of wealth.
>
> **Education**, as a field of study and practice, is concerned mainly with methods of teaching and learning in schools or in school-like environments as opposed to such informal means of socialization as parents' childrearing practices. The discipline also involves the aims, organization, and management of educational institutions.
>
> **Political science** addresses the functions of governments (legislation, administration of the law), voters' behavior, political parties, and the influence of political organizations.
>
> **Psychology** is the science of the mental processes and behavior of individuals and groups, both human and animal. The word *psychology* literally means "study of the mind," and the issue of the relationship between mind and body—or, more precisely, mind and brain—is an intimate concern of this science.
>
> **Sociology** is the human behavioral science that investigates the nature, causes, and effects of social relations among individuals and groups, including social customs, structures, functions, and institutions. (Adapted and condensed from *Encyclopaedia Britannica,* 2006)

Despite the usefulness of academicians' efforts to stake out exclusive territories, the traditional disciplines continue to be much intermingled.

Now why is this observation about academic-discipline domains important for doing theses and dissertations? We think it's significant for two reasons. First, the guidelines for conducting and writing research investigations in different academic departments are much the same, especially within the broad realm of the social sciences and such applied fields as education, social work, and business administration. Therefore, the contents of this book should be suited to the needs of students in a variety of departments. In the titles of research projects that we include throughout the book, we illustrate this commonality among the traditional disciplines.

Second, you may find yourself wanting to adopt methods and theories from more than one traditional discipline, and we believe that doing so is quite proper. We are convinced that the categories of knowledge from which you draw your assumptions, methods, instruments, and theories should be determined by the problem that your work is intended to solve, so you should not be restricted to a narrow interpretation of the main academic discipline in which you are earning a degree.

## THE BOOK'S STRUCTURE

As the table of contents shows, this book is organized according to five major stages in the research and writing process.

**Stage I: Preparing the Way.** The aim of the first stage is to orient you to the tasks ahead by: (1) Identifying resources that can help you in carrying out your project (Chapter 2: Sources of Guidance); and (2) Describing (a) how the professional literature can be of use and (b) how to survey the literature efficiently (Chapter 3: Searching the Literature).

**Stage II: Choosing and Defining Research Topics.** The second stage involves: (1) Selecting the question or problem on which your project will focus (Chapter 4: Sources and Types of Research Problems); (2) Deciding if you wish to create or adapt a theory as part of your project's contribution; and—if you do, indeed, plan to devise a theory—deciding how to go about it (Chapter 5: Building and Adapting Theories); and (3) Clearly delineating your selected problem and creating a rationale that explains what sort of contribution your research will make to the realm of knowledge within which it's located (Chapter 6: Stating the Problem and Its Rationale).

**Stage III: Collecting and Organizing Information.** Once your research question has been specified and its value explained, your next task is to select an effective way to gather the information needed for answering the question. This phase is presented as two substages—*III-A* and *III-B*. The two are typically pursued in parallel, because they are interdependent. That is, collecting data efficiently requires a plan for organizing the data and vice versa. Even though the tasks are performed simultaneously, for clarity of presentation we find it convenient to describe them separately.

**Stage III-A: Collecting Information.** The aim of the first data-collection chapter is to describe a variety of the most useful approaches to gathering information. The purpose is not to inspect in detail the steps that comprise each method. Instead, the intention is to (a) sketch principal features of a method, (b) illustrate the sorts of research questions or problems for which the method is well suited, and (c) point out the method's advantages and limitations. The approaches that are cited include historical accounts, case studies, ethnographies, experience narratives, surveys, correlation analyses, and experiments (Chapter 7: Types of Research Methods and Sources of Information).

The three-part aim of the second data-gathering chapter is to (a) describe popular data-collection techniques and instruments, (b) illustrate research problems for which each technique is particularly appropriate, and (c) note strengths and limitations of each. The techniques and instruments include content analysis, interviews, observations, tests, and questionnaires (Chapter 8: Data-Collection Techniques and Instruments).

Students often encounter problems at the data-collection stage of their project. The third chapter within Stage III-A addresses some of the more common difficulties and offers suggestions about how you might successfully cope with them (Chapter 9: Things That Go Wrong).

**Stage III-B: Organizing Information.** No matter what sort of information you gather to solve your research problem, you need to organize it in a way that enables you to draw comparisons and contrasts, to estimate causes and effects, or to identify trends. For this purpose you require a classification system, such as a chronology, typology, or taxonomy (Chapter 10: Classification Patterns) and a method of condensing the mass of data in an accurate, comprehensible form (Chapter 11: Summarizing Information Verbally, Numerically, and Graphically).

**Stage IV: Interpreting the Results.** At this stage you explain what your collection of classified, summarized information means. This is the "so what?" phase of your project. A single chapter is dedicated to matters of interpretation (Chapter 12: Modes of Interpretation).

**Stage V: Presenting the Finished Product.** In this final stage, you are obliged to describe your completed project to appropriate audiences. Your most immediate audience includes your major advisor and any other faculty members who are assigned to assess your work. Therefore, your first responsibility is to present them with a well crafted written account of your project (Chapter 13: Writing the Final Version). Then, if you are also obliged to defend your project before a committee in an oral examination session, your second responsibility is to fashion a convincing explanation of your research methods and findings (Chapter 14: Mounting a Persuasive Defense).

In addition to receiving their supervising committee's approval, students often wish to communicate their work to a more extensive audience, one that includes fellow students, scholars in the domain of the research problem, practitioners who could find the results of value, and perhaps the general public. Such is the concern of the final chapter (Chapter 15: Reaching a Wider Audience).

The foregoing stages reflect, in a general way, the structure of a typical thesis or dissertation—a structure that often consists of five chapters or parts titled (1) The Problem, (2) The Literature Review, (3) The Methodology, (4) Presentation and Analysis of the Results, and (5) Summary, Conclusions, and Recommendations.

With the above overview of *Theses and Dissertations* now in hand, we move directly to Stage I.

STAGE I

# PREPARING THE WAY

In the earliest phases of planning your research, you will find it useful to estimate the help you will need and to recognize where you can find such help. The dual purpose of Stage I is to illustrate typical kinds of aid from which you can benefit and to suggest sources of aid, including professors, fellow students, you yourself, and the professional literature in your field of interest.

Chapter 2 (Sources of Guidance) describes the most frequently used resources along with their advantages and disadvantages. Since one of those resources—the professional literature—is so important, a separate chapter (Chapter 3: Searching the Literature) is dedicated to explaining (a) multiple ways the literature can serve your needs and (b) efficient methods for surveying published materials.

# TWO

# SOURCES OF GUIDANCE

*"If I'd known he'd be too busy to be of much help, I would have tried to find a better advisor."*

At the outset of your project, it is well to identify potential sources of help and to recognize the advantages and limitations of each. Those sources of most value are usually academic advisors, fellow graduate students, experts outside of your own department or institution, you yourself, and the professional literature.

## ACADEMIC ADVISORS

Policies for assigning faculty members to supervise students' thesis and dissertation projects can vary from one institution to another and even across departments within the same institution.

In some cases, the advisor who guides a student's general academic progress automatically becomes the supervisor of the candidate's work on the thesis or dissertation. Or else the academic department's chairperson or the head of a committee on theses and dissertations may appoint an advisor. Under such a policy, students are relieved of the responsibility of choosing a mentor, but they may unfortunately end up with less than optimal help. In other cases, an academic advisor will not automatically be assigned, but he or she will be only one of a group of several faculty members from whom a student can choose a guide. Under these circumstances, before students announce their choice of a mentor they can profitably collect several kinds of information about the professors who form the pool of potential advisors. Included among the sources of information are fellow students, the professors within the pool, other faculty members, secretaries, research assistants, and the professors' publications.

Institutions and departments can also differ in the number of faculty members assigned to supervise and evaluate a student's research. One common pattern at the master's level is to have a three-member committee for each thesis, with the committee chairperson acting as the candidate's principal supervisor. However, in colleges and universities with large numbers of master's degree students, the entire master's project may be directed and assessed by a single faculty member. At the doctoral level, the supervising committee often consists of three to five professors.

In the following paragraphs, we describe kinds of information to seek about potential advisors. We then suggest useful sources of each kind.

## Kinds of Information to Collect

In learning about the professors in your pool of potential mentors, you will likely find it helpful to discover their (a) fields of interest and expertise, (b) style of advising, and (c) attitudes about appropriate research topics and methods of research.

### *Fields of interest and expertise*

Obviously, the closer an advisor's area of expertise is to your research problem, the better equipped she or he will be to identify difficulties you may encounter, recommend sources of information pertinent to your topic, and guide your choice of methods for gathering and interpreting data. There are several ways to learn about faculty members' specializations—the titles and contents of classes they teach, their published books and articles, the topics of theses and dissertations produced under their guidance, other staff members' opinions, and other students' experiences with those faculty members.

The task of deciding how well a potential advisor's interests and skills suit your needs is likely easiest if you already have a specific research problem in mind, or at least if you have identified the general realm you hope to explore. If you have no inkling of the kind of topic on which your study will focus, then the next of our selection criteria—style of advising—may become your primary concern.

*Style of advising*

Professors vary greatly in how they work with students on theses and dissertations. Those at one end of a monitoring scale closely control each phase of the student's effort, in some cases dictating what is to be done at every step, then requiring the student to hand in each portion of material for evaluation and correction. Advisors at the opposite end of the scale tell students to work things out pretty much by themselves and to finish a complete draft of the project before handing it in for inspection.

Advisors also vary in how available they are when students need them. Some are frequently away from the campus. Some require students to make an appointment with a department secretary several days or weeks ahead of time in order to confer about the individual's research. Others allow students to drop by the office or to phone any time they need help. Some answer queries only in their office. Others permit students to phone them at home.

Professors also differ in the way they offer advice and criticism. Some are blunt about the shortcomings of a student's effort, perhaps derisive and abusive. Others are direct in pointing out weaknesses in the candidate's work, but they do so in a kindly, understanding manner, recognizing that doing serious research is a new endeavor for the student and that mistakes along the way are not only expected but can function as valuable learning opportunities. Yet others are so cautious about potentially hurting a student's feelings that they are reluctant to point out weaknesses in the project and thereby fail to guide their advisees toward correcting the shortcomings of their efforts.

Consequently, you will likely find it useful to learn ahead of time about faculty members' styles of directing theses and dissertations—about how closely they monitor steps in the process, how available they are to offer help, and how skillfully they identify deficiencies and suggest solutions without unduly damaging students' egos.

Your best sources of information about advising styles are usually (a) fellow graduate students who are farther along than you are in the thesis or dissertation process and (b) other professors whom you know personally and who are willing to talk about their colleagues' modes of guidance.

*Attitudes toward topics and methodology*

Faculty members often disagree about what constitutes proper research. Consequently, you might end up with an advisor whose notions of suitable research topics and methods of investigation are at odds with your own beliefs. Therefore, two types of information you may wish to seek are your potential advisors' views of (a) quantitative-versus-qualitative methods and (b) basic-versus-applied research.

***Quantitative-versus-qualitative methods:*** As these terms are generally used, quantitative research involves amounts, which are usually cast in the form of statistics, but qualitative research does not involve amounts in any strict sense. Here are titles of projects that might be categorized under each type:

**Quantitative:**

*Germany's Economic Growth, 1955–2005*
*Rural and Urban Educational Achievement in Oregon*
*Amounts of Public and Private Finance for Welfare Programs*
*Generational Height and Weight Comparisons—Japan and the USA*
*The Growth of Tourism—Florida and Alabama*
*Short-Term Effects of Three Antidepressant Drugs*

**Qualitative:**

*The Philosophical Foundations of Psychoanalysis*
*Silverado—The History of a Frontier Town*
*A Theory of Political Participation*
*One Week in the Life of a Deaf-Mute*
*Judaic Foundations of Islamic Doctrine*
*The Present-Day Relevance of William James's Pragmatism*

Professors who locate themselves exclusively in the quantitative camp demand that students' research involve the compilation of data in the form of amounts. Hence, they reject historical chronicles, philosophical analyses, a line of logic leading to a conclusion, a comparison of the qualities of different societies, the detailed description of an individual's or group's style of life, and the like. Furthermore, adherents of quantitative research sometimes prefer studies that focus on rather large numbers of people, schools, cities, or political constituencies so that broadly inclusive generalizations can be drawn from the research results. Such adherents thus disapprove of studies focusing on one autistic person (single-subject research) or only a few subjects (three autistic children, two schools, four candidates for political office, five neighborhoods) whose results cannot, with confidence, be generalized to a wide range of people or events. Proponents of quantitative studies tend to prefer such research methods as controlled experiments and surveys that employ interviews, tests, systematic observations, questionnaires, and quantitative content analysis. (For arguments supporting the quantitative position, see the following references: Howell, 1997; Shavelson, 1996.)

In contrast, professors who subscribe strictly to qualitative methodology tend to belittle research that involves what they may refer to as "no more than number crunching," which they feel oversimplifies complex causes, dehumanizes evidence, and fails to recognize individual differences among people, among environments, and among events. Advocates of qualitative studies tend to favor such research techniques as historical and philosophical analyses, descriptive observation, case studies, ethnography, and hermeneutics. (For rationales supporting the qualitative stance, see Bogdan & Knopp, 1992; Denzin & Lincoln, 1994.)

There are, in addition to the foregoing two polar positions, a great many faculty members who will accept a wide array of research approaches, quantitative and qualitative alike. We would count ourselves among their number because, in our opinion, the quantitative-versus-qualitative controversy is really off target. The issue, in our minds, should not be: Are quantitative methods better than qualitative, or vice versa? Instead, the issue should be: Which approach—quantitative, qualitative, or some combination of both—will be the most suitable for answering the particular research question being asked? This point of view, which respects the contributions that can be made by all sorts of methods, is the one we espouse throughout this book (Thomas, 2003).

However, to be practical about your own situation as a student pursuing a degree in a particular department, what we as the authors of this book believe about the quantitative-qualitative debate is really not important. What is important is how well your own beliefs match those of the advisors with whom you might conduct your research. Thus, a useful twofold question to ask is: Which research methodologies do the potential members of my research-project committee prefer or even accept? And how well do my own preferences match the opinions of those professors? In effect, establishing a good match promotes efficiency, effectiveness, and goodwill in your work with advisors.

***Basic-versus-applied research:*** When you are seeking to learn the attitudes of potential advisors toward research, you may wish to discover what position they hold regarding a contrast often drawn between (a) *basic* or *pure* studies and (b) *applied* or *practical* studies. These two types reflect different motives on the part of the persons conducting the research. The motive behind basic research is to foster people's *understanding of life,* without intending to apply that knowledge to solving practical problems. Consider these titles of studies designed to enhance people's knowledge of the world.

*Toward a Phenomenology of Perception*
*A Theory of Political Ethics*
*The Rise and Decline of Behaviorism*
*A History of Social Work in Wisconsin*
*The Social-Class System of a Seaside Village*

The researcher's motive behind applied studies is to take *constructive action* toward solving the world's problems, that is, to promote people's welfare by improving their lot. The practical nature of applied studies is often reflected in their titles.

*Reading Instruction as an Aid to Homeless Children*
*Using Computers in Content Analyses*
*The Effectiveness of Drug Treatment for Schizophrenia*
*Moral Commitment as a Platform for Social Action*
*Aptitude Tests versus Letters of Recommendation as Predictors of Academic Success in a Community College*

The motives of *promoting understanding* and *acting constructively* are often linked, in that people's attempts to act constructively are based on their beliefs about how the world and individuals' lives operate. Thus, a research project may be intended to provide the understanding needed for solving a problem. Such could be the aim of studies titled:

*Lifestyles of Blind Adolescents*
*Labor Market Effects of Demographic Change in Four Western States*
*How Working Toward an Understanding of Collaborative Leadership Can Change Small Business Culture*
*The Local Party Caucus as a Political Tool*
*Alternative Forms of Multicultural Education*

In our opinion as authors of this volume, basic and applied topics are equally desirable foci for theses and dissertations. However, not all professors would agree. Some believe that basic research designed to promote understanding is the proper aim of graduate students' studies. However, others insist that projects should always focus on solving problems that confront societies and individuals. Still other faculty members consider both basic and applied issues as worthy matters for master's degree and doctoral candidates to pursue.

Consequently, you may wish to discover the attitudes that potential advisors have about basic and applied studies so that you can try to find members for your research committee whose preferences are in keeping with your own.

As you seek advisors to guide your project, you may profit from considering the traits of an effective mentor and of sources of information that are suggested in Table 2.1.

Once you've obtained a principal advisor, you may discover that he or she is unsuitable, for any of the reasons noted in Table 2.1. To extricate yourself from this relationship, you may find it useful to find another faculty member who would likely be a better advisor. You can explain your plight to this potential "new" advisor and ask that he or she take you on as an advisee. Such an interview is best attempted before you have actually broken your connection with the professor whom you deem unsuitable. The "new" advisor may be willing to help arrange the transition from the "old" to the "new" mentor with as little unpleasantness as possible.

For some students, a key criterion for selecting an advisor is a professor's gender, ethnic origin, or religious affiliation. Such a stipulation can lead to trouble if a chosen professor proves so weak in other desired characteristics that the student fails to get needed help. An example in our own experience involved two women doctoral candidates who wished to write on topics relating to women administrators, and they insisted on having at least one woman on their committee. Unfortunately, the woman they chose was both a micromanager—involving herself in the minutest details of her administrative position—and was frequently away from the campus. She had little or no time for dissertations. As a result, the two candidates' work was delayed more than six months. Thoroughly frustrated, they sought the advice of another faculty member who suggested that they substitute a more accommodating committee member for the inordinately busy administrator. This incident led the doctoral students to realize that technical expertise and availability could be more important for their progress than an advisor's gender, ethnic background, or religious convictions.

However, there are times when it is appropriate to select an advisor—or a member of your committee—as a representative of a gender, ethnic group, political party, religious persuasion, or age category. The intent, in this case, is to have the perspective or life experiences of such a person reflected in your study.

## YOUR SUPERVISING COMMITTEE

As already noted, a committee of three to five professors is typically charged with supervising the preparation of a doctoral dissertation. In some institutions,

**Table 2.1** Traits for Effective Advisors

| *The Best Kind of Advisor:* | *Useful Sources of Information* |
|---|---|
| Is well respected by colleagues and students. | Students who graduated and ones currently working on their projects. Other faculty members whom you know well. |
| Is an expert in the field of your project. | Evaluate the potential advisor's lectures and course syllabi. Read his or her writings to see how pertinent they are for your topic. |
| Supports the research problem you have chosen or helps you find a better problem. | Other students who have had this faculty member as an advisor. Other professors you know well. |
| Will be available to give verbal and written reactions at the time you need them. | Other students who are acquainted with the potential advisor's style. |
| Is a strong, convincing supporter of advisees and has the courage to defend students in front of other professors, which may be necessary during the research process and particularly at the end when the study is submitted for final evaluation. | Other students who have studied under the potential advisor. Other faculty and staff (administrative assistants, technicians, research assistants). |
| Is consistent in giving advice. Does not continually ask for revisions that are to contain new elements. | Other students who have worked with the potential advisor. |
| Works amicably with other members of your supervising committee. Helps you select suitable committee members. | Other students. Other faculty members whom you know well and whose judgments you trust. |

master's theses are also prepared under the guidance of a committee of two or three faculty members. The chairperson of a committee is usually the candidate's chief advisor.

Committee members perform one or more of three functions: (a) give the candidate advice at successive stages of the research and writing process, (b) periodically monitor the progress of the project to help ensure that all is going well, and (c) evaluate the final product to determine whether it is of sufficient quality to warrant awarding the candidate a diploma.

If you, as the candidate, have any control over who will serve on your committee, then there are several items of information you can profitably collect as you decide whom you would like to have as committee members. Those items include the potential members' (a) styles of advising, (b) areas of expertise, (c) attitudes toward different types of research problems and methods of investigation, and (d) attitudes toward each other. Because we have already discussed the first three in this quartet of concerns, we turn directly to the fourth—faculty members' opinions of each other and how those opinions could affect your work.

Two questions to ask about professors' personal relations are: (1) What sorts of disagreements among faculty members can influence their committee membership? (2) What are useful sources of such information?

### Recognizing Faculty Members' Differences

Faculty members sometimes disagree with each other in ways that can affect students' progress. Disagreements can be professional, personal, or some combination of both. A professional difference often concerns such theoretical matters as those reflected in the qualitative/quantitative debate or in the relative importance of heredity and of environment as a cause behind people's behavior. Or a professional difference may center on research techniques—the desirability of questionnaires versus interviews or the appropriateness of a survey versus a controlled experiment.

Personal disagreements are antagonisms seated in people's dislike for each other as individuals. The dislike may derive from insults exchanged in the past, from one professor caustically criticizing another in a faculty meeting or public gathering, from competition between professors over departmental funds or office space, from an exchange of ethnic or religious slurs, from ostensibly immoral behavior, and more. Often the professional and personal become entwined, as when one faculty member incurs another's wrath by identifying the colleague's publications as "fluff" or as "founded on a set of false premises that lead inevitably to asinine conclusions."

Whereas some professors set aside their personal antipathies when serving on a committee and do not let their personality conflicts affect their work with the student, others do not. Whether intentionally or not, they end up using the student's project as an opportunity to strike a blow at the antagonist. The vendetta can affect the student's plan at various stages of the project—selecting a research problem, devising methods of data gathering, interpreting the results, and writing the final version of the study. In nearly all doctoral programs, and in some master's plans, the final step in the dissertation or thesis process involves a meeting in which the candidate defends her or his study before the supervising committee, and the committee then decides whether the product is worthy of the degree the student is seeking. In some instances, rival committee members use the occasion to vent their animosity by disagreeing with each other over elements of the candidate's project. The candidate's hope is that their enmity will not affect the faculty members' objective judgment to the extent of damaging the student's chance of receiving unanimous approval of the project.

One bright PhD graduate, after earning his degree, offered this observation about the dissertation experience:

> Committee members are people, and like all people, have quirks, biases, and ways of thinking that run from the ridiculous to the sublime on occasion. Furthermore, institutions of higher education are like all institutions, with a climate and culture that *must* be recognized. Politics abound, and no doctoral student wants to get hung in the middle. Unfortunately, a student in the dissertation stage can become cannon fodder for political in-fighting.

Whenever faculty members' disagreements, either professional or personal, threaten the fate of a student's thesis or dissertation, two remedies that might be tried are those of (a) proposing changes in the project that would maintain its integrity and purpose and, at the same time, would be acceptable to both of the conflicting committee members or (b) appealing to another faculty member who commands enough respect and influence to compel the contending committee members to accept advice that would resolve the impasse.

Ergo, the work on your project will move along far more smoothly if the members of your supervising committee hold views of research that are compatible with your project and if they don't maintain personal animosities that could influence how your project will be evaluated.

### Sources of Information

As suggested in Table 2.1, the most readily available sources of information about departmental politics are usually those veteran students who have had extended experience in your department, particularly in their roles of teaching assistants and research assistants. They are often well aware of the patterns of friendship and enmity among faculty members. At least in the form of rumor, if not in the form of unquestioned fact, such "old timers" can provide useful opinions about personal-social configurations in your department and can suggest which combination of committee members might benefit you and which might prove awkward or even disastrous.

Other useful sources are professors that you know well and whose opinions you trust. Some of them may not be forthcoming, since they don't want to be accused of meddling in such matters. However, others are willing to offer advice, often in such guarded phrases as "Professor X may not be as sympathetic toward ethnography as a research method as is Professor Q" or "Some students have found Ms. A easier to work with than Ms. B."

## YOUR FELLOW GRADUATE STUDENTS

Not only can fellow students offer useful observations about faculty advisors, but they may also help you in other ways at each stage of your research and writing.

At the beginning, when you are choosing a research problem to pursue, your peers may suggest potential topics and may identify advantages and weaknesses of topics you have under consideration.

As you survey the professional literature that relates to your project, your compatriots may help by suggesting sites to search on the Internet, by sharing relevant articles and books, and by showing you the system they use for taking notes and organizing their references.

During the data-collecting stage, fellow students can be asked to critique the methods (survey, ethnography, experiment, historical analysis) and instruments (tests, questionnaires, interviews, observations) that you intend to employ. They may help you gather data by distributing questionnaires, conducting interviews, or administering tests. They may also help you classify the information you collect by suggesting categories in which to place data or by assessing the strengths and shortcomings of the classification scheme you plan to adopt. Your peers may also be able to suggest appropriate methods of statistical or hermeneutic analysis and perhaps participate in carrying out the analysis.

At the stage of interpreting the classified results, fellow students can be asked to critique your explanations in order to identify weaknesses in logic and to suggest alternative glosses that you hadn't recognized.

During the process of writing the final version of the thesis or dissertation, your peers may be willing to assist by critiquing your plan for organizing the document, by suggesting styles of tabular and graphic displays, and by proofreading the ultimate product.

## EXPERTS OUTSIDE YOUR DEPARTMENT

Most students apparently recognize that they need not confine their requests for aid to the professors on their supervising committee. They realize that they can consult with other faculty members in their department. But students often seem to overlook opportunities to seek help from experts in other campus departments or in other institutions. It thus may be useful for you to extend your purview of sources of aid beyond your immediate setting. There are several ways this can be done.

If the expert you need is on your campus, you can phone to explain the kind of help you desire, or you can make an appointment to meet with the professor at her or his office.

If the person you wish to consult is in another institution, you can submit your request by phone, by fax, by e-mail, or by regular mail. If you do not know the professor's institutional location or address, you may find this information in your campus library's copy of *The National Faculty Directory* (Gale Research Co., Detroit, MI) or in the membership roster of a professional society to which that person belongs. Names, addresses, and phone numbers of such societies are listed in *The Encyclopedia of Associations.* Typical rosters are those of the American Anthropological Association, American Assembly of Collegiate Schools of Business, American Economic Association, American Historical Association, American Psychological Association, American Sociological Association, American Educational Research Association, and Modern Language Association of America. Membership registers not only list professors' institutional addresses but they may include e-mail addresses as well.

When you send your request for help, you should state as specifically as possible exactly what you need. Or, as is often the case, you may wish to receive anything the professor has written in your area of interest. In this event, you can ask for either a list of the expert's writings or, perhaps, reprints of any items that he or she has available. Some faculty members consider such requests just a bother and thus ignore the inquiries or dismiss them with cursory replies of little value. However, many others give serious attention to solicitations from students on other campuses and respond with valuable advice and information.

## YOU YOURSELF

Graduate students, in their haste to complete the thesis or dissertation, often overlook an important source of information—their own experiences. One reason for this is that students have been conditioned in many of the courses they take to locate authority outside of themselves. Textbooks, the professors' lectures, and assigned readings serve as the fount of knowledge. In effect, the student is treated as an empty vessel to be filled with information from external authorities.

Essentialists—those who believe that there is a body of knowledge that contains traditional concepts, skills, and information—argue that there is a canon or body of literature that must be learned by students in a particular discipline. In recent years, constructivists—those who believe that each person creates his or her own body of knowledge—have criticized essentialists for being Eurocentric and male-centered. Consequently, constructivists often encourage graduate students to write down, perhaps in outline form, everything they know and feel about a thesis or dissertation topic before engaging in more systematic scholarship. Another way of saying this is that the *outer curriculum*—the course of study as represented by the text, assigned readings, and lectures—is always a springboard to the *inner curriculum*—what each person experiences as learning settings as cooperatively created (Brubaker, 1994). The tone of constructivism is captured in the title of Gloria Steinem's book, *Revolution From Within* (1992).

Constructivists would, for example, encourage the graduate student to ponder the question, "What within my experience has led me to the selection of this research topic, and how has my research methodology been influenced by such experiences?" For instance, if a researcher is studying at-risk children, she or he might point out in the introduction or in a methodology chapter that the topic was selected because of the writer's personal experiences in trying to reach at-risk children. Or, the researcher might write that she or he was an at-risk student as a child, then add that a case-study methodology was chosen as it seems to be the next best thing to personally "being there." The constructivist as advisor might also encourage the student to personalize the latter part of the final chapter of the thesis or dissertation. As one professor said, "The implications of your findings are where you must spread your wings, for this is the major place in your writing where the committee must know the personal meaning you assign to what you have discovered."

Two warnings to be sounded with regard to constructivism are: (1) Be careful that your attitude toward your own experiences doesn't lead to narcissism, a preoccupation with self that simply compounds your ignorance, and (2) use your experiences as a starting place that leads to a more comprehensive and precise critique of matters you are researching.

## THE PROFESSIONAL LITERATURE

As you know, an enormous body of academic writing has accumulated over the centuries, and it continues to increase today at an exponential rate. A great deal of the help you need to complete a respectable project will likely come from this assemblage of knowledge. Because there are multiple roles that the professional literature can play in your endeavor, and because ways of surveying the literature can be complex, a thorough discussion of such matters warrants a separate chapter. Those concerns become the focus of Chapter 3.

Finally, as a device for immediately applying the topics of this chapter to your own case, we provide a checklist that you may wish to complete.

## PLANNING CHECKLIST

The intent of this checklist is to help you decide what position you wish to adopt regarding a number of the issues raised in the chapter. You can show your response to a question by writing an **X** in the space before each answer that represents your intent.

1. If you do not already have a principal advisor for your project, how do you plan to find one?

    ____ Get other students' opinions about which professors are most helpful.

    ____ Ask faculty members whom I respect for their recommendations.

    ____ Look up the specializations of different faculty members (their courses and publications) to select one whose expertise is close to my academic interests.

    ____ Other (specify)________________________________

2. If you already have an advisor, but you are dissatisfied and would like to find a better one, what do you plan to do?

    ____ Nothing. Trying to change would cause too much trouble.

    ____ Ask the advice of a faculty member whom I trust.

    ____ Ask another faculty member to be my advisor, and take that faculty member's advice about how best to effect the transfer.

    ____ Ask the department chairperson or dean for advice as to how I should handle this problem.

    ____ Other (specify)________________________________

3. If your project is to be supervised by a faculty committee, how will the additional committee members (other than the principal advisor) be selected?

    ____ By me.

    ____ By my principal advisor.

    ____ By agreement between my principal advisor and me.

    ____ By a committee that is authorized to make such decisions.

    ____ Other (specify)________________________________

(Note: In responding to the questions under item 4, write W on the line in front of each choice that tells the kind of help you want, and write E before each choice that shows the kind of help you can probably expect to get. Obviously, in some cases the help you want will be the same as the help you can expect, so both W and E will appear on the same line. In other cases you may want help but you expect it may not be forthcoming, so you'll look forward to living with a discrepancy between want and get.)

4. What kind of help do you want, and what kind of help do you expect to receive from:

4.1 Your principal advisor?

____ (a) None.

____ (b) Suggestions for a research topic.

____ (c) An appraisal of research options I propose.

____ (d) Prompt responses to each stage of my project that I hand in.

____ (e) Sources of information, such as bibliographies, experts to contact, e-mail addresses, reprints of journal articles.

____ (f) Suggestions about methods of data collection.

____ (g) Suggestions about theories on which to base my study.

____ (h) Suggestions about how to classify and organize my data.

____ (i) Suggestions about interpreting my results.

____ (j) Suggestions about the overall organization of my final written product.

____ (k) Proofreading the final product, and correcting typos, grammar, spelling, and usage errors.

____ (l) Preparing me to defend the final project before the examining committee, both in the early stages of the project and at the end.

____ (m) Other (specify)________________________________

4.2 Your other committee members?

(To respond, on the line following **Want**, write the appropriate letters from the list under 4.1 to indicate which types of help you *want*. On the line following **Expect**, write the letters from the 4.1 list to indicate types of help you *expect*. Use this answer system for items 4.2 through 4.5.)

Want ________________________________

Expect ________________________________

4.3 Your fellow graduate students?

Want ________________________________

Expect ________________________________

4.4 Other professors on your campus?

Want ________________________________

Expect ________________________________

4.5 Experts located away from your campus?

Want ________________________________

Expect ________________________________

THREE

# SEARCHING THE LITERATURE

*"This business of searching and reviewing the literature. What literature is that? What am I supposed to find? Exactly what's a 'literature review'?"*

The expression—*the literature*—typically refers to published writings in books, journals, conference proceedings, and Internet websites that relate to the field of investigation within which a student's project lies. Such literature also includes unpublished theses and dissertations. However, there is no universal agreement among professors about (a) what should be contained in the student's review of the literature, (b) what functions such a review should assume in the overall project, or (c) where the review should be located in the finished document. Therefore, you may find it helpful to be acquainted with alternative positions that advisors may hold in relation to such issues.

The first section of this chapter sketches some of the more common viewpoints professors adopt. By understanding those viewpoints, you should be better prepared to discuss the literature review with your advisors and to argue your case if their ideas about the search fail to coincide with your own. The second section of the chapter describes ways that a literature search can be conducted efficiently. The final section describes a pair of avoidable errors of judgment—"lamentably dumb mistakes"—that students occasionally commit.

## FUNCTIONS OF LITERATURE REVIEWS

One popular patterning of chapters in theses and dissertations goes something like this:

Chapter 1: Introduction
Chapter 2: Review of the Literature
Chapter 3: Methodology
Chapter 4: Results/Findings
Chapter 5: Analysis and Interpretation of the Findings
Chapter 6: Summary, Conclusions, Applications, and Recommendations for Further Study

Such a pattern implies that the entire collection of information from the professional literature belongs in Chapter 2. However, whether it's wise to locate all references to the literature within a separate chapter is a matter of debate. Two questions worth answering are (1) What function is material from the literature expected to perform in your project? (2) Where in the final version of your thesis or dissertation can such material most reasonably be located?

A typical answer to the first question is that faculty advisors want your project not only to display your ability to answer the particular question on which your research will focus, but also to demonstrate how skillfully you (a) situated your chosen topic within a relevant body of knowledge, (b) found in the literature a significant quantity of other studies that bear on your topic, (c) evaluated the quality of those studies (their strengths and limitations), (d) identified the linkages between your project and previous studies, and (e) showed what contribution your project can make to the field in which your work is located. Although these five functions can often be conveniently housed within the same chapter, there are also various other functions that the literature review can serve. Hence, it is useful to consider what those functions are and where material bearing on them can suitably be placed. Here are ten such functions. A survey of the literature can:

***1. Suggest ideas for research problems.*** Well before the time you actually start work on your project, you can be on the lookout for potential research topics. While reading a textbook, listening to a lecture, or browsing through a journal, your intuitive reaction to items may signal potential topics. Such reactions can be recognized in your spontaneous response to what you encounter: "That may not be true in all cases" or "Surely that's an oversimplification of a complex situation" or "Now that's an idea worth following up in more detail" or "You can't draw such a broad conclusion from such a limited sampling of people" or "There must be a better way to test that theory." On these occasions, you may find it worthwhile to jot down your reaction and to suggest, even in a vague way, the kind of study that could derive from your response. Adopting this habit enables you to compile a list of research possibilities from which you can select your thesis or dissertation problem.

***2. Identify strengths and weaknesses of others' theories and empirical studies.*** Authors of books, articles, and book reviews in your discipline frequently offer assessments of work in that field. Those analyses can prove useful for your own work by alerting you to weaknesses to avoid and by suggesting good ideas to incorporate in your own study. By pausing in your reading to note these features and to identify the publication in which they appear (author, year, title, volume, number, publisher, page number), you gradually accumulate references that may prove useful for your project.

***3. Identify theories that can be applied or tested.*** The word *theory*, as we use it throughout this book, is a proposal about (a) what variables are important for understanding some phenomenon and (b) how those variables interact to make the phenomenon turn out as it does. Thus, a political theory may be designed to explain why people vote the way they do in elections. A sociological theory may show how and why people within a family may rise or fall on a social-status scale from one generation to the next. An economic theory may explain stock market cycles of advance and decline. An anthropological theory may offer reasons for the appearance of particular religious practices within representative cultures. A psychological theory may identify factors affecting compulsive behavior. An educational theory may propose how teachers' personality characteristics interact with pupils' characteristics to affect pupils' academic performance.

Thus, in the professional literature, you may find theories that your thesis or dissertation will test empirically, extend, revise, or replace. During your reading, as ideas about theories come to mind, you may find it useful to record your thoughts and note the passage or chapter that stimulated those thoughts, along with the bibliographic location of the passage (author, year, title, volume, number, publisher, page number).

***4. Suggest methodological approaches.*** The word *methodology* is used here to mean the steps you will follow in answering your research question, including the kinds of information you collect, how you collect it, and how you classify and interpret the results. The professional literature is a valuable source of methodological possibilities, including the advantages and limitations of different approaches. Such information not only can guide your choice of a research design but also can aid you in devising a defense of that choice. Therefore, as you browse through the literature, you can profitably take notes about (a) the components of a given method, (b) the kinds of research problems for which that method has been used, and (c) the method's strengths and weaknesses.

***5. Explain data-gathering techniques and instruments.*** Each research design includes ways of collecting information, such as analyzing the contents of documents, conducting an opinion survey, observing people's behavior, administering tests, or carrying out an experiment. Journal articles or single chapters of an edited book, because they are restricted in length, may mention the data-collecting methods and instruments but not describe them in detail. You will find this practice satisfactory if the instrument that a writer mentions (such as a test or questionnaire) is a standardized, published document whose specific nature you can discover by obtaining a copy and reading its instruction manual. But authors' tests, questionnaires, or interview protocols are often ones they created on their own and may not be reproduced in the account of their research. In these cases, if it is important that you learn the specific nature of a data-gathering technique, you may need to hunt for the study's original, detailed description (perhaps in a book or dissertation) or else write directly to the author to request a copy of the account.

***6. Provide typologies and taxonomies for classifying data.*** A quantity of collected information—such as historical accounts, survey responses, and test scores—is typically an incomprehensible mess until it's been classified and summarized. The professional literature contains alternative ways this can be done. Taking notes about different approaches, along with each one's advantages and limitations, prepares you for writing the portion of your thesis or dissertation in which you (a) discuss alternative classification schemes, (b) tell which scheme you adopted, and (c) defend the suitability of that scheme by comparing its features with the strengths and weaknesses of other options.

***7. Suggest statistical and graphic treatments.*** Numbers, tables, diagrams, and pictures are among the devices useful for classifying and summarizing data. Therefore, as you peruse the literature, you may benefit from contemplating the kinds of data you intend to collect and from taking notes about authors' statistical techniques, kinds of tables, and graphic displays that you might wish to include in your own study.

***8. Illustrate ways of interpreting research results.*** The word *interpreting* in the present context refers to explaining to readers what your classified information means. This is the "*so what?*" phase of research. The professional literature can help prepare you for the interpretation task by illustrating the diverse conclusions authors have drawn from their data. It's useful for you to note which modes of interpretation in the literature you find most convincing, and why. Conversely, you can also determine which interpretations you consider weak, and why. This exercise can aid you in establishing criteria to guide the conclusions you draw from your own data.

***9. Show ways of presenting the completed research project.*** Throughout the literature, the quality of presentations is remarkably varied. Some authors write well, some moderately well, and others very badly, indeed. The expression *bad writing* as used here refers to research reports that are difficult to understand by the audience for which they are intended. Flaws of presentation can be of various kinds—(a) poor organization, so readers are amazed at what comes next in the report, (b) key words not defined precisely, (c) esoteric terms used when simpler, familiar terms would suffice, (d) convoluted sentences, (e) few, if any, lifelike examples to clarify abstract concepts, and more. As you read authors' accounts, you may wish to note which features of their presentation contribute to ease of understanding and which serve as barriers to meaning. This can alert you to ways you can enhance the quality of your own writing.

***10. Suggest outlets for publishing the completed product.*** You will reach a broader audience with your project if the results can be disseminated in some form other than that of an unpublished thesis or dissertation. That form may be an abstract, a succinct journal article, a microfiche or microfilm version of the entire work, a chapter in someone else's book, an entire book itself, or a website on the Internet. During your review of the literature, you may locate potential outlets for the type of research your project involves. Recording the addresses of those outlets and noting the form that each type assumes can prepare you for contacting sources of publication once your project is finished.

In summary, the professional literature has many potential functions for promoting the quality and speed of your work. Recognizing these functions at the outset of your project, then taking proper notes during the search, helps ensure that you invest your time economically.

## EFFICIENT WAYS OF SEARCHING THE LITERATURE

One useful approach to surveying the literature involves decisions about (a) search strategies, (b) where to hunt, and (c) what to record and how to record it.

### Search Strategies

An approach some students use is the generally-browse-and-peruse strategy. They hunt for books and journals in the broad area of their topic, then read the sources in detail, hoping to find material that might apply to their project. In our experience such a method is very inefficient. A specify-and-look-up strategy is far more productive because it saves lots of time, eliminates wading through pages that will be of no use, and guides you to where relevant material should be located in your project.

When employing a specify-and-look-up approach, you first decide which functions you intend your literature survey to serve. Those functions can be cast as questions you plan to answer, such as

1. What studies have already been conducted about my topic, and what conclusions did the authors draw?
2. What key terms did the author use that can relate to my study, and how were those terms defined?
3. What are methodological strengths and limitations of previous studies relating to my topic?
4. On what theories have previous studies been founded? Or, which theories have been applied in previous studies?

Additional questions of this sort can focus on the other functions we described earlier in this chapter. Armed with your guide questions, you skim through book chapters, journal articles, newspaper accounts, or Internet web pages to find the answers you seek. As a result, you rarely, if ever, read a book straight through. Instead, you hunt up answers to your questions. In some instances this will require a detailed examination of one or more book chapters—sometimes an entire book or monograph—as when you wish to thoroughly understand the theory on which the study was grounded. In other cases, your task consists of hunting only for a key word or phrase in the book's index or on a website (as in learning how an author defined a term that will be important in your project); then you read only the book pages whose numbers appear for that word in the index.

Sometimes your search will be guided by a single question. In other cases, you will find it economical to look up answers to several questions at the same time in order to make the most efficient use of a book, dissertation, or journal that would be difficult or inconvenient to obtain on a future occasion.

*Examples of key words used in a literature search*

Here are two examples of key words whose meanings students might seek in their literature search. The first example is from a project titled *Social-Class Changes in a Southern Town—1945–2005*. The second is titled *Treatment Plans for Attention Deficit Disorder (ADD)*.

***Social-Class Changes in a Southern Town—1945–2005:*** Key terms can be selected either to address the project's topic in general or to focus on a particular function that the literature is expected to serve. General key terms for the study of social class can include *social class, social stratification, socioeconomic status (SES), social structure, upper class, middle class, lower class, minorities, the rich, the poor, wealth,* and *poverty*. Words specific to a function, such as that of generating research methods for the social-class study, could include *social-science research methods, survey techniques, interview techniques, social-class scales, scaling methods,* and *social-class typologies.*

***Treatment Plans for Attention Deficit Disorder (ADD):*** General key words for the study of attention deficit can be *attention, attention deficit disorder (ADD), hyperactivity, attention deficit hyperactivity disorder (ADHD), inattention,* and *distractibility*. If one of the chosen functions of the literature search is that of locating ADD within the general learning-disorders domain of knowledge, then key terms—in addition to the foregoing ones—could include *learning disorders, learning handicaps, disadvantaged learners, special education, remedial education,* and *teaching the handicapped.*

In summary, as you plan your literature review, you will likely find it helpful to decide which functions the review should perform and then to select both general and specific-function terms to guide your effort.

## Where to Hunt

Thanks to personal computers, the Internet, and the World Wide Web, the task of finding suitable resources has been dramatically simplified and the outcome markedly enriched over the past four decades. Prior to the 1980s, researchers—including graduate students—were obliged to hunt for pertinent literature by fingering through library card catalogs, inspecting the references listed in the closing pages of books, questioning professors and fellow students, and hunting through volumes containing abstracts of studies in a given discipline. Today, a student with a personal computer at hand, and access to an Internet server, can discover appropriate literature sources that may be located all over the world. Thus, the best place to begin your search is probably at a computer connected to an Internet server. The server may be located in your own college or university, or it may be a commercial provider.

Some libraries' lists of book holdings are available to anyone with access to the World Wide Web. However, more specialized data banks—such as lists of journal or newspaper articles and their abstracts—require a password available only to certain kinds of users, such as faculty members and students of the school in which you are enrolled. Hence, you can get a password for your own university library's restricted services, but probably not for those services in other institutions' libraries unless you make special arrangements.

In addition to taking advantage of the Internet, you still may—as in "the good old days"—profit from asking the advice of professors, fellow students, and librarians as you pursue answers to your literature-search queries.

The libraries of most higher-education institutions have an open-stack policy. Students are permitted to wander among the rows of shelved books and bound journals, inspect the titles, and look through any volumes they choose. However, some libraries maintain a closed-stack policy. In order to get a book, a user must find the book's call number and title in the library's computerized catalog, write that information on an order card, and hand the order to a librarian who will then have a library employee find the volume and deliver it to the check-out desk. An open-stack policy is much to your advantage, for it permits you to find the sections of the library's holdings that are most relevant to your project and to browse among the titles shelved there to find sources that may be of use. You can then inspect the tables of contents and indexes of those books to locate answers to your search questions. You can also inspect the lists of references at the ends of chapters or ends of journal articles to find resources that bear on your topic.

### What to Record and How to Record It

If you have used function questions to guide your search, then the problem of what to record from the literature is obviously solved. You simply write answers to your questions. It is also the case that, as you survey the literature, the contents of the article or chapter you are reading may suggest further search questions that had not occurred to you before. Thus, you not only record the information you have found but also add to your search strategy the question generated by that information.

The matter of how to record what you find can involve considering both what form to use and how to code what you record.

*The Form*

Which form of recording will be most suitable is influenced by your location, your skills, your facilities, the expense, and the time available. If you are using a book or journal in a library, you may find it most feasible to take handwritten notes. Or if the library has photocopying facilities for patrons' use, you may choose to photocopy passages from a resource. If you have checked a book or journal out of the library and have it at home near your computer, you can enter quotations or summaries of passages by keying them in with your word-processing program.

If you need to quote extensive portions of a book chapter or journal article and then use those quotations as part of your thesis or dissertation, you will find that a scanner that utilizes an OCR (optical character recognition) program is a great boon. Although photocopying a document furnishes you an exact copy of that document, it does not allow you to enter the document directly into the computer file containing the portion of the project on which you are currently working. But by placing the source of the quotation—book, magazine, or photocopied item—in a scanner attached to your computer, and utilizing an OCR program, you can copy pages and save them in the word-processing program you are using. You are then able to treat that material the same as you would if you had typed it into the computer yourself. The quoted material can be edited or moved around however you wish.

Sometimes you may find it convenient to orally enter summaries or quotations into a tape recorder. One advantage is that speaking is usually faster than writing. Obviously, using a tape recorder requires that you be in a situation in which your talk doesn't disturb others, and the location needs to be free from noise that would muddle the recording. There is also computer software available that enables you to speak into the computer and have your speech recorded as written material.

You can save yourself time and grief if, at the outset of your project, you prepare (a) the bibliographic style you intend to use in the final version of your project, (b) the manner in which you will cite references and add notes, and (c) a coding system for indicating where in your project you plan to utilize selections from the professional literature.

***Bibliographic style:*** For the final version of your thesis or dissertation, there are several popular ways of citing the literature resources you have used. One way is to place all of your references in an alphabetical list at the end of your document. Sometimes this list is labeled *Bibliography* and contains sources that you consulted, even ones that you do not cite specifically in the body of your work. Or the list may be titled *References* and limited to items that you mention in your document.

Here are two of the standard forms for listing references. The first is from the *Publication Manual of the American Psychological Association* (Fifth Edition) and is commonly used for works in the fields of psychology, sociology, economics, education, and political science.

**Book:** Washington, G., & Lincoln, A. (2004). *Past presidents' personalities.* Philadelphia: B. Franklin's Press.

**Journal article:** Marx, K. (1934). Sociology in the third reich. *New European Social Thought, 14*(3), 123–142.

The second, from the *Chicago Manual of Style* (15th Edition), is often used for studies in the humanities. It sometimes is also found in educational and certain social-science publications.

**Book:** Raleigh, Walter. *A Complete History of the World.* 62nd ed. London: The Tower Press, 2006.

**Journal article:** Johnson, Ben. "W. Shakespeare and the Kate Who Kissed." *Elizabethan Archives* 8 (1604): 67–82.

Other acceptable variations of each of these forms can be found in the bibliographies and lists of references in books and journals in your field of study.

Since you will need information about the style used for kinds of publications other than books and journal articles (such as unpublished dissertations, newspaper articles, conference proceedings, and personal communications), you will find it helpful to consult such sources as the APA and Chicago manuals.

When you select a style, it is important that (a) it be acceptable to the members of the faculty committee that supervise your project and that (b) you consistently stick to that same style throughout your work. In some universities, the rules governing the form of theses and dissertations are available in a booklet or style sheet available in the central library, in your own department, in the campus bookstore, in the graduate school office, or on the Internet. If your institution has such a publication, you can benefit from obtaining a copy at an early stage of your project.

***Citations and notes:*** Throughout the final version of your study, you are obligated to identify the literature resources from which you have drawn quotations and key concepts. There are several common ways of citing such references. One way that has increased in popularity over recent decades is to note the name of the author and the year of publication in parentheses. Then readers can find the exact title and publisher of the book or article in the list of references at the end of your document. That's the system we use throughout this book.

An alternative approach involves a superscript—a small number raised above the line, like this[1]—which guides readers to the cited source at the bottom of the page. Sometimes the source that is signaled by a superscript is not displayed at the bottom on the page but, rather, is located in a numbered bibliographic list at the end of the current chapter or at the end of the entire document.

You may occasionally wish to add an explanatory note to a segment of your presentation, but you don't want to interrupt the flow of thought of the present paragraph. There are several options for adding informative material. One is to place the added comments in parentheses within the body of the writing. (Such a note then looks like this, which does, indeed, interrupt the flow, but the parentheses show the reader that the inserted comment is simply an *aside.*) Another popular practice is to cast the addition as a footnote at the bottom of the page, signaled by a superscript. Or else the insertion can be an *endnote* in a listing of such notes at the close of the chapter or at the end of the thesis or dissertation. These options and others are illustrated in such resources as the *Chicago Manual of Style.*

***Coding material from the literature:*** The word *coding* is used here to mean attaching code numbers or letters to each passage or set of notes that you take from the professional literature. The code indicates what function you intend the passage or notes to perform in your project. We are thus suggesting that you should not take any material from the literature (quotations, concepts, theories, appraisals) unless you can estimate where in your work that material will likely be used. We believe it's a waste of time to lift passages from a book or journal simply because such material "might be useful someplace or other."

Once you have selected the topic or research problem on which your project will focus, you should be able to predict, at least in a general way, the kind of content and pattern of organization that your thesis or dissertation will assume. To make such a prediction requires that you (a) envision the kinds of questions your project will answer for readers and (b) estimate the sequence of chapters or sections into which your entire document will be divided. One way to accomplish this task is first to list the questions you hope to answer for

---

[1]Washington, G., & Lincoln, A. (2004). *Past presidents' personalities.* Philadelphia: B. Franklin's Press.

the reading audience. To illustrate, here's a list of questions for a dissertation in the field of English literature that will be titled *An Analysis of Traditional and Modern Verse Forms.* The questions need not be listed in the same sequence in which they will be answered in the completed dissertation.

1. What is meant by "verse forms"?
2. How is "traditional" distinguished from "modern"?
3. Why is it worth writing a dissertation about such a topic? What contribution does this work offer to the field of English literature?
4. What material in the professional literature (literary history and criticism) relates to this topic? What is the significance of that material for this dissertation?
5. What alternative definitions of poetry or verse have been proposed in the professional literature? In other words, what characteristics of writing qualify writing as poetry or verse?
6. What criteria or standards have been used for judging the quality of poetry?
7. What foot and meter schemes have been used, when, and by whom?
8. What rhyme schemes have been used, when, and by whom?
9. What specified poetic forms have been used, when, and by whom (such forms as the sonnet, limerick, Alexandrine, heroic couplet, blank verse, etc.)?
10. How have authors of poetic works linked verse forms to the subject matter or themes of their poems and verses?
11. What have been principal trends in the evolution of poetic and verse forms? What have been the causal conditions responsible for such trends?
12. What methods can be used for compiling types of poetry and verse? What are advantages and limitations of each method? Which of those methods has been employed in this dissertation, and why that method?

The way code numbers for the 12 questions can be attached to material taken from the literature is shown in Figure 3.1. Here, the student has photocopied a verse from a book titled *Glimpses of England* and has written at the bottom of the poem the code numbers for three of her guide questions—numbers 7 (foot and meter schemes), 8 (rhyme schemes), and 10 (linking the verse form to its subject matter). To indicate more precisely how she thinks the material might be used, she has noted exact features of 7 (*iambic* foot and *pentameter* meter) and 8 (internal rhyme and end-line rhyme pattern) that she would want to include in her dissertation; and she plans to include the quoted verse about Shakespeare's plays as one example.

On the reverse side of the sheet on which she photocopied the verse, she wrote the bibliographical information that would be needed for the list of references at the end of the dissertation; and she noted the citation that would accompany the verse when she reproduced it in her document.

Not only is it useful to devise a code system at an early stage of your project, but you can also profit from (a) preparing a proposed sequence of chapters or sections into which your final written document will be divided and then (b) locating your coded guide questions in those chapters. For instance, here is such a plan for the dissertation on poetic forms, with the Arabic numerals indicating which of the guide questions would be addressed in the various chapters.

Chapter I: The Significance of Studying Verse Forms (1, 2, 3, 5, 6)
Chapter II: Methods of Investigating Verse Forms (4, 12)
Chapter III: Foot and Meter (6, 7, 11)

Shakespeare Theater Season at
Stratford on Avon

A chance to enter scores of wondrous lives—
Today to bray at Bottom's comic flight.
Tonight, delight with Windsor's merry wives.
Tomorrow, sorrow at the black Moor's plight.
For Lear, a tear at letting madness reign.
Macbeth, the death of virtue and of kings.
Sweet Juliet, beset by passion's pain.
From ordinary Will, such wondrous things.

*(7) Foot and meter—iambic pentameter*

*(8) Rhyme—Internal (today/bray, tonight/delight, etc.)*
*End-line rhyme scheme—ababcdcd*

*(10) Serious subject matter, serious verse form*

**Figure 3.1** Number-Coding a Quotation

SOURCE: Thomas, 1999, p. 2.

Chapter IV: Rhyme or No Rhyme (6, 8, 11)
Chapter V: Established Poetic Forms (6, 9, 11)
Chapter VI: Matching Form to Subject Matter (6, 10)
Chapter VII: Conclusion (3, 5, 6, 11)

The value of coding becomes apparent when you begin to draft one of your chapters. For example, when the author of the dissertation on verse forms prepares to write Chapter III: Foot and Meter, she simply gathers all of her notes that bear the code numbers 6, 7, or 11, and arranges them in the order in which she plans to write about the topics that the different notes address. If she had not coded the notes, she would have needed to inspect every item in her entire collection of references in order to locate the ones that concerned foot and meter.

A second example illustrates a different way of coding material from the literature. The project in this case is a thesis titled *School Principals' Leadership Styles—A Comparative Study.* The focus of the literature search is not a set of questions but, rather, a list of topics. And the code consists not of numbers but of key words. Some researchers prefer key words to numbers because they find it easier to remember what the words refer to than what the numbers signify. Here, then, is the list of topics that are the object of the literature search, with the topics accompanied by their code words.

| *Code* | *Topics* |
|---|---|
| DEFINE | Definitions of leadership, characteristics of leaders. |
| CRITERIA | Ways of distinguishing between good leadership and bad leadership. |
| THEORY | Theories of leadership—the variables that contribute to leadership and how those variables interact to produce good or bad results. |
| STYLE | Leadership-style classification systems (typologies, taxonomies). Advantages and disadvantages of each system. |
| DECIDE | Typical kinds of decisions that principals face. |
| CAUSE | Ways of classifying (typologies, taxonomies) the factors (causes) that influence principals' decisions (thought patterns and actions). Advantages and disadvantages of each way. |
| STRAT | Strategies principals use for improving a school's social climate and efficiency. |
| METHOD | Methods of studying leadership and research instruments used. Advantages and disadvantages of each method. |

Figure 3.2 shows how two photocopied segments of a book titled *Staying on Track* (Brubaker & Coble, 2007) have been coded in the margin adjacent to the passages. For each passage, the book's page number is added below the code word and the full bibliographic reference is written on the back of the sheet.

The same sort of margin notation can be used to identify concepts, theories, appraisals, viewpoints, and the like that are not quoted directly but are summarized in the thesis writer's own words. Here is an example from the leadership-styles project. It's in the form of a note written on a card that includes not only the writer's summary but also the source of the information (Figure 3.3).

| | |
|---|---|
| CAUSE<br>P. 10 | In surveying assistant principals, principals, and central office leaders, we were surprised at the degree of uniformity in their response as to the causes of assistant principal and principal derailment. We have categorized these responses in descending order of frequency as follows: (a) incompetence, (b) external political conflict, (c) internal political conflict, (d) difficulties with leadership processes, (e) diminished desire to learn and improve, (f) legal and/or moral problems, and (g) personal reasons. |
| STRAT<br>P. 36 | If you pick up almost any article or book on curriculum or instructional leadership, you will discover the following two common findings: (a) the formally appointed leader of the organization, such as the principal or superintendent, sets the tone for all within the organization; and (b) staff development or inservice education is a major vehicle the formally appointed leader can and should use as a teacher educator, administrator, or both. |

**Figure 3.2** Word-Coding Passages

As with the dissertation about verse forms, the organization pattern for the thesis about leadership can be predicted at an early stage of the project by the author asking himself two questions:

1. If I knew nothing about school principals as leaders, what would I wish to learn? In other words, what information would I need in order to become well informed about the leadership role of principals?
2. In what sequence should that information be presented so that I would find it easy to understand?

The first question identifies the desired content for the thesis. The second focuses on the manner in which such content can effectively be presented—the sequence of ideas that readers will meet. Estimating ahead of time what a thesis' organizational pattern should be serves to sharpen your focus as you develop your project. In particular, it helps you distinguish among four sources of the contents—(a) the professional literature, (b) your faculty advisors and fellow students, (c) information you may collect directly by means of testing, an opinion survey, an experiment, or the like, and (d) the creative thinking that you must do on your own as you devise hypotheses, theories, methods of gathering data, and interpretations of what you discover from your investigation. Consider the following organization of the school-principals project that the student could preplan, after deciding that the study will focus on the styles of eight representative school principals. The preplan also indicates the intended location of the word-coded material from the professional literature.

| | |
|---|---|
| Theory | Resource-mobilization theory proposes that the best leaders are skilled at collecting the resources needed to do the job. |
| p. 565 | Leaders do this by forming coalitions with existing groups and organizations, getting financial support, and generating effective political pressure. |
| | Turner, Ralph H. (1994). Collective behaviour. Encyclopaedia Britannica (Vol. 16). Chicago: Encyclopaedia Britannica. |

**Figure 3.3** Word-Coding Note Cards

**PART I: A Foundation for Studying Principals' Leadership Styles**

Chapter 1: The School Principal and Alternative Conceptions of Leadership
DEFINE, CRITERIA, THEORY, STYLE

Chapter 2: Principals as Decision Makers
DECIDE

**PART II: The Styles of Eight Principals**

Chapter 3: The Research Design
METHOD, STYLE, CAUSE

Chapter 4: Creating the Interview Plan, Questionnaire, and Observation Plan
METHOD, DECIDE

Chapter 5: Administering the Interview and Questionnaire

Chapter 6: Conducting Observations
METHOD

Chapter 7: Classifying the Responses
STYLE, STRAT, THEORY

Chapter 8: Interpreting the Results
THEORY

**PART III: Implications of the Study**

Chapter 9: Conclusions and Suggestions for Enhancing Leadership Skills
THEORY, STRAT

It should be apparent that such a preplan may require changes as the research progresses. But even in its initial sketchy form, the plan serves as a useful guide to (a) what the professional literature can contribute and (b) where the coded material from the literature can suitably be placed.

Clearly, there is nothing sacrosanct about the two methods of coding illustrated above. They are merely samples. You may prefer to create a system of your own that is better suited to your taste and work habits.

How and where to record material: Prior to the arrival of the photocopy machine and personal computers, the time-honored way of extracting quotations and ideas from the literature was to take handwritten notes on 3-by-5-inch or 5-by-7-inch cards, or on tablet or notebook paper. This may still be a useful method. However, at an increasing rate, researchers are photocopying pages of books and journals and of microfilmed newspapers. If they have a computer at hand as they peruse a book or journal, they take notes or record quotations directly on the computer. In some cases, if their speaking does not disturb other people—as it can in a library or classroom—they enter their notes orally into a tape recorder or into a computer.

Next, consider the advantages of searching the Internet's World Wide Web.

## SEARCHING THE WORLD WIDE WEB

The Internet includes the World Wide Web, which had a collection of more than a 106 million websites by 2007, with thousands of more sites added each week. During 2006, there were 30.9 million new sites on the Web, shattering the record of 17.5 million in 2005 (Netcraft, 2006). Each website is a particular organization's or individual's Internet address at which information can be found. One website may be a university library, listing the books, journals, and reports housed there. Another site may be a newspaper, displaying the articles published recently and in the past. A third site may be the biography of an author and a list of the author's published writings. A fourth may show the articles from an academic journal, current and past. A fifth may contain *blogs*—a collection of one or more person's thoughts about particular topics. And so the variety of sites goes on and on, providing an astonishing, rich storehouse of facts, theories, and opinions that can be valuable resources for students who are writing theses or dissertations.

To take advantage of the World Wide Web's resources, you need (1) a computer that has access to the Internet via (2) an Internet service provider, (3) a browser in your computer, and (4) one or more search engines.

An *Internet service provider (ISP)* connects your computer to the Internet. There are many sources of providers. Some are commercial ventures (such as *ATT Yahoo, America Online, Earthlink, Net Zero, Charter*) for which you pay a monthly fee. Other ISPs are operated by such organizations as educational institutions, businesses, local governments, philanthropic groups, fraternal societies, and more. You may wish to use your own college's or university's service, for which you need not pay a fee.

A *web browser* is a program (software) in your computer that enables you to find printed text, pictures, and other information on a web page at a website on the World Wide Web or on a local area computer network. Popular browsers include *Internet Explorer, Netscape Navigator, Mozilla Firefox,* and *Opera.*

To make your use of the World Wide Web most efficient, you need a *search engine*—a computer program that finds documents related to specified key words and returns to your computer screen a list of the documents found by the key words. Typical search engines are *Google, Ask, Yahoo, Alta Vista,* and *Excite.*

The Internet is rapidly overtaking library holdings as a source of information for theses and dissertations. An Internet search is conducted by the same general method suggested earlier for a library search. That is, key words are entered into a search engine in order to generate a list of websites relevant to those words. Typically, several thousand sites will thus be generated, with the ones that seem most pertinent and recent usually in the early part of the list. Each entry whose title seems useful can then be opened and the contents inspected.

One great advantage of a computer search is that material—such as a journal article or a biography—that appears on the screen can usually be copied, either the entire article or selected passages, and can be pasted into a word-processing file in your computer. Thus, whenever you wish to quote from the stored material, you simply lift out (copy) the segment you want and paste it into your manuscript.

Our earlier suggestions about taking care to accurately record the source of material taken from books and periodicals (author's name, title of the source, date, publisher, page numbers) apply equally to material taken from a website.

One important difference between academic books and Internet websites is that of quality filtering. The process of publishing scholarly books and journals usually includes a quality-assessment component. That is, when editors estimate that submitted manuscripts might be worth publishing, they typically send the manuscripts to be reviewed by people who are regarded as experts in the realm of the manuscripts' subject matter. Those experts are asked to judge the quality of the manuscripts' content from several viewpoints, including (a) the contribution the work makes to the field of knowledge, (b) the factual accurateness of the material, (c) the clarity of the author's prose, and (d) the kinds of readers who might value such a product. Therefore, books and journals that are thus "refereed" by experts can more likely be trusted than materials that do not go through such a filtering procedure. Furthermore, assessments of books also often appear after the books' publication, with such assessments in the form of reviews and letters to the editors of periodicals, such as academic journals. However, the Internet has no such quality-filtering process. People can put anything they wish on web pages to which they have access. Therefore, students who collect information from the World Wide Web must determine for themselves which information—or which sites—can be trusted and which cannot. In effect, greater care in accepting material from the Internet for use in a thesis or dissertation is usually required than in accepting material from books and journals that have been vetted by well-informed scholars.

So, what procedures can students adopt to help ensure that material on websites is trustworthy? In answer, they can usefully consider consistency across websites, author qualifications, and author perspectives.

The phrase *consistency across websites* means how much different websites agree on factual matters. For example, a graduate student whose thesis focuses on the use of elicit drugs by elementary-school children can enter the words "drugs elementary school pupils" into the search engine Google and thereby generate more than a million relevant websites. Some of those sites will include statistics about the frequency of pupils' drug use. The graduate student can then compare the statistics from one site with those from other sites in order to judge how consistent the figures are across sites and thus estimate which data are probably the most accurate.

*Author qualifications* refers to the characteristics of the writer of material on a web page that qualify the author to speak authoritatively about the subject matter of that page. Indicators of expertise can include the writer's official position, educational background, reputation in the subject-matter field, past publications, and awards received. Also useful are the opinions that other people have expressed about the author. For instance, imagine that a doctoral candidate, whose research concerns the societal effects of global warming, is hunting the World Wide Web for estimates of such influence. The estimate on one web page is from a professor of astrophysics in a major American university, a professor who is also a contributing editor to the journal *Science* and the author of two books on global warming published by a university press. Now, compare that web page with another site whose author is a radio talk-show host and standup comic with a high school education. Which of the two websites will likely contain more trustworthy information about societal effects of global warming?

*Author perspectives* are the personal values and interests that creators of web page contents seek to promote through the views they express. Thus, in assessing the material on a web page, it is helpful to consider the vantage point—the bias—from which an author is writing. So, what difference does it make for your research if website material that you use is from an evangelical Christian rather than from an atheist? Or from a Democrat rather than a Republican? Or from the chief executive officer of an international corporation rather than a save-the-wildlife society?

In summary, caution is necessary in using material from websites, because the Internet operates without any monitoring of the quality of the information and opinions posted there. Of course, the same cautions are also applicable to print material—books, journals, magazines, reports—but the dangers of misinformation and unacceptable bias are greater in the case of the Internet.

Finally, it is important to recognize that computer searches can be valuable at all stages of preparing a thesis or dissertation. For example, here is a list of the junctures in the dissertation process at which one doctoral candidate—writing about the management of educational institutions—conducted web searches. The Internet aided her in:

*Selecting a research topic by means of*

Surveying the literature in field of study
Researching areas of special interest
Identifying experts in my field, who were then contacted by e-mail

*Developing methodology by*

Inspecting various methods of inquiry
Reviewing case studies in my field
Reviewing research related to my topic
Identifying possible sites for conducting a case study
Investigating features of the selected site that could affect my project
Reviewing kinds of software suitable for conducting qualitative research

*Collecting data by*

Locating interview and observation sites
Examining online documents describing similar case studies
Reviewing interview and observation strategies
Identifying ways of gaining interviewees' trust

## ERRORS OF JUDGMENT

Three sins authors may commit when citing published sources are those of (a) overloading their review of the literature, (b) plagiarizing, and (c) failing to keep complete, accurate bibliographic information, and then attempting to fill in missing information by guessing.

## Overloading a Literature Review

When a student's plan for a project includes a chapter dedicated to a survey of the professional literature, some students—perhaps many—hate to leave out any item they unearthed during their search. They feel it a shame to omit any reference that took them hours to locate and digest. They also believe that the more citations, the better. The longer their list of resources, the greater the chance that readers will credit them with being a thorough, painstaking scholar. But such an approach may well give quite the opposite impression. Mindlessly including everything even remotely related to the research topic is apt to produce an ill-organized, puzzling conglomeration whose contribution to the project is difficult to imagine. If your supervising committee members are astute and careful in their assessment of your work, they will regard an overloaded review as evidence of incompetence.

You can avoid this error if you specify precisely what your review is intended to accomplish and then assiduously apply that intention as you select what to include and what to exclude. For example, if the purpose of the review is to locate your study within a relevant domain of literature, then you are obligated to (a) clearly define the nature of that domain by describing the criteria you use for determining what sorts of studies belong within that body of work and (b) show how your study meets those criteria—that is, explain how your work relates to the other theories and empirical investigations that you have found in the specified domain. Items from the literature that fail to meet your standards should be left out. Consequently, readers of your finished product should never be puzzled about the function that any of your literature references perform in your study.

## Plagiarizing

Plagiarism is the act of claiming to be the author of material that someone else actually wrote. The most obvious form of plagiarism in theses and dissertations is the inclusion of passages that ostensibly are the student's own words but actually have been copied from someone else's work. Readers get the impression that the student is claiming to be the original author whenever passages are not placed within quotation marks (or not indented on both the right and left) and are not accompanied with the name of the original author of the material.

Academic plagiarism is nothing new. But what has been new since the latter years of the twentieth century is the ease with which writings on virtually any topic can be misappropriated with little risk of detection. The principal instrument responsible for a recent rapid rise in academic plagiarism has been the Internet, which John Barrie (a developer of software for detecting web plagiarism) calls "a 1.5 billion-page searchable, cut-and-pasteable encyclopedia" (cited in Bartlett, 2001). When thesis or dissertation writers, while searching the World Wide Web, happen on a particularly felicitous phrasing of ideas that are useful for their project, they may be tempted to lift the passage verbatim and insert it into their manuscript without acknowledging the source of the material. This practice is particularly egregious when the stolen passage is extensive or when the student steals numerous passages. Two ways to avoid plagiarizing are to (a) place the material in quotation marks and cite the original source or (b) rephrase the sense of the passage, without using quotation marks. But even with the rephrasing, it is appropriate to cite the source.

Whereas plagiarism has become far easier these days as a result of the Internet, it is also the case that members of thesis and dissertation committees have become increasingly adept at discovering word theft. And students caught passing other people's writing off as their own need to recognize that they are placing their academic careers in jeopardy. Not only are professors who are experts in a field of knowledge likely to recognize the original sources of writings lifted from that field, but present-day computer technology has equipped faculty members with web-plagiarism checkers or verifiers.

The typical web checker is an Internet service that works the following way. A student's thesis or dissertation is entered into the checker's website. The website is programmed to compare the contents of the manuscript with the contents of thousands of documents on the World Wide Web. A report is then sent back to the professor, showing how much of the student's work is identical to, or highly similar to, documents on the Web; and the report identifies what those original documents were.

One of the dangers of even a limited amount of plagiarism is that it alerts the student's advisor and committee members to the possibility that considerably more of the student's work has been the product of someone else's brain. As a British colleague of ours has warned, "The thirteenth stroke of the clock casts doubt not only on itself but on the other twelve strokes as well."

**Filling In by Guessing**

Accurately recording bibliographic information is not always a simple task when you are obliged to survey scores of books, periodicals, and Internet websites while pressured by time and competing responsibilities. Thus, you may either neglect to record the source of a quotation or piece of information or fail to include all elements of a source—the author's initials, the year of publication, the location of the publishing company, or the page numbers for a chapter in a book of collected works. Thus, when preparing the final version of your bibliography, you can find yourself scurrying to the Internet or the campus library to retrieve the missing information. Your problem is compounded if the book you need has been checked out by another of the library's clients or if the volume originally had been furnished to you by another university via the interlibrary-loan service. Under these conditions, students sometimes feel tempted to create the missing data by guessing. They estimate what the author's initials or the chapter page numbers might have been. They may rationalize this behavior by reasoning that "Nobody's going to use my references to find the book" and "No one will discover what I've done, and it's insignificant anyway."

There are at least two difficulties with thus yielding to temptation. First, the essence of research and scholarship is to be as truthful as possible. You expect the authors of the books and periodicals you read to be honest and as accurate as they know how. Therefore, as a scholar, you bear that same responsibility. Other people may, indeed, use your bibliography in their own search for resources, so they suffer whenever your citations are inaccurate.

Second, you may get caught at falsifying information. Some members of your faculty advisory committee are likely to be well acquainted with the body of literature from which you have drawn material included in your project. So when they review your list of references, they may spot items containing false information. These items are usually viewed as the result of carelessness, like typos and misspellings, and you will be asked to correct them. But readers may also suspect that you manufactured the erroneous material, and this makes them wonder about the accuracy of the entire thesis or dissertation. In sum, if your project is to make a proper contribution to the world of scholarship, it's worth your time and energy to be as correct as possible in identifying the sources of material derived from your survey of the literature.

## PLANNING CHECKLIST

As an aid in applying the contents of this chapter to your own thesis or dissertation, you may find it helpful to carry out the following activities.

1. In the following list, place an **X** on the line in front of each function that your search of the literature is intended to perform:

    ____ Help me find a suitable research problem.

    ____ Locate my study within a field of related knowledge.

    ____ Demonstrate my command of that field of knowledge.

    ____ Identify inadequacies of knowledge in that field.

    ____ Show what contribution my study can make to a specified domain.

    ____ Identify hypotheses or theories to apply or to test in my study.

    ____ Suggest methods and instruments for gathering information for my study.

    ____ Identify strengths and weaknesses of different data-gathering methods.

    ____ Suggest ways of classifying my data (typologies, taxonomies).

    ____ Suggest statistical or graphic treatments for my data.

    ____ Suggest ways of interpreting the results of my study.

    ____ Suggest practical applications of the results of my project.

    ____ Illustrate the form that my final report can profitably assume.

    ____ Other (specify)________________________________

2. For each of the functions that you checked under item 1, make a list of key terms you plan to use to guide your search of the literature.

3. Specify the bibliographic form you will adopt for listing references at the end of your thesis or dissertation. For each type of resource that you will use in the literature, prepare a sample reference to guide note-taking during the literature search. Specifically, prepare a sample for (a) a book by a single author, (b) a book by multiple authors, (c) an edited book, (d) a journal article by a single author, (e) a journal article by multiple authors, (f) a periodical article with no specified author, (g) an encyclopedia entry, (h) a newspaper article, (i) an unpublished conference paper, (j) an unpublished thesis or dissertation, (k) a personal communication to you (letter, phone call, e-mail), (l) a report on the Internet, and any other type of resource you plan to use.

4. Specify the form in which you will cite references within the body of your thesis or dissertation. Create a sample of this form for each type of literature resource that you intend to consult.

5. In the following list, place an **X** on the line in front of each method or medium you intend to use in searching the literature:

 ____ Books in the campus library (titles, tables of contents, indexes)

 ____ Loose and bound journals in the campus library (inspect article titles, read articles' abstracts, inspect studies cited, read research methods, inspect research instruments, read final conclusions)

 ____ Books and periodicals in public libraries

 ____ Personal computer (at home or in a campus office) with access to the Internet.

 ____ Computer terminal in the campus library, my academic department, or the student center so as to search the Internet and World Wide Web

 ____ Professors' collections of books and periodicals

 ____ Friends' collections of books and periodicals

 ____ Newspapers and periodicals to which I or my acquaintances subscribe

 ____ Other (specify) ________________________________

6. Do you plan to use a code system for identifying the functions that material from the literature is expected to perform? If so, describe the form that the codes will assume, and specify the meaning of each item in your code system.

7. Do you intend to prepare a tentative outline of the likely contents of your thesis or dissertation and the sequence in which those contents will be presented in the final document? If so, describe the sections or chapters into which the document will be divided, give the title of each section or chapter, tell what it will contain (what its function will be in the overall project), including what kind of material from the literature will be located in each chapter (this can be shown by code numbers or letters).

8. In the following list, place an **X** on the line in front of each method you intend to use for recording information that you extract from the literature:

 ____ Handwritten note cards

 ____ Handwritten notes on tablet or notebook paper

 ____ Typewritten notes

 ____ Entries in a computer, saved on a hard disk and/or floppy diskettes

 ____ Photocopied passages of publications

 ____ A computer attached to a scanner that is equipped with optical-character-recognition software to copy passages of printed material into a word-processing program so the material can be formatted and edited

## STAGE II

# CHOOSING AND DEFINING RESEARCH TOPICS

The three chapters at Stage II focus on a pair of tasks—selecting the problem you intend to study and devising a proposal that enables your advisors to judge the suitability of your problem and the way you propose to solve it.

Chapter 4 (Sources and Types of Research Problems) reviews a variety of sources from which you can generate research topics and proposes ways to distinguish between good and bad options.

Sometimes, as an important part of their research problem, students wish to create or adapt a theory, but they say they don't know how to go about it. Chapter 5 (Building and Adapting Theories) is intended to help meet that need.

Chapter 6 (Stating the Problem and Its Rationale) moves beyond identifying an appropriate topic to the next step of casting the problem in the form of a research proposal that makes clear why your problem is a good one and how you plan to resolve it.

FOUR

# SOURCES AND TYPES OF RESEARCH PROBLEMS

*"I've gone through a lot of the literature, and it seems that all the good research topics have been used up. What's left for me to work on?"*

One long-honored tradition in academia is that of professors assigning thesis and dissertation topics to their advisees instead of having students create topics of their own. Or, if faculty supervisors don't actually assign topics, they may at least suggest what their advisees might study. There are both advantages and disadvantages to assigned research problems. Perhaps the most obvious advantage of adopting a professor's proposal is that you ensure that your mentor enthusiastically endorses your project. Assigned topics are often part of a faculty member's own research program, with each student's topic representing one piece of a complex puzzle the professor is trying to solve. And if the research is funded by a financial grant, you may get paid for working on the portion that involves your thesis or dissertation. If a report of the research is published in a journal or in conference proceedings, you may also be credited as a coauthor. Or your mentor may acknowledge your participation in a footnote to a journal article or book chapter. Furthermore, accepting a topic that is part of someone else's research not only relieves you of hunting for a research problem, but it may also lighten your burden of devising a design, creating data-gathering instruments, and interpreting the results. Those tasks may already have been performed by the professor or by his or her staff. However, depending so heavily on others for a research problem robs you of the opportunity to work out such matters for yourself. So, from the standpoint of gaining experience generating and solving problems on your own, an assigned topic that is accompanied by assigned research procedures may get you your degree with less pain, but it may not serve as the best preparation for future research you wish to pursue on your own.

Now, what about this chapter? If you have already been assigned a problem, you may wish to skip the chapter and move on to the next. Or, if you already have chosen a topic of your own, you may want to move directly to Chapter 6. However, if you are still in the market for a problem to investigate, then the following pages may prove useful.

The purpose of Chapter 4 is to answer two questions:

1. To what sources can I turn to find a good problem on which to focus my thesis or dissertation?

2. How can I distinguish between appropriate and inappropriate problems? In other words, how can I tell a good problem from a bad one?

## SOURCES AND KINDS OF PROBLEMS

There certainly is no shortage of worthy research problems if you know how to hunt. Perhaps the best way to generate problems is to cultivate the habit of critical reading and listening. This means constantly bringing questions to mind while you are poring over books and journals and while you witness lectures and discussions. The sorts of questions you pose identify kinds of problems to investigate. Beyond critical reading and listening, a further source of topics is that of problems met on the job, either on your own job or someone else's. In order to illustrate how such search strategies work, the following examples demonstrate specific ways of using critical reading/listening and on-the-job problems for discovering suitable topics.

### Critical Reading and Listening

Questions you ask about what you read or hear can concern (a) the significance or focus of an author's research topic, (b) the applicability of an author's results to other populations, times, or places, (c) a researcher's methods of collecting information, (d) ways data have been classified, (e) an author's theory of what causes events to occur as they do, (f) applications of theories, or (g) some combination of several of these matters.

### *Topic significance or focus*

An article you read or a lecture you attend may make you wonder: "Isn't that just trivia? Who would ever take that seriously? What's the importance of studying such stuff?" But can you then think of some way the topic could be recast to render it worth investigating? If so, you've generated a potential research topic.

### *Results applicability*

In all research, the information an investigator collects encompasses only a limited number of people, objects, activities, or events. For instance, a case study may focus on a single mentally gifted girl in Bavaria. A questionnaire survey may involve responses from 1,022 Labor Party members in Liverpool, England. An ethnographic investigation may focus on family structure in two Central American Mayan villages. An achievement-testing program may involve 37,000 students from schools in Hong Kong, Singapore, South Korea, and Taiwan. A historical account may trace the evolution of weaponry in Europe during the period 1700–1900.

Sometimes researchers are content to restrict their summaries and interpretations to only those people, institutions, and events they have directly studied. But authors frequently view such people and events as representatives of a broader class of phenomena, so the conclusions drawn from this sample are cast as generalizations applying to other phenomena that were not directly investigated—to other gifted children, to other Labor Party members, to other Indian villages, to other Asian students, or to other nations' weaponry during other time periods. Consequently, when you read such studies, you may wonder whether conclusions reached in a given context actually hold true for other places and times than those directly investigated. You may, therefore, choose to devise a *replication study,* adopting the same methods of gathering information that were used in the original investigation but applying those methods to a different sampling of people, institutions, or events. In doing so, you are conducting *comparative research,* identifying the likenesses and differences between the results of the original study and your own.

Two questions to guide your reading and listening as you search for replication possibilities are these: "Would the same conclusions result from studying a different sample of people, institutions, events, or time periods? What kind of sample might yield different results, and why?"

*Methods of collecting information*

There is usually more than one method of compiling information to answer a research question. Thus, one way to choose a research problem is to seek an answer to a question someone else has studied, but to employ a different method of gathering data. For example, consider the questions in Table 4.1 and some alternative ways to answer each question.

Now, imagine that you have read four different studies in an academic journal, with those studies designed to answer the four questions in Table 4.1. In each investigation, the method of gathering data was the first of the alternatives listed in the table. Imagine, also, that you select one of these questions as your thesis problem, because you believe a different data-collection procedure than the one used in the journal report would yield more informative results. Hence, for your project, you choose to answer the same question as the one in the published study, but you intend to adopt a different alternative for gathering information, or perhaps a combination of several alternatives. Consequently, the innovative contribution made by your thesis can be threefold. You will (a) introduce the academic community to your data-collection technique, along with a description of its strengths and limitations, (b) show how the results obtained with your procedure compare with the results reported in the journal, and (c) offer your estimate of why the outcomes of the two studies were similar and/or different.

Questions that can direct your hunt for potential research opportunities that relate to information-gathering methods include: "Would the outcomes of the study that I'm now reading have been different if another data-collection procedure had been used? In what way might the outcomes have differed? What other data-collection procedure might I use that could produce more valuable—or at least different—results?"

*Ways of classifying information*

Each time you collect information to answer a research question, you must organize your data in a form that permits a description, analysis, and presentation of the results to your intended audience. This means you must adopt a system for classifying your information. Such systems are often referred to as typologies or taxonomies. Therefore, one way of finding a research problem can be that of substituting a scheme for classifying data that differs from the scheme used in an existing study. In effect, you produce a methodologically innovative thesis or dissertation.

For example, let's assume that you've read a report of people's attitudes about government controls over individuals' rights to own guns. The woman who conducted the survey had compiled opinions by means of interviewing

**Table 4.1** Data-Collection Options

| *Research Questions* | *Alternative Data-Collection Methods* |
| --- | --- |
| What roles within the family are typically found in traditional Zuñi Indian villages, how do family members learn their roles, and what sanctions are applied to those who fail to perform their roles properly? | ____ Observe representative families over a three-month period.<br>____ Interview Zuñi villagers of different ages.<br>____ Analyze published writings about Zuñi family life.<br>____ Collect questionnaire responses from residents of a variety of villages. |
| How do critical incidents in the lives of young adolescents (ages 12–14) affect their personal-social adjustment? | ____ Observe ten 12-year-olds for a period of two years.<br>____ Interview 14-year-olds about critical incidents in their lives over the past two years.<br>____ Conduct a questionnaire survey of 12- to 14-year-olds to identify critical incidents and results of those events.<br>____ Interview parents of adolescents.<br>____ Analyze published studies of adolescents' problems. |
| How do voters react to negative political advertising on television (negative means attacking opposing candidates' policies, wisdom, integrity, or moral character)? | ____ Compare the percentage of each candidate's negative ads with the percentage of votes each candidate received in the election.<br>____ Conduct an experiment by showing only negative ads to one group of respondents, only positive ads to a second group, and a mixture of positive and negative ads to a third group. Then ask respondents how they would vote in an election involving the candidates who sponsored the ads.<br>____ Interview voters by telephone.<br>____ Interview voters face to face.<br>____ Collect voters' questionnaire answers. |
| In what ways, and to what degree, are schools' curriculum contents (the subject matter and skills taught) influenced by liberal as compared to conservative school board members? | ____ Attend a series of school board meetings to witness discussions of curricula.<br>____ Analyze minutes of school board meetings.<br>____ Interview school administrators.<br>____ Interview board members.<br>____ Summarize the results of published studies of school board activities. |

respondents over the phone. She then reported her results in terms of (a) males versus females and (b) the strength and direction of each respondent's attitude in terms of four categories—*strongly in favor of controls, somewhat in favor, somewhat opposed,* and *strongly opposed.* However, when you read the study, you were dissatisfied with the interpretation of the results. You believed the work would have been far more valuable if a different system of classifying answers had been used. For instance, perhaps you would like to learn how respondents' attitudes about gun controls might be related to their (a) age, (b) level of formal education, (c) family status (married versus single, having children versus being childless), (d) occupation, (e) religious affiliation, and (f) gender. Therefore, in your own study, you plan to conduct a telephone survey in which you gather these six kinds of information about respondents when you ask their opinions of gun controls. Because an interpretation that can be drawn from the results of any research venture is constrained by the classification system used, you will be equipped to draw a more sophisticated, detailed set of conclusions than those drawn by the author of the published study.

*Creating or revising theories*

As suggested earlier, a theory in its most basic form is (a) a description of components, variables, or factors and (b) a description of how those components interact to (c) produce some outcome. Thus, theories are explanatory in that they propose how and why things happen as they do. In your survey of how other scholars have diagnosed problems in your field of interest, you may be dissatisfied with the explanations they offered, so you try to think of a better way—or at least an alternative way—to account for what occurred. In other words, you create a theory of your own or perhaps a variation of someone else's model. As a result, your thesis or dissertation takes the form of an explication, and perhaps an application, of your theory. The following two examples illustrate ways to invent a research topic of this sort.

The first example is the case of a hypothetical doctoral candidate interested in the fate of educational reforms. After reading a host of evaluations of educational reform efforts, large and small, he realizes that educational innovations often become bogged down, with some of them dying completely and others falling well short of the success envisioned by their proponents. Our doctoral student is particularly curious about how analysts account for reform failures. In other words, he's interested in theories of the success and failure of educational innovations. In his survey of the professional literature, he discovers a variety of factors that ostensibly account for the outcomes of educational change efforts, such factors as (a) available financial resources, (b) ways of presenting reform proposals, (c) the qualities of the people responsible for implementing a reform, (d) how many people will be affected by the innovation, and more. But one factor that he thinks has been overlooked is that of the risk people face when they are expected to participate in an educational change. Therefore, as his dissertation problem, he takes on the challenge of formulating a *risk theory* to explain, at least partially, why some educational innovations succeed better than others. His risk theory is founded on the following proposition:

> The word *risk* means the likelihood that undesirable consequences will result from an action. The term *educational risk estimate* refers to people's expectation that they will suffer some sort of loss if they accept a role in an educational-change project. *Positive potential* is the opposite of risk. Positive potential refers to the likelihood that people will experience personally desirable consequences from their participation in an educational reform. The amount of effort they will exert, either to support or to defeat an innovation, is determined by the relationship between the amount of risk and amount of positive potential they expect. Thus, a person's effort can be computed by the formula $E = p - r$. In other words, positive potential minus risk equals the effort an individual will expend.

Now, the student's task in developing his dissertation consists of (a) proposing variables or conditions that influence people's perception of risks and of positive potentials, (b) defending those variables with logical analysis and empirical evidence, and (c) explaining how such variables interact to determine (d) the amount of effort individuals expend to support or to thwart an intended educational change.

A second example illustrates one way a current social concern may motivate a student to focus her dissertation on theory construction. A doctoral candidate in anthropology, inspired by the recent feminist movement, reads accounts of women's roles in Dakota Indian societies and disagrees with several interpretations she finds there. She believes the writers have given too little attention to how Dakota women's social contexts and events in their lives have altered their roles over the twentieth century. In an effort to correct these oversights, she plans to write a dissertation titled "An Ecological, Significant-Events Theory of the Evolution of Women's Roles in Dakota Cultures." The ecological aspect is based on the fact that Dakota women live in different social settings, which influence the roles they assume. Some live on reservations, some in small towns, some in cities. Each of these environments affects women's roles in different ways. The significant-events aspect derives from the doctoral candidate's conviction that changes in women's roles are not properly understood in terms of time periods, such as one decade compared to another, but are best viewed in terms of events that alter women's lives. Thus, the dissertation will not be divided into chronological periods but, rather, into sequences of significant events. Some events are societywide, such as the extension of voting rights to women in 1920. Others are individual and come at different times in different women's lives, such as marriage, the birth of a child, or moving to a new location. Therefore, the two principal variables on which the student's theory is built are *social contexts* and *significant events.* Each of these variables will be divided into subcategories—(a) types of social settings in which women live and (b) types of events that significantly alter women's roles. To gather evidence about such matters, the researcher plans (a) to read accounts of life in Native American cultures during the twentieth century (particularly Dakota cultures) and (b) to spend the summer interviewing Dakota women—those living on a reservation and those living in a town or city.

The foregoing pair of examples illustrate only two approaches to theory building. A more detailed description of how to create or adapt a theory is offered in Chapter 5.

*Applying theories*

Whereas some students' projects involve creating theory, far more consist of applying existing theory to new situations. Here are four examples.

***A seven-factor theory of intelligence:*** The model of human ability offered by Harvard University psychologist Howard Gardner proposes that intelligence is not a singular, unified personal power that operates with equal effectiveness in all aspects of life. Instead, intelligence is more accurately conceived to be seven separate types of ability or *intelligences* that make their separate contributions to the adequacy of people's performance in life's endeavors. The seven focus on (1) use of language, (2) logical-mathematical analysis, (3) spatial representation, (4) musical thinking, (5) the use of the body to solve problems or to make things, (6) an understanding of other individuals (a form of social intelligence), and (7) an understanding of oneself (Gardner, 1993).

An elementary school teacher, for her master's degree in education, creates activities for third-grade pupils that offer them practice in each of Gardner's seven types of intelligence. The aim of the activities is to promote children's development in all seven types of aptitude. She entitles her project "A Frames-of-Mind Curriculum for Third Graders."

***Social-exchange theory:*** According to social-exchange theory, an individual who benefits from another person's acts is obligated to reciprocate by furnishing benefits to that person in turn. For many common types of social interaction, proper exchange is dictated by cultural tradition in the form of expectations about fairness, expectations that assume the form of *exchange norms.* Such norms are adopted in a culture as devices for coercing the parties in a social transaction to abide by what is considered fair. Members of society impose social pressure to encourage people to comply with those norms. The extent to which people abide by exchange norms influences their status in the society's hierarchy of respect, prestige, and power. "When fairness does not occur [that is, when the norms are violated], the norms compel the party who fails to be fair to accept a degradation of status in the group as compensation for the imbalance" (Eve, 1986, p. 189).

A doctoral student in sociology intends to use social-exchange theory as the lens through which to study the rules that guide social interaction among members of a college sorority and among members of a college fraternity. The purpose is to discover (a) ways in which the sorority and fraternity are alike and different in their social-exchange attitudes and (b) individual differences among members within each of these societies in their social-exchange practices.

***A theory of historical revisionism:*** This theory is founded on the proposition that whenever a radical change of political power occurs, the newly installed leaders seek to revise historical records in order to legitimatize their right to govern and to cast their organization and efforts in a highly favorable light.

As an application of the theory to a new case, and to reveal conditions that affect the way the theory manifests itself in a particular instance, a political-science student plans to inspect histories of Cuba written by Cubans prior to Fidel Castro's rise to power and ones written in Cuba after he became head of the government.

***Site-based-management theory:*** A graduate student in the field of administration has become especially interested in the presently popular leadership theory that organizations should be flattened, shared decision making should be adopted, and power should be decentralized. The student has informally observed several organizations in which such site-based-management theory has been applied; and she recognizes that, instead of reducing the power of the officially appointed head of the organization, the plan gives the head even more power. For example, the chief executive officer (CEO) can use site-based-management advisory committees as scapegoats who are blamed when things go wrong in the organization. The CEO can also use consultation with advisory committees as a means of delaying the decision-making process. At the same time, all documents released by the CEO and the advisors laud site-based-management theory, avoiding any mention of the theory's shortcomings. It is also apparent that such documents can function as historical revisionism, enabling CEOs and their close associates to remap the administrative territory in a way that serves their political interests. Consequently, the student decides that this contrast between site-based-management theory and its practice is a hot topic worthy of formal research.

## Problems Encountered on the Job

Theses and dissertations are sometimes designed to solve problems met either in people's vocations or in their avocational pursuits. In the following discussion, the phrase *on the job* refers to either of these sources of research topics. The following examples illustrate a range of problems from on-the-job sources.

As a topic for her dissertation, a teacher on leave from an inner-city high school created a "next-step decision-making program" by which students who were doing poorly in school could follow a systematic plan for analyzing their difficulties and identifying (a) alternative next steps they might take and (b) the likely outcome of each alternative. Upon returning to her school for the upcoming academic year, the teacher intended to test the effectiveness of her model by trying out her scheme with failing students and, on the basis of the tryout, to evaluate and refine her program.

A political-science doctoral candidate, while serving as a volunteer in an election campaign for a state senator, planned to compare three methods of conducting pre-election polls. The aim was to determine how accurately each method predicted the outcome of the coming election. His polling methods involved three different methods of choosing the sample of respondents who would be asked to tell for whom they planned to vote.

For his master-of-business-administration degree, an employee in a stock-broker's office intended to analyze television advertisements sponsored by brokerage companies. His purpose was to learn (a) the kinds of investors at which different types of ads were aimed, (b) how ads sought to attract potential investors' attention, and (c) how the ads attempted to convince viewers that the company was trustworthy and efficient.

The daughter of the owner of a toy and hobby store planned to write her thesis on trends in the games that children and adolescents in the local region had played over the past half century. She would distribute questionnaires to local residents of different age levels, seeking information about (a) the games respondents had played during their childhood and adolescent years and (b) their knowledge of the terminology and rules associated with different games (such as marbles, hopscotch, run-sheep-run, Monopoly, baseball, soccer, Dungeons and Dragons, and Nintendo).

A student majoring in human development was asked her advice about which of two nursery schools was the more suitable for children ages two through four. Each school was identified with a local church—one with the Church of Latter Day Saints (Mormons) and the other with the Christian Science center. This inquiry about the two preschools influenced the student to take—as her research problem—(a) analyzing likenesses and differences in the underlying philosophies of the two religious persuasions (by studying

Joseph Smith's *The Book of Mormon* and Mary Baker Eddy's *Science and Health*), (b) identifying likenesses and differences in the conduct of the two schools (by observing ongoing activities in each school), and (c) comparing each school's philosophical foundation with its activities.

A high school counselor, pursuing a master's degree in clinical psychology, intended to trace, over a six-month period, the progress of four teenagers who were being treated for drug abuse. The purpose of the study was to delineate the interaction of factors in each youth's life that appeared to influence how well he or she recovered from drug use and initiated steps toward a constructive future.

While visiting an aunt, a sociology student attended a birthday party for the aunt's 90-year-old neighbor, a Black man who had served in the U.S. Army during World War II and subsequently played a key role in Martin Luther King's civil-rights movement. As various guests at the party described events in the man's career, the student recognized that the story of the neighbor's life would serve as an important document of African Americans' efforts to assume their rightful place in American society. Therefore, as his thesis the student chose to narrate the tale of the neighbor's career against a background of political and social events during the past 90 years, casting much of the work in the neighbor's own words as tape-recorded during a series of interviews that the student would conduct.

In summary, questions that come to mind as you pursue your occupation or engage in leisure-time activities may suggest a focus for a thesis or dissertation.

## HOW TO DISTINGUISH A GOOD TOPIC FROM A BAD ONE

We suggest nine criteria for judging the desirability of research problems.

### The Nine Criteria

The nine standards can be cast in the form of questions about your supervising committee, "true" research, the expected outcomes of your study, the feasibility of your methods, time constraints, skills and knowledge, equipment, personnel, and funding.

#### *Committee approval*

Do the members of your supervising committee approve of your proposed research problems?

When you submit your proposal to your major advisor and other committee members, it's not sufficient to give them only a title or a question that your project is intended to answer. In addition, you need to offer a rationale telling why your problem is a good one and what methods you plan to use for gathering and analyzing your data. This synopsis furnishes the information the professors need to judge your proposal. (Ways to define your topic and support it with a rationale are described in Chapter 6.)

If any of your committee members consider your proposal unacceptable, you either need to change your problem or need to replace dissenting committee members with ones who approve of your topic.

The following standards are among those that faculty members typically include in judging the worth of thesis and dissertation topics.

*True research*

Is the task you propose for yourself really research, or is it something else?

As noted in Chapter 2, faculty members often differ in their worldviews. For instance, positivists and postmodernists can disagree vehemently over what constitutes suitable research topics and methods of investigation. Therefore, it is important that your definition of research coincides with that of the faculty members who supervise and evaluate your work.

Furthermore, students' intentions, as reflected in how they phrase their project proposals, can suggest that they are not seeking an answer to a significant question but, rather, are trying to get readers to accept a belief that those students already cherish and wish to propagate. Such an intent can be implied when they introduce their project with such a phrase as "My purpose is to prove that . . ." or "I will demonstrate that . . ." or "This study will make it clear that. . . ." Therefore, if you know at the outset exactly what conclusions will be drawn at the end of your project, then the project qualifies as propagandizing or salesmanship rather than research.

*Outcome significance*

Will the results of your research be considered significant by the readers for whom your project is intended?

A topic that you select may qualify as research, yet still not be considered a suitable thesis or dissertation problem. One reason is that the task you pose for yourself may be too simple, in that it fails to represent the complexity and level of expertise expected of a person who deserves a graduate degree.

A second reason is that the answer you hope to derive from your investigation appears to be insignificant, so readers' would respond to your results with "So what?" or "Who cares?" Therefore, in originally presenting your topic, you are obliged to indicate for whom—and why—an answer to your research question is important.

*Feasible methodology*

Does your research problem appear solvable with the methods of investigation you have in mind?

Chapter 6 illustrates how to describe your research question in a fashion that convinces readers that the methodology you plan to adopt will produce credible answers.

*Time constraint*

Can the project be completed within the available time period?

In the dim past, some graduate school wag created the ABD academic degree (All-But-Dissertation), which might be awarded to that large corps of doctoral candidates who completed all the course work but never finished their dissertations. Consequently, faculty advisors are often concerned about how well students' research projects fit within the time constraints imposed by (a) the college or university (some schools set a limit of five years for completing a master's program and seven years for completing a doctorate) and (b) other time-consuming responsibilities in students' lives (a job, a family). Therefore, in presenting your project proposal to your advisors, you might profitably include a schedule of the phases that the project will involve and an estimate of the time required to complete each phase.

*Required knowledge and skills*

Do you already have the knowledge and skills required for completing your project? If not, how and when do you intend to acquire them?

Typically, doing a thesis or dissertation is a valuable learning experience, in that students are not expected at the outset to command all of the knowledge and skills required for completing their project. They gain that knowledge and skill as the project evolves. Thus, when you present your proposal to faculty members, you should be prepared to explain which knowledge and skills you already possess and which you will need to acquire. Sometimes it's not feasible for you to learn every specialized skill you need, such as complex computer programming or a foreign language, so you must depend on others for such services. Hence, it is well to estimate ahead of time what those services will be and where you intend to find them.

*Equipment and supplies*

What facilities will you need to carry out your project, and how do you intend to acquire them?

Although a description of needed equipment and supplies is usually not included in the written project submission, it is useful to have that information in mind in case it is requested by a professor who reviews your proposal.

*Personnel*

Who will perform each of the jobs required for carrying out your project?

Sometimes the student who creates the project will be the sole participant in the research and perform all the necessary tasks alone. But other projects require outside help—people to serve as interviewers, test correctors, statistical analysts, and more. Because faculty committee members may inquire about the personnel who will be involved in your research, you may wish to be prepared ahead of time to answer questions about whatever assistants you will need.

*Funds*

What expenses do you expect to incur, and how do you expect to pay for them?

Your principal advisor or other members of your supervising committee may ask how much your project is expected to cost and where the money will come from. In some instances they will ask only for a likely total amount. In others they will ask for a list of activities and equipment, along with an estimated cost of each. Even if your professors do not require a written expense projection, it is well to have in mind an estimated cost and source of funds.

To summarize, when you submit your research proposal to your advisors, you will typically be expected to furnish a written synopsis that defines the research problem or issue, suggests why it's important to study, and explains the methods you intend to use for resolving the problem or question. Members of supervising committees may also ask about the time period within which you expect to complete your project and the sources of the needed knowledge, skill, equipment, supplies, personnel, and funds required in your plan. Whether or not you include these additional matters in your written proposal, it's well to have answers to such queries in hand when your plan is being inspected.

## PLANNING CHECKLIST

Completing the following checklist may help you recognize the stage at which you now find yourself in selecting and describing your research problem.

1. Place an **X** on the line in front of each source that you intend to use (or have already used) for finding a research problem.

    ____ A faculty member who assigns or suggests topics

    ____ Questions that come to mind from my reading

    ____ Questions derived from what I heard in a lecture

    ____ Questions derived from class discussion

    ____ One or more of my fellow students who suggest a topic

    ____ Problems or issues met in my vocation or avocation

    ____ Other (specify)________________________________

2. On the line next to each of the following criteria, write the letter that best reflects how confident you are that your research proposal meets that standard.

    The code letters and their meanings are

    V = very confident D = doubtful

    S = somewhat confident U = unknown at this time

    ____ Outcome significance. The results of my work will be considered significant by the audience for which the project is intended.

    ____ Feasible methodology. My research problem can be satisfactorily solved by the investigative methods I plan to use.

    ____ Time constraint. I can complete the project within the expected time frame.

    ____ Required knowledge and skills. Either I already have the knowledge and skills required for completing my project, or I have a plan for acquiring them, or I know people who can provide them.

    ____ Equipment and supplies. I know what materials I will need to carry out my project and how to acquire them.

    ____ Personnel. I know who will perform each job required in the project.

    ____ Funds. I know what the cost of the project will be and how I will pay the costs.

    ____ Advisors' approval. My proposal is acceptable to my faculty advisors who will supervise and/or appraise my project.

FIVE

# BUILDING AND ADAPTING THEORIES

*"As an important part of my project, I'd really like to devise a theory, or at least I'd like to adapt one, but I don't know how to go about it."*

As already noted, the word *theory,* as we use it throughout this book, is a proposal about (a) what variables are important for understanding some phenomenon and (b) how those variables are related to each other. In previous chapters we have distinguished between (a) classification systems and (b) theories that involve propositions about what causes events to turn out as they do. However, in the present chapter we subsume both of those matters under the topic building and adapting theories and then differentiate between the two by calling the former classificatory theories and the latter explanatory theories. The two can be considered theoretical matters because both fit our generic definition. Each concerns variables important for understanding some phenomenon, and each proposes how those variables relate to each other. However, the two have different functions, as reflected in the second part of the definition—how variables relate to each other. Classificatory theories (classification systems, typologies, taxonomies) consist of categories into which phenomena (people, institutions, events) can be placed so their likenesses and differences can be compared and contrasted. Explanatory theories consist of proposals about how phenomena interact to produce an observed outcome. Thus, classificatory schemes emphasize comparison, while explanatory schemes emphasize cause. You may wish to create a new—or to revise an existing—classificatory or explanatory theory as part of your thesis or dissertation. Your theory may even be the central focus of the project.

The fourfold purpose of this chapter is to suggest (a) how to identify the need for a new or revised theory, (b) how to devise a classificatory theory, (c) how to devise an explanatory theory, and (d) how to revise an existing theory.

## THE NEED FOR A NEW THEORY

The need for a new or revised theory is revealed in your dissatisfaction with the classification systems or causal explanations you have found so far. Such dissatisfaction is generated by the discrepancy between what you have observed and what existing theories offer.

### Classificatory Theories

First, consider discrepancies that come to mind when you recognize that a classification system doesn't do justice to people or events you know about. For instance, in the field of politics it is common to categorize politicians as *conservatives* versus *liberals* or as *right-wingers, middle-of-the-roaders,* and *left-wingers.* But critics have complained that such divisions fail to depict the actual policies and practices of many politicians. Where do you place a politician whose economic proposals seem *conservative,* social-welfare policies *liberal,* and views of international relations *middle-of-the-road?* Hence, a better system is called for. That better system could take the form of a doctoral dissertation.

Problems are also found in categorizing people by ethnic status. One common system in the United States involves these divisions: Anglo, Black, Hispanic, Native American, Asian, and Pacific Islander. But what about people from European or Middle-Eastern heritage who are not of Anglo-Saxon stock, such as Italians, Romanians, and Arabs? Where do they belong? And if a woman has an African American father and an Anglo-American mother, is that woman to be classified as Anglo or Black? Again, a better typology is needed.

Another source of dissatisfaction may be your experience in trying to fit data into a classification system. Imagine that you have gathered cases of wrong-doing and now wish to classify them. You try a system found in New York State law, a system that includes such types as felony, misdemeanor, minor infraction, and the like. However, when you begin dividing your cases among the types, you find that many fit none of the categories, so you end up with a heavily populated class titled *miscellaneous* or *unclassifiable* in which you are obliged to place a great number of cases. Something is wrong with a classification scheme that fails to accommodate all cases. A better scheme is needed.

In summary, whenever you inspect a taxonomy that fails to provide classes that accommodate all of your data, you now have the opportunity to create a new classificatory theory or to revise an existing one.

### Explanatory Theories

In a similar manner, you may be dissatisfied with the causal explanation that a theory offers to account for a phenomenon. This is likely to occur when you have observed an event, either directly or vicariously in a newspaper or book or television newscast, and then hope to explain the outcome by means of a theory; but you find the explanation some theorist has proposed is unconvincing. To illustrate, assume that you have read about a pair of students who brought automatic pistols to their high school and shot nearly two dozen classmates. A theory proposed by a criminologist traces the cause to the interaction of three variables: (a) a lack of teachers' awareness of danger signs in students' behavior, (b) inadequate communication among school personnel, and (c) inadequate cooperation between school personnel and law enforcement bodies. However, you consider this analysis too simple, for it fails to address a variety of other causal factors that you think are relevant, such as parents' supervision over their children's activities, the patterns of social relationships among students, and more. Thus, as a thesis problem, you choose to propose a theory that includes more variables and envisions a more complex pattern of interrelationships among variables to explain such events as the school shooting.

Your dissatisfaction might also come in the midst of a study you are conducting. Imagine that you have collected 40 interviews with elderly residents of retirement communities. Your purpose has been to learn retirees' opinions about proposed changes to the U.S. government's social security provisions. With the tape-recorded results of your interviews in hand, you now need a theory that will explain why retirees didn't all agree in their judgments about the suggested changes. However, your hunt through the professional literature fails to reveal a theory that suits your need, so you decide to create your own model.

A third condition that motivates researchers to design explanatory theories is the researchers' simply wondering why something happens as it does.

"I'm wondering what caused him to lose the election, when he looked like a sure winner?" (political science)

"Why do some people consistently save money, while others spend every cent they get their hands on?" (economics, psychology)

"Under what conditions are children likely to tease or abuse their peers?" (psychology)

"What are games intended to accomplish in different cultures?" (anthropology)

"Why do some disadvantaged people go on welfare while others don't?" (social work)

If such events motivate researchers to create or revise theories, then how can they go about that task? The following paragraphs suggest a solution.

## BUILDING A CLASSIFICATORY THEORY

Apparently the most common approach to constructing a classification system consists of gathering a quantity of data (items, cases, examples, responses) within a defined domain, then seeking to create categories (a) into which all of the items can be fitted (no items are left over) and (b) that will convey a useful meaning when the categories are compared.

To illustrate one way this can be done, we draw on our own experience with a project conducted to reveal the consequences people would recommend for the misconduct of individuals involved in six cases of wrongdoing. We use this example because we have an insider's view of the approach used.

The six cases varied from wartime crimes to adolescents' lawbreaking and to automobile accidents. Here is the target question the research was expected to answer:

> In such moral incidents as those depicted in the six cases, what diverse rationales or types of moral reasoning will people adduce to support the consequences they would suggest for the wrongdoers in the incidents? (Thomas & Diver-Stamnes, 1993, p. 1)

A more specific aim of the study was to compare the responses to the cases by six different groups of students, ones from (a) a California inner-city high school located in a socioeconomically depressed neighborhood, (b) a Catholic high school in a medium-sized California city, (c) high schools and universities in Saudi Arabia, (d) a junior college in Honolulu, (e) a high school in a small Hawaiian community, and (f) a teacher-education program in Northern California. A classification system would be needed to categorize respondents' answers so that the six groups could be compared. Because no established system was available to perform this task, we generated a system out of questionnaire replies from the 542 questionnaire respondents. The process was as follows:

We began with no preconceived organizational categories into which we would fit people's rationales for their suggested consequences. In other words, we chose to be led by the data, extracting categories inductively by listing the respondents' answers from the questionnaires.

As a first step, answers that were either identical or seemed clearly an alternate phrasing of the same idea were combined as one item in the list. For example, such responses as "*Make the person suffer for the offense*" and "*The person should feel what it's like to be hurt*" formed a single item. Even with such combining of answers, the list was very long, extending to more than 200 items. In effect, although respondents were reacting to only six moral incidents, they provided a great diversity of moral-value rationales.

As a next step, the items that appeared similar in *intent* were conceived to form a cluster, and a word or phrase was created to reflect the apparent essence of that cluster. To illustrate, the two responses *"She was too young to know better"* and *"In the society he comes from, what he did was not considered improper"* were both placed in a category titled *Awareness of Right and Wrong.*

Finally, the labeled clusters were cast into five major groupings that appeared to represent broader generalizations than did the clusters. For instance, clusters labeled *Prevent Future Offenses by the Actor, Deter Others from Misconduct,* and *Wreak Revenge* were collected under the title *The purpose of the consequences.* This process resulted in five overarching categories that represented the general framework for the taxonomy, (1) moral values, (2) purpose, (3) conception of causality, (4) consequence feasibility, and (5) agent qualifications. Such a scheme enabled us to propose that the consequences people recommend for wrongdoing are the product of a pattern of thought that:
Usually includes:

*Moral values*—A set of values composed of moral principles (30 types) and the conditions under which those principles apply (44 types).

*The purpose of consequences*—A conviction about the function the consequence is intended to perform (15 types).

Occasionally includes:

*Conceptions of causality*—Beliefs about what caused the wrongdoing (15 types) and/or why the recommended consequence would likely accomplish its purpose (2 types).

*Consequence feasibility*—An estimate of how feasibly a suggested consequence could be implemented (6 types).

*Agent qualifications*—A belief about which individuals or agencies have the right and responsibility to assign consequences for wrongdoing (6 types).

> We thus judged that such a five-element scheme, with its subsumed clusters and types, would be useful for deriving a well-informed interpretation of (a) why people think their recommended consequences are just and practicable and (b) how the beliefs of one individual or one group compare with those of another. (Thomas & Diver-Stamnes, 1993, pp. 19–20)

The final version of the typology featured three levels of specificity. The first, most general level consisted of the above five major categories. The next, more specific level consisted of the clusters under a major category. The third, most specific tier contained particular types within a cluster. This scheme can be illustrated with the class titled *moral values,* which was divided into two sections: (a) principles and (b) conditions affecting the application of the principles. On Level I, Moral Values Conditions subsumes eight clusters that form Level II. The number of Level III types that appear under each Level II cluster is indicated in parentheses following each cluster title.

I. (b) Moral Values—conditions affecting the application of principles

Character traits (5)
Prior circumstances (2)
Concurrent circumstances (15)
Post-incident circumstances (12)
Extent of damage (4)
Legal considerations (1)
Value compatibility (1)
Fair chance (4)

On Level III, the way that types of conditions were described within a cluster can be illustrated with three items in the *fair chance* cluster (Table 5.1). Each type was cast in two parallel forms: (a) conditions warranting less severe aversive consequences on the left and (b) conditions warranting more severe aversive consequences on the right. A quoted example from statements by participants in the study is included with each type as a more precise guide for people who are applying the taxonomy in classifying respondents' opinions.

The typology resulting from the foregoing process was then used to classify the answers offered by the 542 participants in the moral-reasoning study.

**Classification Systems' Resources**

Books illustrating typologies in the social sciences and humanities include:

American Psychiatric Association. (1994). *Diagnostic and statistical manual of mental disorders* (4th ed.). Washington, DC: Author.

Bailey, K. D. (1994). *Typologies and taxonomies: An introduction to classification techniques.* Thousand Oaks, CA: Sage.

Bloom, B. S. (1956). *Taxonomy of educational objectives: Cognitive domain (Handbook I).* New York: McKay.

Crovello, T. J. (Ed.). (1992). Classification, scientific. In *World Book Encyclopedia* (Vol. 4, pp. 653–656). Chicago: World Book.

Fleishman, E. A., & Quintance, M. K. (1994). *Taxonomies of human performance.* New York: Academic.

Krathwohl, D. R., Bloom, B. S., & Masia, B. B. (1964). *Taxonomy of educational objectives: Affective domain (Handbook II).* New York: McKay.

Thomas, R. M. (1995). *Classifying reactions to wrongdoing: Taxonomies of misdeeds, sanctions, and aims of sanctions.* Westport, CT: Greenwood.

## BUILDING AN EXPLANATORY THEORY

There are many ways to go about building a theory. We will demonstrate one way that draws on the definition of explanatory theory that we have adopted in this book. We start with a definition of explanatory theory.

> An explanatory theory identifies (a) the variables important for understanding some observed outcome and (b) explains how those variables interact to produce that outcome.

To illustrate this theory-generating process, we chose to devise a theory of *cultural self-identity,* meaning how persons view themselves in terms of cultural groups. Here are the general steps to take:

1. Select some phenomenon that you want to explain (in this case it's *cultural self-identity*), in the sense of proposing the causes that have brought that phenomenon about.
2. Decide which variables or components apparently contribute to why the phenomenon turns out as it does, and cast those variables in the form of propositions.

**Table 5.1** Sample Items From a Moral-Values Typology

| *Conditions Warranting Less Severe Aversive Consequences* | *Conditions Warranting More Severe Aversive Consequences* |
|---|---|
| **Fair Chance:** A decision to be lenient in applying sanctions may be affected by a proposer's convictions about how to be fair to transgressors. | |
| *Second Chance:* Everyone should be allowed an occasional mistake, so an offender should not suffer severe consequences for the first misdeed. | *Sanction Consistency:* Any time a person commits an offense, he or she—without exception—should experience consequences deemed proper for that type of offense. |
| "If it was the woman's first accident, then they shouldn't put her in jail." | "Unless sanctions are applied without exception, people won't learn to obey the law." |
| *Reparation Opportunity:* Less severe punishment enables the person to provide reparations to the victims of his or her misbehavior. | *Absence of Reparation Opportunity:* There is no reason to expect that the person would provide more reparations to the victims if the person were given less severe punishment. |
| "Jail time would keep the driver from being able to pay for the medical bills of the injured parties and thus would cause them more suffering." | "The guy's insurance will pay the woman's doctor bills, so it's okay to put him in jail." |
| *Self-Improvement Opportunity:* The consequence should be adjusted to permit the transgressor to engage in constructive self-improvement. | *Self-Improvement Opportunity Unwarranted:* There is no reason to think the transgressor would engage in self-improvement if the sanctions were less severe. |
| "The girl should be in detention only during summer vacation, so she won't miss any days at school." | "If the boy just goes to regular school and isn't put in detention, he's not going to learn how to behave. He needs discipline." |

SOURCE: From *What Wrongdoers Deserve* by Thomas, R. M., & Diver-Stamnes, A. C. 

3. Envision how the variables interact during the process of self-identity development, and illustrate the process with lifelike examples.

4. Propose a scheme for evaluating or measuring the causal factors.

5. Find or create the specific assessment instruments and methods to use in gathering information about each variable.

6. Apply the evaluation scheme to a real-life situation to test how well the theory explicates the phenomenon it is designed to explain.

## An Illustrated Process of Theory Building

We now demonstrate those steps with our hypothetical theory.

### *Step 1: Select a phenomenon to explain*

Imagine that we've read about couples from different cultural backgrounds who bear children of mixed cultural heritage. In our reading, we have encountered such passages as the following:

> All my life I've been aware of being half and half. I feel like I'm on the fringes of things in a lot of ways. I'm half Jewish and half Christian. I was raised as a political radical, but I don't really have any politics. I don't have any geographical roots. I just feel there are a whole lot of ways I don't belong. I've wanted to know who I was ever since I was a teenager. (Cowan & Cowan, 1987, p. 246)

> [My white maternal grandfather] wasn't exactly thrilled when he heard my mother was about to marry a black man. "I want to crawl inside a hole," he had said. (Funderburg, 1994, p. 9)

> Don [white American] and Cherry [Japanese] lived in Australia. . . . Don forbade Cherry to speak Japanese to their girls or teach them anything about Japan. "If they grow up to speak Japanese, they'll speak it to each other at school," he said. "That will make them different. They stand out among the other kids as it is. But they're not Japanese, they're Australian, and they're going to speak English." In response to such pressure, Cherry counseled her daughters, "You're not Jap, you're Australian girl. I'm Australian, too." (Spickard, 1989, p. 147)

Imagine, as well, that these passages are relevant to one of our interests, which is people's self-identities and the ways those identities are formed. We consider self-identity to mean a person's conviction about "who I am." Part of self-identity consists of an individual's feelings about "the cultural groups I really belong to, the groups whose members accept me as one of their own." Such groups can be defined by ethnicity, religion, social class, age, language, and more. We are particularly curious about the development of identity in bicultural individuals—in persons whose parents come from different cultural origins. Unfortunately, we have been unable to locate a formally organized explanation of that process, so we propose to create our own theory of bicultural self-identity development. In the following description of our approach, we identify the mother's original culture as culture A and the father's as culture B.

*Step 2: Identify causal factors*

From our reading and personal observations we estimate that three variables are particularly significant in forming a bicultural person's sense of cultural belongingness: (1) perceived comparative advantages (desirability) of cultures *A* and *B,* (2) the treatment that the bicultural individual receives from family members of the two cultures (*A* and *B*), and (3) the treatment the individual receives from other people of the two cultures (*A* and *B*). We recognize that these three are not the only causal factors, but we think they are powerful and will thus contribute significantly to our understanding how personal identity evolves. Our next task is to cast the factors in the form of propositions or hypotheses that reflect the influence we think each factor exerts.

***Proposition 1:*** Bicultural individuals tend to adopt characteristics of the culture (*A* or *B*) that would appear to offer them greater advantage in terms of personal welfare. If one culture appears to be more desirable in one aspect of life and the other in a different aspect, then the individual's self-identity will be an amalgam of features from the two cultures.

***Proposition 2:*** The better the bicultural person is treated by relatives, the more likely the person will identify with the culture of those relatives. If treated well by relatives of both *A* and *B,* the person will incorporate features of both cultures into his or her self-identity. But if treated well by relatives on only one side of the family, then characteristics of that culture will be featured in the person's identity. If treated badly by relatives on both sides of the family, the individual will suffer identity confusion and distress.

***Proposition 3:*** Influential, but somewhat less significant than family members' treatment (particularly in childhood), is the treatment the bicultural person receives from nonfamily members of cultures *A* and *B.* If treated well by people of both cultures, the person will adopt features of both cultures. But if treated well by people from only one of the two cultures, then characteristics of that culture will be featured in the person's identity. If treated badly by people of both cultures, the individual will suffer identity confusion and distress.

So, we are proposing that our three factors are causal variables that we think contribute significantly to the outcome variable—the bicultural person's self-identity.

*Step 3: Trace interactions among variables*

We now speculate about how the causal variables interact in the process of self-identity development. We imagine that the interaction follows the pattern proposed in Figure 5.1. The diagram shows what we estimate happens when a bicultural person participates in an event that influences how that person (a) perceives comparative advantages of cultures *A* and *B* and/or (b) is treated by relatives from *A* and *B* and/or (c) is treated by nonfamily members of *A* and *B*.

The pattern begins at the top with events in daily life that involve one or more of the three causal variables, events that serve as influential life conditions. For instance, a bicultural 16-year-old girl observes the quality of language usage by classmates from cultures *A* and *B,* she newly meets a relative from culture *A,* and she attends a high school social club's rush party where there are girls from both culture *A* and culture *B.* She is warmly greeted by her newly met relative from culture *A,* and at the rush party is treated well by girls from culture *A* but snubbed by ones from culture *B.* Thus, we predict that these experiences strengthen her tendency to adopt the language usage of culture *A* in preference to the usage typical of culture B.

Therefore, we propose that the girl interprets each event in a way that affects her welfare—her happiness, sense of confidence, disappointment, or distress. As indicated by the arrow pointing from the girl's welfare to *influential life conditions,* the girl's experiences feed back to influence the three life-condition factors, altering them a bit or else confirming her original conception of them. For example, the rush-party experience may confirm her expectation that being identified as a member of culture *A* is more advantageous than as a member of culture *B.*

The results of the round-cornered box at the top (life conditions interacting with self-interpreted welfare) influence the person's self-identity ("who I am culturally" and "the groups to which I truly belong"). This revised or confirmed concept of self influences how the person subsequently acts (individual's behavior)—confident, diffident, aggressive, submissive, friendly, antagonistic, or such. Other people respond to such behavior (others' responses). Then the individual interprets those responses as praise, criticism, acceptance, rejection, approval, disgust, reward, punishment, or the like. That interpretation serves as a factor feeding back to the beginning of the cycle.

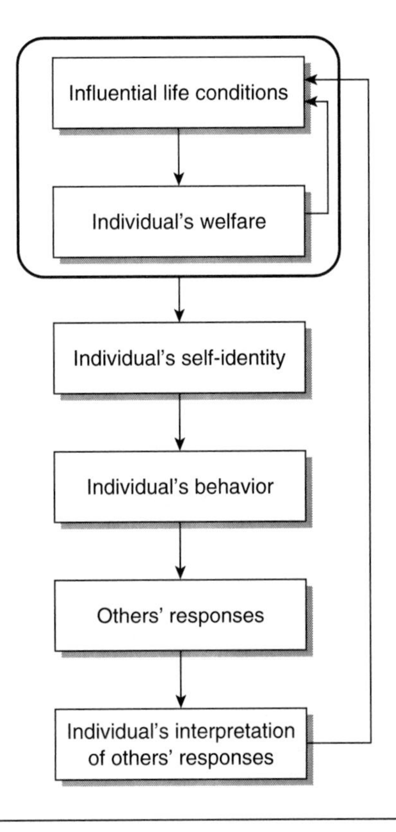


**Figure 5.1** An Envisioned Process of Self-Identity Development

In effect, by depicting a process of development, we have added four additional factors or components that affect self-identity—(a) the bicultural person's interpretation of how life conditions affect her or his welfare, (b) the individual's behavior as influenced by self-identity, (c) other people's reactions to such behavior, and (d) the individual's interpretation (feedback) of such reactions.

*Step 4: Propose a scheme for evaluating causal variables*

If we are to render our theory useful for judging bicultural people's self-identities and in understanding the process through which those identities evolve, we need to establish a way to assess the status of the three life-condition variables and the four additional process variables.

To begin, we assume that each of those variables represents a scale and that a bicultural person's perceptions can be located at a particular place on

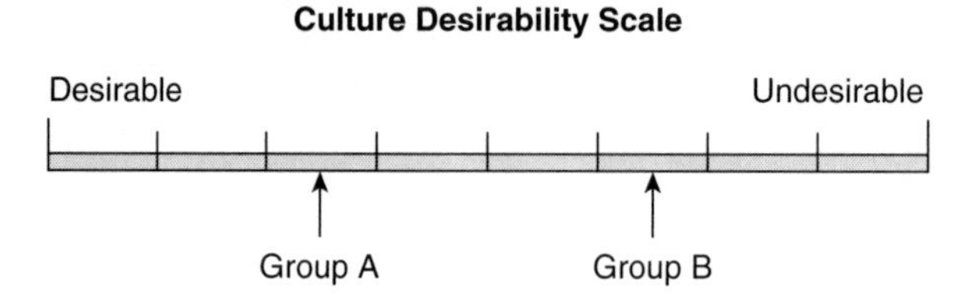


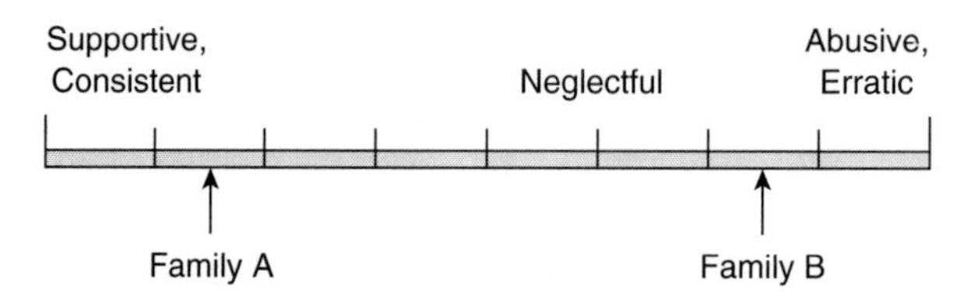


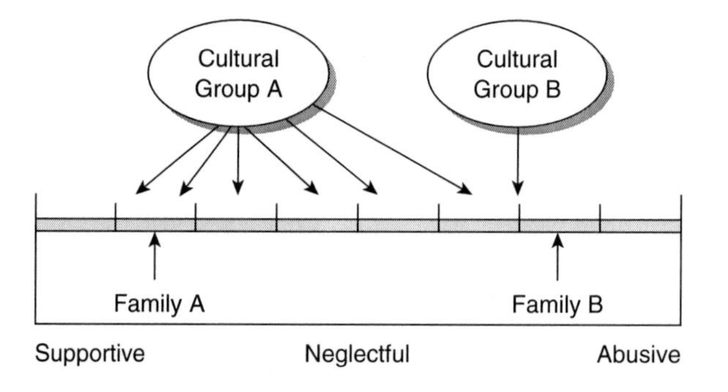


**Figure 5.2** Causal-Factors Scales

each scale at any given time of life. In Figure 5.2, we diagram the first three scales and demonstrate how they may serve to display different individuals' perceptions of the three causal factors. We illustrate the use of the scales by showing how hypothetical information could be charted. For instance, we can show how, in the eyes of a bicultural boy,

(a) his mother's culture (Group A) is seen as more advantageous than his father's (Group B),

(b) his mother's relatives (Family A) treat him better than do his father's relatives (Family B), and

(c) nonfamily members of his father's culture (Cultural Group B) are more consistent in their treatment of him than are nonfamily members of his mother's culture (Cultural Group A), some of whom treat him well, some moderately well, and some rather badly.

We can then create similar scales for displaying the additional variables: (a) the bicultural person's interpretation of how life conditions affect her or his welfare, (b) the individual's behavior as influenced by self-identity, (c) other people's reactions to such behavior, and (d) the individual's interpretation of such reactions.

*Steps 5 and 6: Devise and apply assessment methods*

Finally, the task of rendering our theory operational by creating specific techniques for evaluating the variables and their interactions and applying those techniques to bicultural people's self-identity is a daunting assignment that we won't attempt here. Instead, we will simply note that a thesis or dissertation may either consist of performing only the first three steps of the theory development process or consist of all five steps. The latter option is obviously the more difficult, but it produces more useful knowledge.

## Explanatory Theory Resources

The following books illustrate explanatory theories in various academic fields.

Chafetz, J. S. (1978). *A primer on the construction and testing of theories in sociology.* Itasca, IL: Peacock.

Demaine, J. (1981). *Contemporary theories in the sociology of education.* London: Macmillan.

Hall, C. S., Lindzey, G., & Campbell, J. B. (1998). *Theories of personality.* New York: Wiley.

Hilgard, E. R., & Bower, G. (1981). *Theories of learning* (5th ed.). Englewood Cliffs, NJ: Prentice Hall.

Miller, P. H. (1993). *Theories of developmental psychology* (3rd ed.). New York: Freeman.

Thomas, R. M. (1997). *Moral development theories—secular and religious.* Westport, CT: Greenwood.

Thomas, R. M. (2004). *Comparing theories of child development* (6th ed.). Belmont, CA: Wadsworth.

## ADAPTING AND REVISING THEORIES

Less demanding than the task of creating a new theory is that of revising an existing theory so as to provide either a more satisfactory classification system or a more adequate explanation of phenomena.

Revising a classification system usually consists of (a) adding new classes, (b) dividing existing classes into more precise subtypes, or (c) rearranging the hierarchy of classes so that major and minor categories assume a different pattern.

Revising an explanatory theory can involve any one or more of the following adjustments: (a) adding new causal factors, (b) dividing existing causal factors into more precise components, (c) proposing a different weighting of factors (assigning more importance or power to certain factors and reducing the significance or strength of others in their influence on the outcome variable), and (d) describing a different pattern of interaction than the pattern proposed in the original theory.

A further way to adapt an explanatory theory is to accept the original author's factors and mode of interaction, but to devise different techniques for appraising the factors and their interactions than those used in the original version. For instance, you might substitute an interview system for the original author's questionnaire approach to data collection. Or you might create a rating scale for recording observations of people's behavior rather than depending on the original author's method of using people's self-reports.

## PLANNING CHECKLIST

Completing the following checklist may help you identify the roles that you will assign to classificatory and explanatory theories in your project.

1. Write an **X** on the line in front of each item that tells what classification system or systems (typologies, taxonomies) you intend to employ in your project.

    ____ No classification system needed, since nothing will be classified.

    ____ How many classification systems will you use? Indicate number _____.

    ____ On a separate sheet of paper, describe each classification system you intend to use by explaining the following:

    What will be classified?

    If it is an existing system, what are its title and its source?

    If you plan to revise an existing system, what revisions do you plan and why?

    If you intend to create a new system, why do you need a new one? Why won't an existing system meet your needs?

    If you intend to create a new system, what steps will you follow in developing the system?

2. Write an **X** on the line in front of each item that tells what explanatory theory or theories you intend to use in your project.

    ____ No theory needed, since no proposals about causes of phenomena will be included.

    ____ How many theories will you use? Indicate number _____.

    ____ On a separate sheet of paper, describe each theory you intend to use by explaining the following:

    What will be explained?

    If it is an existing theory, what are its title and its source?

    If you plan to revise an existing theory, what revisions do you plan and why?

    If you intend to create a new theory, why do you need a new one? Why won't an existing theory meet your needs?

    If you intend to create a new theory, what steps will you follow in developing it?

## ⁜ SIX ⁜

# STATING THE PROBLEM AND ITS RATIONALE

*"I'm not quite sure about what I should put in my proposal when I give it to my advisors for their approval."*

Once you've selected the problem you plan to study, you can profit from casting it in a form appropriate for submitting it to your advisors. Although professors may not all agree on exactly what should be in your proposal, most of them will at least want a clear statement of your research problem, your reasons for choosing it, and a concise description of how you hope to find a solution. They also may want to know how you define the key terms that are at the heart of your project. Chapter 6 addresses these matters in the following order: (a) stating the problem to be investigated, (b) defining key terms, (c) supporting your choice of a topic with a convincing line of reasoning, and (d) briefly describing your intended research methods.

## STATING YOUR RESEARCH PROBLEM

Two popular ways to state a research problem are as a question and as a hypothesis. To illustrate, consider three graduate students' projects. The first concerns academic aptitude, the second family functions, and the third political theory.

By casting a problem in the form of a question, the researcher suggests the kind of answer being sought, with that suggestion then serving to guide decisions about the methods of investigation to employ.

______ What is the comparative effectiveness of four ways to assess high school students' academic ability—(a) high school grades, (b) teachers' letters of recommendation, (c) multiple-choice aptitude tests, and (d) achievement tests that students answer in essay form?

______ What changes have occurred in the structure and functions of Mexican American families during the latter years of the twentieth century, and what trends do such changes reflect?

______ Which aspects of a political party and what interactions among those aspects adequately explain the party's success in local elections?

A hypothesis represents a probable answer to the research question, but the probability that the answer is correct still needs to be tested through further investigation.

______ The most effective method of assessing high school students' academic ability is by multiple-choice aptitude tests. The next most effective is by high school grades, then by essay tests, and the least by teachers' recommendations.

______ Over the twentieth century, trends in the structure and functions of Mexican American families have included (a) a decrease in the use of Spanish as the language of communication in the home, (b) husbands' continued dominance in deciding important family issues, (c) a rising divorce rate, and (d) a continuation of younger family members sharing household tasks.

______ Predictions about a political party's success in local elections are most accurate when based on the analysis of the following components and their interactions: (a) fund-raising practices, (b) training methods for party workers, (c) a clearly stated position on locally important issues, (d) name-recognition of party candidates, and (e) activities that attract the attention of the news media—especially local television, radio, and newspaper reporters.

Now, which of these approaches is preferable—a question or a hypothesis? In what circumstances is one better than the other?

There are at least two conditions under which you might favor the hypothesis over the question. One is when there is good reason to believe that a proposed solution to the research issue is correct, but that belief still needs to be corroborated or refuted by evidence. The other is when you intend to apply a statistical test to the data you collect, and casting the problem as a hypothesis renders statistical testing more convenient.

However, the vast majority of problems can be expressed as questions that involve who, how, which, why, what, when, where, how much, how frequently, or several of these.

- Who were the original founders of Laver City, and what role did each play? (*history*)
- How do supermarkets set their selling prices for produce and, in particular, how much does the spoilage of produce affect pricing? (*economics, business*)
- Which method of teaching beginning reading best equips first-graders to infer the meanings of new words? (*education*)
- Why did Albania and North Korea become such closed, doctrinaire communist societies? (*political science*)
- What characteristics are most significant in differentiating people of the upper class from those of the lower class in Kentwood County? (*sociology*)
- When (during the day, month, and year) do people most frequently suffer feelings of depression, and why at those times? (*psychology*)
- Where did the counterculture movement of the 1960s in California begin, and who led the movement? (*history, sociology, anthropology*)
- How frequently do immigrants from Britain compared to immigrants from China apply for U.S. citizenship, and what are the reasons for the differences between the two groups? (*social psychology*)

Frequently a topic is best expressed as two or more questions, sometimes with minor questions subsumed under major ones.

1. In India, what was the extent of "brain-drain" migration of talented citizens to the United States over the period 1969–1999?

   1.1 In what fields had emigrants specialized before leaving India?

   1.2 What reasons did emigrants give for leaving their homeland?

   1.3 What expectations did emigrants hold for their new life abroad?

2. In what parts of the United States did immigrants from India settle?
   - 2.1 What occupations did immigrants enter?
   - 2.2 How well were immigrants' expectations fulfilled in their new environments?

To summarize, two important purposes are served by your being obliged to state your topic precisely. First, the statement guides you in charting the steps to take toward solving the problem. Second, it makes clear to your advisors what you intend to do, thus expediting their task of evaluating your proposal and offering advice.

## DEFINING KEY TERMS

Much misunderstanding in human communication results from people bringing different meanings to the words they use in speaking and writing. Effective researchers seek to avoid this difficulty by clearly explaining the meanings they assign to key terms in their investigations.

If, early in the research process, you define precisely what you intend by words and phrases crucial to your project, (a) you help identify appropriate methods of gathering and interpreting data and (b) your advisors can judge at the outset how well they agree with your definitions, thereby saving you possible trouble during subsequent stages of your project.

The terms *key words* and *key phrases* refer to concepts at the core of your study, concepts that must be unambiguous if you are to conduct your research with proper care and if the procedures and outcomes are to be properly understood by your reading audience. Among the most basic terms are those found in a project's title or topic question. To illustrate key words, in the following examples we have italicized each term that calls for a definition:

______ What is the *comparative effectiveness* of four ways to *assess high school students' academic ability*—(a) high school *grades,* (b) *teachers' letters of recommendation,* (c) *multiple-choice aptitude tests,* and (d) a*chievement tests* that students answer in *essay form?*

______ What *changes* have occurred in the *structure* and *functions of Mexican American families* during the twentieth century, and what *trends* do such changes reflect?

______ Which *aspects* of a *political party* and what *interactions* among those aspects *adequately explain* the party's *success* in *local elections?*

Different ways that researchers define key terms are those of (a) offering no definitions, (b) providing synonyms, (c) furnishing sentence descriptions, (d) citing shared experience or knowledge, and (e) defining by the operations used in conducting the research. Implications of using each of these methods can be demonstrated with examples of terms in the above questions.

## No Definitions

It's probably apparent that neglecting to explain what is intended by *political-party aspects* or *success* is unacceptable, because those terms obviously can convey so many different meanings. But the need to specify what is intended by *academic ability, high school students,* and *family structure* may not be so obvious, since we often find individuals using those terms without any clarifying explanation, apparently on the assumption that the words mean the same to everybody.

First consider *academic.* Are mathematics, history, English literature, Spanish language, home economics, auto repair, guitar instruction, and floral arranging all equally *academic?* If not, then what distinction should be drawn among them? And what about *ability?* On what evidence should judgments of ability be based—intelligence test scores, grade point averages, teachers' judgments, or people's performance in such games as Scrabble, Trivial Pursuit, and Monopoly?

How about *high school students?* If we are judging their academic ability, is it important to know who they are in terms of socioeconomic status, ethnic background, home language, parents' education, and whether they are in private schools or in public schools?

Now consider *family.* Is *family* supposed to mean only a pair of parents and their biological offspring? Or does it mean people living together, whether or not they are biologically related? Or does it encompass all of a person's legal relatives, no matter where they reside?

What is *family structure?* Is it the set of roles that different family members play? Is it the manner in which authority and power are distributed among family members? Or is it the pattern of communication among members?

In summary, we conclude that leaving key terms undefined is not acceptable in theses and dissertations.

### Synonyms

At first glance it might seem that a synonym could clarify the meaning assumed for a key word or phrase. However, for the precision needed in research, synonyms rarely suffice, because too frequently they carry as many different meanings—or as many vague meanings—as the words they are supposed to elucidate. In the main, the only occasions on which synonyms are suitable are ones in which a new, unfamiliar word can be adequately clarified with a familiar word or phrase. This can occur with places (Kalimantan = Borneo, Vanuatu = New Hebrides, Myanmar = Burma), people (Muhammad Ali = Cassius Clay), institutions or agencies (State Department = foreign relations department), or conditions (Down's syndrome = mongolism).

### Sentence Descriptions

A single sentence, or a few sentences, may be enough to explain the meaning the author assigns to the use of a term within the boundaries of the author's project.

> The words *comparative effectiveness,* as intended throughout this thesis, refer to the relative accuracy of four methods of predicting high school students' later success in college.
>
> The term *Mexican American family* in this study means a group of people of Mexican heritage, currently living in the United States, who are related by blood, and are members of the same household.
>
> *Political party aspects* on which the present investigation focuses are (a) amount of money spent on a local campaign, (b) the amount spent on different forms of advertising, (c) the number of active party workers, and (d) the socioeconomic composition of the registered party membership.

Sentence definitions often contain words that require further clarification in the form of additional sentences. Such is true of the terms *high school students* and *later success in college* in the first of our examples. It is also the case with *Mexican heritage* and *related by blood* in the second example and *forms of advertising* and *active party workers* in the third example.

Sometimes it is desirable to tell not only what a key word is intended to mean, but also to explain what it is not intended to include. The purpose is to rule out unintended meanings that readers might reasonably assume unless they are told otherwise.

> The phrase *currently living in the United States* refers to individuals who spend at least six months consecutively in the household, so the phrase does

not include short-term visitors or family members who shuttle in and out of the household during a six-month period.

The word *advertising* means presenting to the public information and appeals by means of paid-for space in newspapers and paid-for time on radio and television. Party workers going door to door to solicit votes is not *advertising* in the sense intended here, nor does a report or editorial in the news media about a candidate or a political party qualify as *advertising.*

## Shared Experiences

Sentence definitions can sometimes be usefully enhanced with lifelike examples that serve as clarifying experiences shared by author and reader.

The purpose of an *aptitude test* is to estimate the capacity of people to succeed at some endeavor, such as to predict their ability to succeed in college. On the other hand, the purpose of an *achievement test* is to judge how well people have mastered knowledge or skills they have already studied or practiced. Sometimes the same test can serve both purposes. To illustrate, assume that two high school students take an algebra test. Their scores will reflect their achievement up to that time—what they have already learned about algebra. But their scores can also be used to estimate how well they will succeed with future studies in mathematics. A student scoring at the 95th percentile will, in the future, probably do better in math than a student at the 27th percentile.

The expression *family functions* refers to what family life contributes to the individuals who comprise the family. For instance, children—because they are members of a family—receive food, shelter, clothing, medical care, affection, and instruction in cultural traditions (language, customs, values). Parents—because they head a family—gain satisfaction for having produced offspring, receive affection and gratitude from their children, and enjoy the approval of outsiders for performing their childrearing duties in a responsible manner.

## Operational Definitions

Defining a key term operationally consists of specifying the techniques used for measuring or assessing the characteristic that the term signifies.

In this study, *academic aptitude* is defined by the scores students earn on the Educational Testing Service's computerized version of the *Scholastic Aptitude Test*, edition 2007.

*Degree of success in elections* is defined as "the percentage of votes a candidate receives out of the total number of votes cast."

The term *high school grades* refers to a student's grade point average as computed by the following formula "[*(SLGE) (CPPW)]*" CPPW where SLGE = student's letter-grade equivalent (A = 4, B = 3, C = 2, D = 1, F = 0) and CPPW = number of class periods per week for a course.

### Conclusion

It is not necessary to limit yourself to only one of the above ways of defining terms. You may often find it best to cast one definition as a sentence, another as several sentences elaborated with lifelike examples, and a third as the procedures used for measuring the variable that is being defined. Which methods you choose can depend on (a) which type you believe will be most precisely understood by readers and (b) which type guides you most accurately in selecting data-gathering techniques and interpreting the data.

## PROVIDING A RATIONALE

A rationale typically consists of a line of reasoning that performs two principal functions. It describes a context within which to locate the intended project and suggests why doing such a study is worthwhile. A further function can be that of justifying the methods you plan to use for solving your research problem.

### Roles for the Rationale

The rationale plays a role at two stages of your project: (a) when you first submit your research proposal to your advisors for their advice and approval and (b) when you write your final version of the thesis or dissertation so readers will understand the contribution to knowledge or the contribution to practice that your work represents.

#### *Placing your work in context*

Locating your study in a context consists of identifying a domain of life into which the research fits. One popular way to accomplish this is to introduce a label that you assume is familiar to your readers. Labels can be on different levels of specificity. To illustrate with our hypothetical study of Mexican American families, consider three alternatives that descend from the general to the specific. The first label—*social change*—places your work within a very broad field. The second—*family structure*—identifies a more limited realm. The third—*trends in family structure and function among Mexican Americans*—represents a very narrow field, indeed. Your rationale might start with the label that signifies the field in which you think your work belongs.

- Among theories of social change, the most prominent types . . .
- The literature on family structure can be divided into . . .
- Investigations of trends in family structure and function among Mexican Americans treat such issues as . . .

Your next task is that of showing how your project fits into the selected realm. Here is one way that could be done for the second option—family structure.

> The literature on family structure can be divided into six categories focusing on (1) family members' roles, (2) types of human needs met within different family structures, (3) nuclear and extended forms of family, (4) lineage and governance (i.e. patrilineal, matrilineal), (5) explanations of family structural change over time, and (6) cross-cultural comparisons. The present study links the second and fifth of these categories by addressing the question: What changes have occurred in the structure and functions of Mexican American families during the twentieth century, and what trends do such changes reflect? In addition, by centering attention on a particular ethnic group—Mexican Americans—the study provides material useful to people interested in the last of the categories, that of cross-cultural comparisons.

*Identifying your intended contribution*

Perhaps the most important function of an author's rationale is the explanation of how the project can contribute to knowledge (*basic research* that corrects or expands people's understanding of the world) and/or to practice (*applied research* that improves the conduct of some aspect of life). This function is typically performed by the author's identifying shortcomings in the existing body of knowledge or practice that could be remedied by the proposed research. As noted in Chapter 1, contributions can be of various kinds, including

- Evidence about kinds of events, individuals, groups, or institutions not studied before
- Outcomes derived from applying existing theories or methods of investigation to events, individuals, groups, or institutions not yet studied in such a fashion

- The use of new data-gathering methods or instruments for studying phenomena
- A novel theoretical view of familiar events
- New interpretations of existing data
- Conclusions drawn from combining the results of similar studies (*meta-analysis*)

The following examples illustrate two ways of wording research proposals so that they (a) specify the question to be answered, (b) locate the study in a domain of knowledge or practice, and (c) identify the study's intended contribution.

The first description begins with the domain of the project (cognitive development), then cites a shortcoming in the literature related to a particular theory within that domain. The author ends the proposal by specifying the research question, which implies what the project should contribute to the body of knowledge about cognitive development.

> In L. S. Vygotsky's theory of children's cognitive development, a feature that has attracted increasing attention among psychologists and educators has been his *zone of proximal development,* which can be defined as "the set of actions that the child can perform when helped by another person, but which are not yet available to the child in his individual acting" (Valsiner, 1987, p. 233). Although Vygotsky's proposing such a zone has been widely praised, the present writer's survey of the literature on learning suggests that very little is known about how to recognize when a child has entered such a zone of readiness for instruction. But if the people who bear responsibility for children's learning are to profit from the notion of a zone of proximal development, they need guidance in how to recognize when a child is within that zone. The purpose of this dissertation is to help fulfill that need by seeking answers to three questions: (1) What are the potential indicators of the zone of proximal development? (2) How accurately can each indicator predict a learner's readiness to acquire a particular skill or type of knowledge? (3) Which characteristics of teaching methods are most effective for promoting learning in the zone of proximal development?

The second example opens with the research problem, cast in the form of a hypothesis, which is followed by the domain of knowledge (social stratification) and a rationale suggesting how the author's project could add to that domain. The proposal has been rendered more elaborate than the cognitive-development example by this author's bolstering the presentation with several citations from the professional literature and defining two key terms.

This thesis is designed to test the hypothesis that the class structure of a society is a social construction which is perceived differently (a) by people at different levels of the structure and (b) by different age cohorts.

My aim in conducting such an investigation is to help settle a controversy in the field of social stratification about the defining characteristics of social-class structures. A large body of theory and empirical research has been devoted to identifying dimensions of social class (Allsworth, 1973; Bennel & Masovic, 2004; Garcia, 1982; Mendoza, 2001; Swenson, 1986). However, the issue of how people in the social system perceive the structure continues to be muddled and controversial (Johnson & Haxton, 1996; Pontius, 2003). Furthermore, there is a lack of information about how the variable *age-cohort* may influence perceptions of class. My intention is to help clarify these matters by studying social-class perceptions of residents of the city of Mapleton.

For the purpose of this thesis, the concepts *social construction* and *age cohorts* are defined in the following manner:

*Social construction* refers to the belief that social class is not an objective reality, in the sense of a necessary relationship among people based on their possessions, abilities, or accomplishments. Instead, social class is an agreement (a mental construction) among people about (a) where individuals belong in terms of their relative prestige and (b) the characteristics that contribute to that prestige.

The term *age cohort* refers to the period of time (such as the year or cluster of a few years) during which a particular group of people were born. For example, all persons who are now age 14 form one cohort, and all who are now age 27 form another.

## DESCRIBING YOUR DATA-COLLECTION METHODS

Some faculty advisors will be satisfied to have you submit your proposed study initially as a topic and a rationale, as illustrated in the cognitive-development and social-stratification examples. But before giving final approval to your plan, they will usually wish to learn what methods you intend to use for collecting and analyzing your data. This means that you may wish to submit your proposal in two stages.

The first stage consists of describing your research question and supporting that choice with a rationale. Your intention at this juncture is to solicit your advisor's opinion about the suitability of your topic before you go to the trouble of working out a data-gathering plan. Then, if your topic and its rationale are judged acceptable—either in their original state or in a revised version—you move ahead to specifying your methodology. At the first stage, your advisor may wish to suggest which methods will and which will not be suitable for answering your research questions. Subsequently, in the second phase of your submission on a later occasion, you describe your intended data-gathering techniques and perhaps the mode of interpretation you hope to employ.

However, at the time that you first submit your proposal, some advisors will want you to specify your methodology as well as your topic and supporting rationale. The following excerpt illustrates one way that might be done. In this example the author (a) begins by identifying a domain (high school vocational counseling), (b) then explains that his intended contribution consists of a theory generated out of other researchers' work (cited in brackets) and that the project is designed to test hypotheses derived from that theory, and (c) finishes by describing the intended methods of data gathering and interpretation. In this instance, the research question (Why do the effects of high school vocational counseling on students' subsequent careers vary from one school to another?) is implied rather than stated outright.

> Writers have often proposed that the influence of high schools' vocational counseling procedures on students' subsequent careers varies among schools, but none has offered a compelling theory for why such effects occur [Hanks, Stuart, & Alpert, 2001; Lindsey, 1994; Risutto, 2005]. I use existing knowledge about counseling effects to develop hypotheses for between-school differences in counseling outcomes. Building on the work of Stevens [1987], I argue that the impact of vocational counseling varies according to the vocational opportunities in the community. I also consider claims that counseling produces different effects in public and private schools [Galloway & Burton, 1999; Portia & Vandenberg, 2003]. I plan to test these hypotheses by applying methods of multi-level contextual analysis to data on vocational counseling and later job placement in a national sample of high schools.

## A Final Comment

In order to cover a lot of ground and offer diverse examples within the space of a few pages, we have described research problems and their rationales in an unrealistically brief form. In actual thesis and dissertation proposals, such descriptions are far more detailed. To show how a more true-to-life, extensive proposal looks, we have included in the appendix at the end of this volume the outline of a dissertation proposal by Robin Ganzert.

## PLANNING CHECKLIST

In planning your thesis or dissertation, you may find it helpful to answer the following queries:

1. In which form do I intend to state my research problem?

 ____ As a question

 ____ As a hypothesis

2. Will the statement be in the form of a single problem or of more than one problem?

 ____ A single problem

 ____ Two or more problems at the same level of specificity

 ____ Two or more problems, with constituent subproblems subsumed under more general ones

 ____ State the problem or problems ____________________

 ______________________________________________

3. In the above statement of my problem, I underline each *key word* or *key phrase* that needs to be assigned the meaning intended in my research. Then, on the following lines, I list each key word or phrase beside the form of definition I plan to use for that term.

 ____ No definition (the meaning is obvious) ____________________

 ____ Synonym ____________________

 ____ Single sentence ____________________

 ____ Several sentences____________________

 ____ Shared experiences/knowledge____________________

 ____ Operational definition____________________

4. What functions do I intend to include in the rationale I prepare?

 ____ Identify a domain in which the study is located

 ____ Suggest how the study can contribute to knowledge or practice

 ____ Identify sources of other studies or of controversies related to my study

 ____ Identify one or more theories or hypotheses to be tested by the study

 ____ Other (describe)____________________

5. Will the proposal I submit to my advisors include a description of the research methods I plan to use?

 ____ Not in the first submission of the proposal

 ____ Yes, but only in a subsequent second submission

 ____ Yes, the first time I submit it

STAGE III-A

# COLLECTING INFORMATION

Much of the work on every thesis and dissertation consists of gathering information. Data-collection tasks can vary markedly from one project to another. Such tasks may include distributing questionnaires, interviewing respondents, poring over documents, administering tests, observing public events, searching the Internet, conducting experiments, and more.

The process of collecting information can consist of five phases:

(a) identifying the kinds of information needed to answer the research questions
(b) identifying potential sources of that information (books, journals, public documents, people to question or test, kinds of experiments to conduct)
(c) choosing among the sources
(d) devising efficient methods and instruments for gathering the information
(e) compiling the desired data by means of those methods and instruments

Chapter 7 (Types of Research Methods and Sources of Information) and Chapter 8 (Data-Collection Techniques and Instruments) focus on these matters.

During the process of gathering data, students often encounter frustrating problems. Chapter 9 (Things That Go Wrong) identifies some of the most common difficulties and suggests ways of solving them.

SEVEN

# TYPES OF RESEARCH METHODS AND SOURCES OF INFORMATION

*"It's not clear whether I should get all my information out of the published literature or else conduct an opinion survey or maybe do an experiment."*

The two activities inspected in this chapter are those of identifying (a) popular research methods and (b) ways of gathering information for answering research questions. The chapter is divided into three sections. The first section introduces guide questions for four hypothetical studies that graduate students might plan. The second section—by far the longest—describes diverse methods of collecting information to answer research questions. The third section tells which of those methods we think might be suitable for answering the guide questions posed for the four studies in the first section.

The chapter's structure, in effect, offers you the same experience researchers may have when they are deciding which methods of data collection are best suited for answering their focal questions. Therefore, you may wish to read the chapter in this manner: (a) in the first section, note the guide questions for the four envisioned studies, (b) keep those questions in mind as you survey the methods in the second section, so as to estimate which approach would likely produce convincing answers to which question, and (c) in the third section compare your decisions about suitable methods with the ones we suggest for the four studies.

## SPECIFYING THE DESIRED DATA

As already noted, the key to the information you need is the set of questions your research is designed to answer. In way of illustration, consider the questions posed in four envisioned projects.

Project title 1: *One Size Fits All: State and Federal Legislators' Solutions for Students' Unsatisfactory School Achievement*
Guide questions:

- How do educational experts (teachers, school psychologists, researchers) diagnose and treat students' problems of unsatisfactory achievement?
- How do legislators, as reflected in laws they pass, propose that students' unsatisfactory achievement be diagnosed and treated?
- How well do the solutions recommended by educational experts match the solutions proposed by legislators?

Project title 2: *Destined to Preach the Gospel: A Social-Psychological Study*
Guide questions:

- What factors in the life of Reverend Delevon Johnson determined that he would become a lifelong missionary in Africa?
- How did the causal factors in Reverend Johnson's life compare with those in other African missionaries' lives?

Project title 3: *The Comparative Effectiveness of Same-Sex Therapists Versus Opposite-Sex Therapists With Teenage Drug Users*
Guide question:

- In counseling teenage drug users to stop using illicit drugs, is greater success achieved when the counselor is of the same sex as the client than when the counselor is of the opposite sex?

Project title 4: *The Dynamics of Choosing Candidates to Run for Political Office in Adams County*
Guide questions:

- Who were the candidates that ran for political office in Adams County over the past 12 years?
- What other individuals were potential candidates but were not selected to run?

- By what processes were candidates selected to run for different offices?
- What inferences can be drawn about those processes' effect on the quality of political officeholders in Adams County?

## GENERAL RESEARCH METHODS

For convenience of discussion, it is useful to separate (a) general approaches or methods of gathering and presenting information from (b) specific techniques and instruments of data collection. We are using the term *general method* or *general approach* in reference to a principal type and source of information, whereas the term *techniques and instruments* refers to the specific steps and devices used in compiling the information. Chapter 7 is concerned with general methods. Techniques and instruments used within those methods are reviewed in Chapter 8.

The following overview assumes the form of a cafeteria of information-collection methods from which researchers might choose one or more that suit their needs. Every method is described in a pattern intended to facilitate readers' quickly scanning the approaches to find answers to their questions. That is, almost all descriptions address the same eight elements:

1. *Method label:* a typical title for the method.
2. *Method definition:* a typical description of the method.
3. *Purpose:* the intent of the method, and kinds of research questions for which it can provide answers.
4. *Procedure:* a typical sequence of steps followed in employing the method.
5. *Sample projects:* titles of theses or dissertations in different academic disciplines for which the approach is well suited.
6. *Advantages:* Strengths of the method in regard to (a) how effectively it can furnish answers to the research questions, (b) how easy it is to gather data, (c) how acceptable the method is likely to be for potential readers, and (d) how broadly the generalizations drawn in a study can be extended to other groups and settings.
7. *Limitations:* Weaknesses of the method in regard to the same characteristics as those listed under Advantages.
8. *Resources:* Books, journal articles, and other materials that (a) describe, analyze, or evaluate the approach or (b) illustrate its use.

The types of methods surveyed in this section are subsumed under six major headings—(a) historical accounts, (b) case studies and ethnographies, (c) experience narratives, (d) surveys, (e) correlation analyses, and (f) experiments. Subtypes are identified under several of these headings.

Even a casual inspection of the types reveals that they are not mutually exclusive but, rather, they often overlap. A particular thesis or dissertation may employ several of the types as dictated by the research questions to be answered.

## Historical Accounts

Four kinds of historical methods are described—descriptive chronicles, interpretive histories, biographies, and autobiographies.

### *Descriptive chronicles*

***Defined:*** A descriptive chronicle traces events over a period of years in the life of a family, organization, ethnic group, region, kind of occupation, social movement, or the like. Authors of descriptive chronicles attempt objectively to depict what occurred, sticking to the facts without speculating about why events happened as they did.

***Purpose:*** The dual aim of a descriptive chronicle is (a) to record a succession of events so they will not be lost to posterity and (b) to inform readers of what actually took place, showing which conditions changed and which conditions stayed the same with the passing of time.

***Procedure:*** One way of preparing a chronicle consists of the researcher:

1. Delimiting the entity on which the chronicle will focus, that is, specifying a particular organization, social movement, occupational group, or such.
2. Determining the time frame to be encompassed by the chronicle.
3. Specifying the questions to be answered by the information that is sought.
4. Identifying sources of information to be used (libraries and archives to be searched, documents to be analyzed, individuals to be interviewed).
5. Collecting information from the sources as directed by the guide questions, and verifying the accuracy of the information (seeking multiple

accounts of each significant event, resolving discrepancies between accounts).

6. Organizing the obtained information by (a) selecting the events that will be recounted and (b) placing those events in chronological sequence.

7. Writing the final narrative.

***Sample projects:*** Representative titles of chronicles include

*The Evolution of Studies of Perception* (psychology)
*A History of Clifton College* (education)
*England's Child Labor Laws—1750–1950* (sociology)
*Changes in Iroquois Myths Over Time* (anthropology)
*Public Land Laws in Minton County—1900–2000* (political science)

***Advantages:*** By compiling and ordering events from the past, chronicles preserve information that otherwise would be lost to future generations. Chronicles that are strictly descriptive are easier to produce than interpretive histories because they do not require theoretical analyses, estimates of cause, or the evaluation of events.

***Limitations:*** Many readers are not satisfied with only a retelling of events. They want the author also to suggest what the affairs mean, such as (a) why events occurred as they did, (b) how events might have happened in some other manner if conditions had been different, (c) who was affected by the happenings, or (d) what the recounted events portend for the future.

***Resources:*** Issues relating to writing chronicles are discussed in

Gilderhus, M. T. (2002). *History and historians: A historiographical introduction* (5th ed.). Upper Saddle River, NJ: Prentice Hall.

Lambert, P., & Schofield, P. (Eds.). (2004). *Making history: An introduction to the practices of history*. New York: Routledge.

*Interpretive histories*

***Defined:*** An interpretive history not only traces incidents over a period of years, but includes the author's estimate of what that collection of happenings means. Various kinds of meaning can be assigned to the data. One popular kind is explanatory, an estimate of what caused events to occur in the pattern reflected in the author's narrative. Another is evaluative, a judgment of whether events produced good or bad outcomes, whether people behaved responsibly or irresponsibly, whether organizations were efficient or inefficient, and the like. A further kind of meaning assumes the form of inferred lessons, which are generalizations derived from a historical account that can serve as guiding principles for the future, on the assumption that history repeats itself—at least partially.

***Purpose:*** Like descriptive chronicles, interpretive histories are intended to (a) record a succession of events so they will not be lost and (b) inform readers of what actually took place, showing which conditions changed and which ones stayed the same with the passing of time. However, as suggested above, interpretive histories include a substantial measure of the author's beliefs about what the events signify. Authors differ markedly in the amounts and types of interpretation they include. Some histories are long on description and short on interpretation, leaving to the reader the task of estimating what the events "mean." Other histories are quite the reverse, with authors suggesting at great length what the recounted happenings disclose.

***Procedure:*** Here is one series of stages in the preparation of an interpretive history. The author

1. Selects an area of emphasis for his or her own study (public schooling, farming practices, political conventions, criminal law, dreaming, bank policies, or the like).
2. Searches through history books and journals (particularly those related to the author's field of emphasis) to discover theories on which historians have based their works; then adopts or creates a theoretical vantage point from which to view events, that is, creates a theory of cause-and-effect and/or a set of standards for evaluating events.
3. Delimits the location (city, state, nation, world) and the time period on which the study will focus.
4. Specifies the questions to be answered by the information that is sought, including questions about causal relations among events as determined by the chosen theoretical position.
5. Identifies sources of information to be used (libraries and archives to be searched, documents to be analyzed, individuals to be interviewed).

6. Collects information from the sources as directed by the guide questions, and verifies the accuracy of the information (seeking multiple accounts of each significant event, resolving discrepancies between accounts).
7. Revises the interpretive theory or the evaluation standards as suggested by the information that has been compiled. (Collecting data can alter the author's original scheme for estimating causal relations among events or for evaluating events.)
8. Organizes the obtained information by (a) selecting the events that will be recounted, (b) placing those events in a sequence suited to the way events will be interpreted, and (c) assigning an interpretation to the events.
9. Writes the final narrative.

***Sample projects:*** Titles of interpretive histories can include

*The Rise and Decline of a Pioneer Dynasty—1845–1915* (history)
*Conditions Leading to Prison Reform—Britain and USA* (sociology)
*A Revered Elder's Version of Mendingka History* (anthropology)
*Cause and Effect in the Success of Napoleon's Campaigns* (history)
*Stock Market Boom, Bust, and Boom Again—1925–1995* (economics)

***Advantages:*** Interpretive histories provide the researcher an opportunity to speculate about why events happened as they occurred. That opportunity includes the chance to apply the writer's particular conception of historiography, to illustrate the application of a novel theory, or to correct earlier versions that the author believes were flawed.

***Limitations:*** Perhaps the most serious shortcoming of interpretive histories is their heavy dependence on sources of information that can be incomplete or badly biased. When the data on which researchers base their conclusions are not complete or are fraudulent, the validity of those conclusions is obviously in doubt. Thus, authors of historical studies face the challenge of ensuring that the account they write is an accurate portrayal of what happened in the past. That challenge derives from the fact that historians are limited to the accounts of the past they happen to find. How authentically such materials represent the events they depict may be open to serious question. And the farther back in historical time that the events occurred, the greater the question about the accuracy of the records that remain.

A variety of factors contribute to the distortion and loss of records. Over the centuries, valuable books and letters are destroyed by fire, flood, and invading armies. Victors in revolutions and political elections replace the defeated side's accounts of events with their own version of what happened. Manuscripts, letters, books, and periodicals are lost through the neglect or ignorance of people who fail to recognize the potential future importance of those materials. And the absence of scholars in certain cultures or in illiterate segments of the social-class structure results in a lack of records of happenings in such people's lives.

Finally, researchers themselves can be at fault, either by failing to search thoroughly for records or by manipulating the records in a manner that favors a bias they bring to their task.

In view of the risks to the authenticity and balance of available knowledge about the past, conscientious historians adopt several safeguards to promote the accuracy of their work. One way is to obtain multiple accounts of an event to determine how closely different versions match. Another is to locate the account within the sociopolitical atmosphere of its day; the researcher attempts to find convincing evidence that a given description of an incident reasonably reflects what would be expected to occur in the context of those times. A third method is to estimate the reliability of a source by its status as an official document or by the reputation of its author.

***Resources:*** Conceptions of interpretive history include

Appleby, J. O. (1994). *Telling the truth about history.* New York: Norton.

Bailyn, B. (1994). *On the teaching and writing of history: Responses to a series of questions.* Hanover, NH: University Press of New England.

Clark, E. (2004). *History, theory, text: Historians and the linguistic turn.* Cambridge, MA: Harvard University Press.

Iggers, G. G. (1997). *Historiography in the twentieth century: From scientific objectivity to the postmodern challenge.* Middletown, CT: Wesleyan University Press.

Kutler, S. I. (Ed.). (1994). *American retrospective: Historians on historians.* Baltimore, MD: Johns Hopkins University Press.

Lüdtke, A. (Ed.). (1995). *The history of everyday life: Reconstructing historical experiences and ways of life.* Princeton, NJ: Princeton University Press.

Marszalek, J. F., & Miscamble, W. D. (1997). *American political history: Essays on the state of the discipline.* Notre Dame, IN: University of Notre Dame.

Novick, P. (1988). *That noble dream: The "objectivity question" and the American historical profession.* New York: Cambridge University Press.

Rawls, J. (2006). *California: An interpretive history.* New York: McGraw-Hill.

Shapiro, H. (1988). *African American history and radical historiography.* Minneapolis, MN: MEP Publications.

*Biography—descriptive and interpretive*

***Defined:*** A biography is a written account of another person's life. Like chronicles and interpretive histories, biographies can be solely a description of incidents in an individual life, or they can include the author's interpretation of those incidents. Various sorts of interpretation can be offered, such as (a) an estimate of themes, interests, or problems that figured prominently in the person's life, (b) judgments about how other people affected the biographee's development, (c) appraisals of the person's decisions at key junctures in his or her life, and (d) speculation about how the biographee was affected by the physical environments that she or he inhabited. In effect, interpretive biography refers to the studied use of documents that describe critical incidents or defining moments in people's lives—including such documents as autobiographies, biographies, letters, diaries, oral and personal histories, and obituaries (Denzin, 1989, 1997).

***Purpose:*** Biographies can be designed to serve such functions as

- Preserving a record of the personal development and the contributions of a unique or prominent person.
- Correcting previous accounts by presenting a revised portrait of an individual who earlier had been depicted as a different sort of person.
- Through the medium of one individual's life, teaching readers lessons about wise and unwise ways of living.
- Tracing backstage and onstage actions of the biographee, with particular attention to ways in which that individual reconciled or failed to reconcile contradictions, thereby illustrating how contradictions affected the individual's fate and events of the time (Pfitzer, 1991).
- Demonstrating person-environment-interaction theory by showing how significant events are the result of a fortuitous match between (a) the biographee's particular characteristics and location and (b) societal conditions at a given time.

**Procedure:** The stages in writing a biography can be much the same as those followed in producing an interpretive history.

***Sample projects:*** Project titles can include the following:

*The Life Story of a Native American in Eastern North Carolina* (anthropology)
*Gilman Ostrander's Historical World* (history)

*The Political Life of a Woman in a Southeastern City: Making a Difference in the Twenty-First Century* (political science)
*Rural Leadership of a Transplanted American* (social psychology)

***Advantages:*** Perhaps the most important advantage of biographies is their ability to display the unique character of the biographee's life—a life which, in its details and pattern of development, is unlike anyone else's. A biography can serve readers by identifying persistent themes, consistencies, and inconsistencies in the subject's life and by illuminating the historical and cultural contexts in which the subject's life took place. Readers may also derive lessons about life that are inferred from behavior revealed in a biographer's account.

The process of writing a biography may also contribute to authors' own lives by obliging them to clarify their own historiographical persuasions, that is, their beliefs about the worth of different styles of analyzing and presenting historical accounts. In addition, the process may further biographers' intergenerational and intragenerational understandings and, perhaps, promote their self-understanding by comparing their own lives with those of the people they write about.

***Limitations:*** Because interpretive biography involves researchers drawing inferences about the intentions, goals, beliefs, values, and feelings of the people they write about, there is the danger that those inferences may be in error. It's not unusual for a biographer to miss finding all of the evidence needed to support conclusions. As a result, the author may be criticized for being too subjective, basing interpretation on inadequate sources or—out of an ulterior motive—adopting a biased perspective that results in an account that is unduly favorable to the subject (too "soft") or unreasonably critical (too "harsh"). If the author is hasty, thereby drawing conclusions from an incomplete search for evidence, critics may charge that he or she has produced "blitzkrieg ethnography," a lightning exploratory account of a misleading nature.

There also is the danger of authors using conclusions drawn from studying a single life as the basis for generalizing about other people's lives, thereby regarding one person as an exemplar of a group of people, when in fact the person studied is unique and not representative.

***Resources:*** Approaches to writing biographies are reflected in

Atkinson, R. (1998). *The life story interview.* Thousand Oaks, CA: Sage.
Denzin, N. K. (1989). *Interpretive biography.* Thousand Oaks, CA: Sage.
Denzin, N. K. (1997). *Interpretive ethnography.* Thousand Oaks, CA: Sage.
Kridel, C. (Ed.). (1998). *Writing educational biography.* New York: Garland.
Magarey, S., Guerin, C., & Hamilton, P. (Eds.). (1992). *Writing lives: Feminist biography & autobiography.* Adelaide, Australia: University of Adelaide.

Morris, E. (1999). *Dutch: A memoir of Ronald Reagan.* New York: Random House.
Parke, C. N. (1996). *Biography: Writing lives.* St. Leonards, Australia: Allen & Unwin.
Young-Bruehl, E. (1998). *Subject to biography: Psychoanalysis, feminism, and writing women's lives.* Cambridge, MA: Harvard University Press.

### *Autobiography—traditional and mediated*

***Defined:*** An autobiography is a person's written account of her or his own life. Two sorts of autobiography can be distinguished—the traditional and the mediated.

A traditional autobiography is entirely the work of the person whose life is depicted. Examples would be Benjamin Franklin's *Autobiography* (1771–1788/1951) and Winston Churchill's *Memories and Adventures* (1989).

A mediated autobiography is a cooperative effort that involves the person whose life is being depicted and a writer responsible for casting the work in a suitable form. Sometimes the writer—as the mediator between the person and the reading audience—is identified and sometimes not. Thus, a collaborator may be relegated to the silent-partner role of ghostwriter. Usually the collaborator has been asked to participate in the venture because the person whose life is being portrayed lacks the time, patience, or expertise to create a well-crafted narrative. Examples of mediated autobiographies are *Gretzky: An Autobiography* (1990) by Wayne Gretzky with Rick Reilly and *I, Rigoberta Menchú: An Indian Woman in Guatemala* (1984) by Rigoberta Menchú with Elisabeth Burgos-Debray.

Theses and dissertations are rarely in the form of autobiographies. There apparently are two main reasons for the paucity of such works. First, within the tradition of positivism that dominated academic research throughout the twentieth century, a person writing about himself or herself did not fit the image of a proper scholar who objectively analyzes events from an outsider's vantage point. Consequently, the subjective introspection that permeates autobiographies has generally not been seen as respectable thesis and dissertation fare. Second, the content of a graduate student's life, or the manner of presenting that life, is usually not seen by faculty advisors as sufficiently interesting or instructive to serve as the focus of scholarly attention. However, in the postmodern atmosphere within certain realms of academia over recent decades, autobiographical theses or dissertations are not merely tolerated but warmly welcomed.

***Purpose:*** The typical intent of autobiography is to furnish readers an insider's view of a life by describing how events are interpreted by the person who has lived those events and who is the product of their influence. Hence, autobiographies are intentionally subjective, designed to reveal the motives, plans, ambitions, values, joys, disappointments, fears, and sorrows that help explain the author's behavior.

***Procedure:*** In one apparently common approach to writing a traditional autobiography, authors search through their memories of the past to locate key events (critical incidents) and influential people that affected the course of their lives. The autobiographer's task becomes one of linking together those incidents and people to form a chronological chain of cause and effect intended to explain why such a life assumed its observed pattern.

There are several ways that mediated autobiographies can be fashioned. As one alternative, the collaborator brings to the task a structure for the narrative that consists of a pattern of topics or questions that define the matters to be addressed in the work. The autobiographee's role is then one of providing answers to the questions, either orally or in written form. Answering the questions may also include furnishing letters, diaries, newspaper clippings, photographs, and memorabilia from which the writer can draw information.

A different approach to mediated autobiography consists of the writer intentionally avoiding to prepare a structure of questions ahead of time but, instead, asking the person whose life is being depicted to talk or write at great length about her or his life history, describing the incidents and people that come to mind as significant influences. The collaborator then searches through this wealth of raw material to locate distinctive themes, decision points, and strands of cause that characterize that life. In short, the writer does not come to the project with a preconceived structure but, rather, "follows the data." Finally, the writer creates a narrative that enables readers to understand the themes and influences.

***Sample projects:*** Traditional autobiographies accepted as thesis or dissertation proposals are ones submitted by graduate students (a) whose lives have been sufficiently unique to warrant scholarly attention or (b) whose manner of depicting their lives represents a theoretical or methodological contribution to the professional literature.

*Growing Up in an Inner-City Ghetto*
*An Insider's View of the New York Stock Exchange*
*A Critical-Incident Analysis of the Reformation of a Delinquent*
*The Autobiography of a Child Musical Prodigy*

Mediated autobiographies that serve as the objects of theses or dissertations are usually about the lives of prominent individuals or ones who typify a culture or way of life that is not generally well understood. The task of the graduate student is that of collecting and organizing the individual's life story, then presenting it in a readable form, adding little or no interpretation. Thus, if the person whose life is being described contributes the great majority of the content in his or her own words, then the product qualifies as mediated autobiography. But if the product contains a significant amount of the graduate student's phrasing and interpretation, the work is more accurately labeled *biography.*

*The Life Story of a Pioneering Feminist Activist*
*Reminiscences of a Samoan Talking Chief*
*Political Tactics as Seen by a Secretary to the President*
*Through the Eyes of a Cured Neurotic*

***Advantages:*** The value of autobiographies lies in their depicting an individual's life from the writer's own perspective, thereby revealing motives, goals, beliefs, emotional reactions, and interpretations of events that might not be discovered by an outsider functioning as a biographer.

***Limitations:*** A threat to the validity of autobiographies derives from the fact that they are likely to be self-serving. An autobiography gives its author a chance to concoct a partially fictional account, portraying the author as a more adventuresome, noble, influential, creative, or self-sacrificing individual than is deserved. Thus, the vision of reality conveyed in the narrative may, either intentionally or unwittingly, be somewhat at odds with the truth.

***Resources:*** Styles of autobiographical writing are described in

Anderson, L. R. (1997). *Women and autobiography in the twentieth century: Remembered features.* New York: Prentice Hall & Harvester Wheatsheaf.
Andrews, W. L. (Ed.). (1993). *African American autobiography: A collection of critical essays.* Englewood Cliffs, NJ: Prentice Hall.
Eakin, P. J. (Ed.). (1991). *American autobiography: Retrospect and prospect.* Madison, WI: University of Wisconsin Press.
MacNeil, R. (2003). *Looking for my country: Finding myself in America.* New York: Doubleday.
McCourt, F. (2005). *Teacher man.* New York: Scribner.
Mitchell, A. (2005). *Talking back.* New York: Viking.
Reed-Danahay, D. E. (Ed.). (1997). *Auto/ethnography: Rewriting the self and the social.* New York: Berg.
Stone, A. E. (Ed.). (1981). *The American autobiography: A collection of critical essays.* Englewood Cliffs, NJ: Prentice Hall.

## Case Studies and Ethnographies

Although in the following section we subsume ethnographies under the title *case studies,* it is not unusual for authors to distinguish between the two. Here is the distinction they draw: Case studies are intended to reveal the individualistic attributes of a particular person or institution, while the purpose of ethnographies is to identify beliefs and customs shared by members of a social system. In other words, case studies emphasize features that make one person or group different from others, whereas ethnographies emphasize the commonalities that unify members of a culture.

### *The nature of case studies*

***Defined:*** A case study is a detailed examination of a single person, group, institution, social movement, or event. For convenience of discussion, case studies can be divided into two main types, with each type divided into a pair of subtypes. The first of the main types focuses on an individual's behavior and experiences. The second concerns the operations of a group, institution, or social movement. Under each of these types, a researcher can assume the role of either an outside observer or a participant-observer.

A case study in which the researcher serves as a participant-observer within a group or institution qualifies as a typical ethnographic study, when *ethnography* is defined as the "descriptive study of a particular human society or the process of making such a study. Contemporary ethnography is based almost entirely on fieldwork and requires the complete immersion of the [researcher] in the culture and everyday life of the people who are the subject of the study" (Ethnography, 1994, p. 582).

***General purpose:*** Case studies are differentiated from historical research, biographies, and autobiographies chiefly by their time frame and emphasis. Whereas historical studies, biographies, and autobiographies typically encompass a span of several decades, case studies center attention on a limited time range—from as short as an hour to as long as several months, but seldom more than a year or so. In terms of emphasis, the intent of histories, biographies, and autobiographies is usually to trace cause-and-effect relationships as they develop across the years, whereas the aim of the typical case study is to show how—during a restricted period of time—people interact and relate to their physical/social environments.

*Studying a single person from outside*

***Purpose:*** One well-known example of this subtype is Roger Barker's book *One Boy's Day* (1951), which depicts the way the different environments that a boy inhabited during a typical day affected his behavior. Another example is a master's thesis by Christine Williams titled *A Modern "Ship of Fools": An Account of One Boy's Journey Through the Mental Health System* (1981). Each of these reports the experiences of a person as recorded and interpreted by a researcher who has followed the individual around to observe his or her transactions with the people and environments he or she encountered.

***Procedure:*** In conducting an outsider's view of a subject, a researcher can gather information by observing the subject directly, by interviewing other people who know the subject, by analyzing items produced by the subject (diaries, letters, reports, art objects), and by inspecting documents in which other people offer appraisals of the subject's behavior and traits (school report cards and cumulative records, social workers' reports, medical records, police files).

In approaching the data-collection task, researchers can either (a) start with a mind-set (such as a theory) that guides what they should notice and record or (b) start with no preconception of what to look for.

An illustration of the theory-guided strategy is Barker's ecological scheme that conceives of people occupying successive behavior settings (the person's physical/social environment at a given time) that are composed of two components: (a) the typical ways people act (*standing patterns of behavior*) and (b) the *milieu* that itself involves two elements—*physical things* (a restaurant's dining room or a high school classroom) and *time boundaries* (a two-hour dinner party or a 50-minute class period) (Barker & Gump, 1964; Barker et al., 1970). These components direct the observer's attention to what should be noted. Other mind-sets that focus researchers' observations can concern the studied person's interests, avoidances, likes, dislikes, problem-solving techniques, work habits, friendship patterns, and more.

The opposite approach of intentionally beginning with nothing in particular to look for is intended to reveal life from the viewpoint of the person being examined. The investigator's hope is to produce a case study unblemished by preconceptions. Thus, the researcher tries to record everything that occurs during an event, and then later hunts through the collected records to locate patterns to be used as the themes around which the case-study report will be organized. In practice, however, it is unlikely that researchers can approach their task with a completely open mind. Everybody apparently brings some variety of preconceptions to a case. But at least investigators can try to be open minded, thereby recognizing circumstances they had not expected; thus they are equipped to include those features in their analyses. Important in the conduct of case studies is the researcher's description of the context in which people make decisions and seek to resolve issues. Stake (1995, p. 33) suggests that "the best research questions evolve during the study."

***Sample projects:*** Representative titles include

*One Week in the Life of a Chicago Social Worker* (sociology)
*A Stock Broker's Activities on Bullish and Bearish Days* (business administration)
*Teaching in a Sioux Reservation High School* (education)
*The Role of a Fulani Chieftain* (anthropology)

***Advantages:*** The study of an individual from an observer's perspective can reveal the unique persona that the individual displays to the world and can show how that person's behavior affects other people and vice versa.

***Limitations:*** What the portrait by an outsider does not reveal is the subject's secret ambitions, motives, pleasures, fears, and ways of interpreting events. Furthermore, by focusing solely on one individual, the researcher can, only at great risk of error, infer generalizations from the case and apply those generalizations to the lives of other people.

***Resources:*** Guidance in carrying out case studies, and examples of such studies, can be found in:

Kidder, T. (1989). *Mountains beyond mountains.* New York: Random House.
Stake, R. (1995). *The art of case study research.* Thousand Oaks, CA: Sage.
Yin, R. K. (2002). *Case study research: Design and methods* (3rd ed.). Thousand Oaks, CA: Sage.

*Studying a single person from inside*

***Purpose:*** The aim of the introspective case study is to disclose how events are interpreted by the person experiencing those events.

To qualify as a thesis or dissertation, an insider's case study needs to represent either a person's experiences that are unique enough to represent a contribution to knowledge or else a style of depicting those experiences (such as a novel theoretical perspective) that is of scholarly import.

***Procedure:*** As with autobiographies, case studies from the insider's perspective can be composed solely by the insider (traditional) or can be produced in collaboration with someone else (mediated). If the subject of the study works alone in composing the account, the choice of what to include in the study will be directed either by that person's principal interests and concerns or by a formula for doing case studies derived from someone else, thus modeled on such existing reports as Barker's *One Boy's Day.* If the study is a cooperative effort involving the subject and a collaborator, the sorts of information to be compiled may be guided by a model that the collaborator provides.

***Sample projects:*** Illustrative titles of insider's studies can be

*Precinct Workers' View of Local Party Politics* (political science)
*Life on an Automobile Assembly Line* (anthropology)
*Six Months in Jail* (social psychology)
*The Homes of a Foster Child* (social work)
*An Infantryman's War* (social psychology)

***Advantages:*** Insider case studies can inform readers of the motives, values, beliefs, and interpretation of events of an individual who has participated in those events.

***Limitations:*** Again, by focusing solely on one individual, a researcher can err in applying generalizations from that case to other people's situations. Hence, authors of an insider's view, in order to extend their interpretations to others' lives, need to offer evidence in addition to their own experiences to support those extensions.

***Resources:*** Five examples of this sort of study are

Brinkley, D. (1988). *Washington goes to war.* New York: Ballantine. (An insider's view of Washington, DC, as the nation prepared for World War II.)

Conroy, P. (2002). *My losing season.* New York: Random House. (An insider's view of the Citadel's basketball season by a member of the team.)

Ehrenreich, B. (2005). *Bait and Switch: The (futile) pursuit of the American dream.* New York: Metropolitan Books. (An insider's view by an undercover person living the life of a low-wage worker.)

Goffman, E. (1959). *The presentation of self in everyday life.* New York: Doubleday Anchor. (Much of the information for this classic sociological study of people in the Shetland Islands was collected in restaurants.)

Yankoski, M. (2005). *Under the overpass: A journey of faith on the streets of America.* Sisters, OR: Multnomah. (The tale of two friends, posing as homeless people, spending five months wandering the streets of five cities—Denver, Phoenix, Portland, San Diego, San Francisco, and Washington, D.C.)

Cautionary guidelines for writing mediated autobiographies are offered in

Causer, G. T. (1998). Making, taking, and faking lives: The ethics of collaborative life writing. *Style, 32*(2), 334–338.

*Studying a group or institution—outsider versus insider*

In producing a case study or ethnographic account of a group or organization, the researcher's relationship to the operation of that social entity can vary from distant to intimate. Although in our introduction to this section we dichotomized the researcher's role as that of either an outsider or insider, in practice the relationship of observer to the observed is usually somewhere between those extremes. For instance, a psychologist studying the dynamics of a drug therapy group could view the operation of the group from any of several vantage points that extend along a scale from (a) the most distant, least involved to (b) the least distant, most involved. The researcher could assume any of the following roles, which range from distant to intimate:

- Sometime after the end of the group session, view the group's activities as recorded on videotape.
- View the group's activities via a one-way-vision screen at the time the group is meeting.
- Sit in the meeting room at a distance from the group, attempting to appear as inconspicuous as possible.
- Sit among the group members, but take no part in the proceedings.
- Participate with the group as an observer who is studying the group process and is welcome to make comments.
- Participate in the group as one of those seeking help for a drug-abuse problem, but not revealing one's role as a researcher.

Wolcott, as an anthropologist seeking to produce "a generalized description of the life-way of a socially interacting group," has noted advantages and disadvantages of being a participant-observer at different points along the distant/close scale.

> Ordinarily an outsider to the group being studied, the ethnographer tries hard to know more about the cultural system he or she is studying than any individual who is a natural participant in it, at once advantaged by the outsider's broad and analytical perspective but, by reason of that same detachment, unlikely ever totally to comprehend the insider's point of view. The ethnographer walks a fine line. With too much distance and perspective, one is labeled aloof, remote, insensitive, superficial; with too much familiarity, empathy, and identification, one is suspected of having "gone native." (Wolcott, 1988, pp. 188–189)

***Purpose:*** Case studies of groups can have various aims. One is to identify the cultural characteristics that typify the group. The study becomes comparative whenever two or more groups are observed and conclusions are drawn about ways in which the groups are similar and different.

*A Minangkabau Wedding Ceremony* (anthropology)
*A Silicon Valley Office Party* (anthropology)
*Choosing a Chief—Tahitian and Fijian Practices* (political science)
*Sunday Church—Roman Catholic, Unitarian, Salvation Army* (sociology)

Another aim is to trace the dynamics of a group's inner workings—exposing the roles different people play, the power and prestige relationships among group members, interpersonal problems that arise, strategies adopted to resolve problems, and more.

*Community Building at the Atlanta Union Mission* (social psychology)
*Competition and Cooperation in a College Basketball Team* (social psychology)
*The Dynamics of an Alternative High School Classroom* (education)
*Power Relationships in a Business Office* (business management)
*Settling a Management/Labor Dispute in the Grape Industry* (economics and political science)
*The Internal Workings of a Feminist Organization* (social psychology)

***Procedure:*** The intention that a researcher brings to collecting data for a case study can be at any point along a scale that extends from (a) a specific theory or precise question to answer to (b) no expectations at all about what to observe or how to interpret the results. That intention determines to a great extent the steps in the procedure that will be adopted. At the precise-question end of the scale, viewing a group or institution through the lens of a preconceived structure defines exactly what to look for and what to ignore. In contrast, at the other end of the scale, the task of observing a group is approached with an attitude of "I'll give attention to everything that happens. I'll not decide ahead of time which events and actions are most important. In other words, I'll try not to be biased by expectations I bring from my own culture. Instead, I'll attempt to see life from the viewpoint of the group's participants in order to identify their beliefs and values that explain why they behave as they do."

These two extreme positions can be illustrated with a pair of anthropological investigations, one in the South Sea Island nation of Tonga and the other in West Africa.

*Specific preconceived questions.* In a journal article titled "Dealing With the Dark Side in the Ethnography of Childhood: Child Punishment in Tonga," Helen Kapavalu described the role of physical discipline as an instructional device in contemporary Tongan society (Kapavalu, 1993). The content of Kapavalu's description implies that the following kinds of questions guided her research.

> *The target variable:* What role does physical punishment play in traditional Tongan child rearing, on what rationale is such punishment founded, and what consequences result from that practice?
>
> *Guide questions defining the domain of the case:* What is the authority structure (the system of controllers and the controlled) in Tongan society? How is this structure reflected in the broader community, the family, and the school? What characteristics determine a person's place in the authority hierarchies? What personal-social qualities are valued in Tongan culture? What methods are used by authority figures to foster those qualities in children and youth? Upon what rationale and perception of child nature are these methods founded? How do children and youths respond to such methods, particularly to the use of physical punishment? What significant consequences appear to result from physical punishment—consequences for individuals and for the conduct of Tongan society? What changes, if any, are occurring in the techniques used for socializing the young; what are the likely causes of those changes; and what are the probable consequences of such changes for the welfare of individuals and for the traditional Tongan social system?
>
> How does the role of physical punishment as a child-rearing device in Tonga compare with its role in a typical Australian community? What problems can occur for people from a Tongan background when they enter Australian society, and vice versa?
>
> *Sources of answers to the guide questions:* Incidents of punishment in the daily routine of life in Tongan homes, schools, church sessions, markets, playgrounds, recreational events, and work sites. Ethnographies and accounts

of life in Tonga written over past decades by missionaries, anthropologists, and visitors to the islands.

*Methods of collecting answers:* Observations of child-rearing practices in Tongan settings. Interviews with Tongans in Tonga to learn their perceptions of physical punishment as an instrument of child socialization. Interviews with non-Tongan observers of life in Tonga to gather incidents of physical punishment and the observers' assessments of the desirability of such punishment. (Thomas, 1998, pp. 97–98)

*No preconceived guide questions.* An Indiana University anthropologist, Michael Jackson, identifies his approach to data gathering as phenomenological anthropology, which he defines as

> the scientific study of experience. It is an attempt to describe human consciousness in its lived immediacy, before it is subject to theoretical elaboration or conceptual systematizing. . . . [It consists of] prioritizing lived experience over theoretical knowledge. . . . Phenomenology seeks a corrective to forms of knowledge and description that, in attempting to isolate unifying and universal laws, lose all sense of the abundance and plenitude of life. (Jackson, 1996, pp. 2, 6, 7)

In effect, the researcher avoids forcing the events of people's daily lives into a preconceived theory of cause, such as offering an estimate of how hereditary and environmental factors have contributed to or "caused" an event. Instead, the investigator seeks to judge the meaning of events in terms of the question: What were the experiencing person's thoughts and actions that appeared during—or as a result of—those events?

> The phenomenologist suspends inquiry into the hidden determinants of belief and action in order to describe the implications, intentions, and effects of what people say, do, and hold to be true. (Jackson, 1996, p. 11)

To illustrate this attempt to understand life from the experiencing person's perspective, Jackson offers an example from his experience with the Kuranko people of Sierra Leone in West Africa. He describes a class of women in Kuranko society who were self-proclaimed witches facing imminent death.

> One must consider how the beliefs [in witches] are actually used by the women who confess to witchcraft during terminal illness—as desperate stratagems for reclaiming autonomy in a hopeless situation. The self-confessed witch . . . actively uses the imagery of witchcraft to give voice to long-suppressed grievances, coping with suffering by declaring herself the author

> of it. . . . Thus, she determines how she will play out the role which circumstance has thrust upon her. She dies deciding her own destiny, sealing her own fate. (Jackson, 1996, pp. 11–12)

As a further example, Jackson asserts that storytelling among the Kuranko serves the function of "reconfiguring" people's perceptions of their lives, thereby enabling them to bear the dilemmas and tensions of their daily existence. However, this is not what the Kuranko directly told him. Rather, it's Jackson's interpretation—his inference. Therefore, he has not adhered strictly to presenting his subjects' view of life in their own words. He seems to recognize this by admitting "it is difficult to capture the kinds of transformed awareness that storytelling or ritual effect" (Jackson, 1996, p. 21).

***Advantages:*** Ethnographic research can perform several useful functions. It can reveal those characteristics shared among members of a group that make the group's culture distinctive, thereby contributing to the understanding of why one group differs from another. Case studies can also reveal the internal operations of a group or institution by identifying the relative influence of different members, tracing routes of communication, suggesting the sources of proposals that determine the group's activities, showing how people achieve and maintain their membership, exposing the sanctions used to ensure that members abide by group standards, and more.

The case study is useful as a flexible approach that can be applied to diverse academic disciplines and in varied contexts. In addition, cases that trace happenings in detail allow readers to vicariously experience events as they actually occurred. As instructional devices, case studies provoke discussion that can lead to new learnings and lines of inquiry.

***Limitations:*** To disabuse people of the notion that a case study can be a portrayal of the "objective truth" about a group or organization, Denzin (1997, p. 3) has proposed: "Ethnography is that form of inquiry and writing that produces descriptions and accounts about the ways of life of the writer and those written about." Thus, although authors may assert that they have simply recorded "what really happened," their account of the case is inevitably a rendition filtered through their particular mental lens, so versions of events produced by different investigators will necessarily paint a somewhat different picture. This observation about multiple visions of the same group or same series of events is a disadvantage for readers who were hoping to learn a single "real truth" about a case. However, if a number of different researchers conduct independent studies of a group or institution, the resulting diverse products can be considered advantageous by readers who accept Denzin's proposal that different "truths" result from different accounts of an episode.

Conclusions drawn in one ethnographic study can be applied to other ethnographic studies only at considerable peril because of the unique conditions that may determine the fabric of life in each setting. Furthermore, participant-observers can become so intimately immersed in a society that they diminish the objectivity of perception they sought to bring to the study. If, on the other hand, participant-observers fail to engage themselves intimately in the life of the society—and thus obtain a faulty grasp of the language, cannot view religious rites from a native perspective, or the like—they are apt to convey an inaccurate picture of what life in that setting means to the people who inhabit it.

***Resources:*** Guidance in producing ethnographic research is offered in the following volumes:

Angrosino, M. (2004). *Projects in ethnographic research.* Prospect Heights, IL: Waveland.

Denzin, N. K. (1997). *Interpretive ethnography.* Thousand Oaks, CA: Sage.

Denzin, N. K., & Lincoln, Y. (Eds.). (1994). *Handbook of qualitative research.* Thousand Oaks, CA: Sage.

Gray, A. (2002). *Research practice for cultural studies: Ethnographic methods and lived cultures.* Thousand Oaks, CA: Sage.

Hammersley, M. (1992). *What's wrong with ethnography?* London: Routledge.

Jessor, R., Colby, A., & Shweder, R. A. (Eds.). (1996). *Ethnography and human development.* Chicago: University of Chicago Press.

Madison, D. S. (2005). *Critical ethnography: Methods, ethics, and performance.* Thousand Oaks, CA: Sage.

Examples of the case study approach include

Bussert, J. (1986). *Battered women: From a theology of suffering to an ethic of empowerment.* New York: Division for Mission in North America, Lutheran Church in America.

Doress, P. B., & Siegal, D. L. (1987). *Ourselves growing older: Women aging with knowledge and power.* New York: Simon & Schuster.

Hiss, T. (1990). *The experience of place.* New York: Knopf.

Hochschild, A. (1989). *Second shift: Working parents and the revolution at home.* New York: Viking.

Kozol, J. (1991). *Savage inequalities: Children in America's schools.* New York: Harper.

Mead, M. (1975). *Male and female: A study of the sexes in a changing world.* New York: Morrow.

Shulman, L. (1992). Toward a pedagogy of cases. In J. Shulman (Ed.), *Case Methods in Teacher Education* (pp. 1–30). New York: Teachers College Press.

## Experience Narratives

Such narratives consist of relatively brief stories of influential events in people's lives.

### *The nature of personal stories*

***Defined:*** In recent decades, individuals' descriptions and interpretations of their personal experiences have been increasingly accepted as suitable versions of research by academicians of a postmodern persuasion. In the following section, while we recognize that biographies and case studies often include a large measure of personal views of life, we are limiting the meaning of experience narratives to accounts focusing on a particular time (in contrast to the extended time sequence of biographies) and on a more restricted body of subject matter than that found in most case studies.

***Purpose:*** The aim of experience narratives (or *personal stories*) is to reveal individualistic perceptions of selected life events. The emphasis is on differences among people in their experiences and their ways of viewing their lives as conveyed in their own modes of communication—words, gestures, songs, dances, symbols, art works—rather than in a researcher's modes. In other words, the people who are the objects of the research are mainly the ones who do the telling. The researcher acts chiefly as an organizer and compiler of the narratives. Studies of this sort are thus cooperative efforts in which the compiler (the thesis or dissertation author) and the informant (the person whose narrative is being reported) are credited with being co-researchers.

***Procedure:*** A typical approach to experience narrative research involves such steps as the following:

1. The compiler explains to the informant the realm of life experiences that is the focus of attention, such as the informant's (a) present conception of God, (b) becoming an abused wife, (c) most dramatic sexual episode, (d) suffering discrimination, (e) encounters with a particular ethnic group, or the like.
2. The compiler describes (a) the informant's expected role and why the informant's narrated experiences are valued and (b) the compiler's own role.
3. The informant speaks freely about the topic as the compiler records the narration verbatim, preferably through the use of an audio or video

recorder so the account will be accurate. When such equipment is unavailable or the informant objects to its use, the compiler must depend on notes written at that time or as soon as possible after the session.

4. During the narration, the compiler may feel it necessary to offer prompts that keep the informant on the topic and encourage an elaboration of aspects that have been unclear or inadequately developed. For example, when investigating a respondent's conception of God, a compiler may ask, "What do you feel is your relationship to God?" or "Does God ever help you? And if so, how?"
5. In presenting the recorded narrative in the thesis or dissertation, the compiler prefaces the narrative with a description of:
   5.1 The research topic, that is, the aspect of life that has been the focus of the informant's story.
   5.2 Who the informant was and why such an informant was a suitable source of information.
   5.3 The division of labor between the informant and the compiler in the conduct of the research.
   5.4 The context of the narrative session.
   5.5 Conditions that may have influenced the outcome of the session.

An experience-narrative project can assume a comparative form if more than one person's account is included in the study. Under those circumstances, the author may present the informants' stories without adding any analysis so that the narratives stand on their own. Or else the author may discuss themes, similarities, and contrasts observed among the several accounts.

***Sample projects:*** Illustrative titles of experience narratives include

*Participants' Perceptions of the Woodstock Concert*
*Incidents of Grieving Among the Cree*
*What Basques Talk About at Home*
*A Zulu Shaman's Interpretation of His Work*
*Four-Year-Olds Tell Jokes*

***Advantages:*** Narratives offer two opposite advantages. First, they can show differences among people, enabling readers of research reports to discover and to "celebrate" the uniqueness of individuals' experiences and the curious ways they interpret events. Second, narratives can show similarities among people through demonstrating how ones who live under very different circumstances may have much in common when they display similar desires, emotions, and responses under dissimilar life situations.

***Limitations:*** Narratives do not provide what many consumers of research are seeking, including

- information about how characteristics of people are distributed throughout a population
- generalizations that can be applied to understanding people other than those whose stories have been collected
- ways to correct undesirable personal or social conditions

***Resources:*** Guidance in producing experience narratives is offered in

Clandinin, J., & Connelly, F. M. (2004). *Narrative inquiry: Experiences and story in qualitative research.* San Francisco, CA: Jossey-Bass.

Denzin, N. K., & Lincoln, Y. (Eds.). (1994). *Handbook of qualitative research.* Thousand Oaks, CA: Sage.

Durr, M. (1998). Oral narrative research with black women. *Gender & Society, 12*(6), 766+.

Lieblich, A. (1998). *Narrative research: Reading, analysis, and interpretation.* Thousand Oaks, CA: Sage.

Ruthellen, J., Lieiblich, A., & McAdams, D. (2002). *Up close and personal: Using ourselves in research.* Washington, DC: American Psychological Association.

## Surveys

*General definitions*

Survey methods involve gathering information about a topic from a variety of sources, then reporting a summary of the findings. One useful way to classify surveys is to place them in two broad categories—*direct-data types* and *research-literature types.*

A direct-data survey involves collecting information from individuals, groups, or institutions by means of interviews, questionnaires, opinionnaires, or observations. A research-literature survey involves compiling studies that others have conducted, then interpreting or evaluating those studies from a novel perspective.

*Direct-data surveys*

***Purpose:*** The direct-data type is the kind people usually intend when they use the term *survey.* The aim of such investigations is to reveal the status of some phenomenon within an identified class of people, organizations, or regions at a particular time. Over past decades, thousands of surveys have provided information collected from a wide range of sources. To suggest something of the variety of topics on which surveys can focus, Table 7.1 offers a minuscule potpourri of topics (*Information about*), of sources (*Information sources*), and of devices for directly collecting information (*Data-gathering techniques and instruments,* such as those inspected in Chapter 8). Table 7.1 illustrates only five foci of surveys—*achievement, customs, opinions, policies,* and *status.* Other kinds would have served equally well as illustrations—such as surveys centering on laws, regulations, habits, plans, practices, theories, traditions, worldviews, lifestyles, leisure pursuits, possessions, artistic pursuits, social systems, and more.

***Procedure:*** Direct-data surveys can be conducted in many ways. The following example illustrates one pattern of steps that can be adopted.

1. The researcher's guide question (or questions) defines the survey's focus.
2. Potential people, organizations, or regions to survey are identified.
3. Criteria are established to guide the choice of which options from among the potential ones at step 2 will actually be used.
4. The criteria are applied to the options to arrive at the actual people, organizations, or regions to be studied.
5. Potential instruments and methods of collecting survey data (as described in Chapter 8) are identified.
6. Criteria for selecting the most suitable instruments and methods are established.
7. Specific instruments and methods of data collection are created or adopted.
8. A small sample of people, institutions, or regions that will not be used in the final survey is chosen for testing the instruments and methods in a pilot study in order to discover possible weaknesses in the methodology.

9. The instruments and methods are tried out on the small sample.
10. The results of the pilot study are examined; and the instruments and methods are revised to correct weaknesses found during the pilot study. If many shortcomings were identified, or if the researcher is not confident that the corrections have been sufficient, a second cycle of steps 7–10 may be carried out with a different sample of people, institutions, or regions (which will not participate in the final survey).
11. In most surveys, the entire population that is being studied does not take part. Instead, for practical reasons, only a portion of that population (a sample) is chosen to be studied. Thus, at step 11, a system for drawing the sample is adopted; and a decision is made about which people, organizations, or regions will be asked to participate. (The next segment of this discussion reviews alternative sampling procedures.)
12. The survey instruments and methods are administered.
13. The survey responses are tabulated and classified.
14. The classified results are interpreted to suggest what they mean in relation to the researcher's original guide questions.
15. A description of the study is written in the form of a thesis or dissertation.

***Problems of sampling:*** Sometimes researchers intend to apply the conclusions drawn from their survey solely to the sources of information (people, documents, events) that directly participated in the survey. For instance, a sociology student interviews all members of a local truckers' union to learn their opinions of a proposed change in truck safety regulations. The results are then reported as representing only the viewpoints of those members, with no speculation about how truck drivers in general, or those in other union locals, might have answered the interviewer's questions. The results of such a study can be referred to as descriptive conclusions.

Even though some researchers draw generalizations only about the actual participants in their survey, far more wish to extend their conclusions to embrace people or events that were not included in the study. In effect, the survey's subjects are considered to be only a portion—no more than a sample—of the population to which the research findings will be applied. Thus, on the basis of testing the reading skills of 1,500 high school seniors, a graduate student in the field of educational psychology may draw conclusions about the reading abilities of all 136,000 of an entire region's seniors. This application

**Table 7.1** Examples of Survey Topics

| *Information About* | *Information Sources* | *Data-Gathering Techniques & Instruments* |
|---|---|---|
| **Achievement:** | | |
| academic | school records | test scores, grades |
| athletic | teams' record sheets | content analysis |
| financial | income tax returns | content analysis |
| political | election returns | content analysis |
| | magazines, newspapers | content analysis |
| scientific | science journals | content analysis |
| theatrical | magazines, newspapers | content analysis |
| **Customs:** | | |
| clothing | people's appearance | direct observation |
| | photos, drawings | content analysis |
| dietary | restaurants | nutrition rating scales |
| | people's self-reports | |
| governance | constitutions | content analysis |
| | people's experiences | interviews, questionnaires |
| | history books | content analysis |
| housing | housing sites | photographs |
| | magazines, books | content analysis |
| **Customs:** | | |
| marriage | marriage ceremonies | direct observation |
| | academic journals, books | content analysis |
| religious | religious services | direct observation |
| | religious publications | content analysis |
| | anthropological studies | content analysis |
| social interaction | social situations | direct observation |
| | social-psychology books & journals | content analysis |
| **Opinions about:** | | |
| human rights | people | interviews, opinionnaires |
| politicians | people | interviews, opinionnaires |
| | newspapers, magazines | content analysis |
| social behavior | people | interviews, opinionnaires |
| taxation | people | interviews, opinionnaires |

*(Continued)*

**Table 7.1** (Continued)

| *Information About* | *Information Sources* | *Data-Gathering Techniques & Instruments* |
|---|---|---|
| **Policies about:** | | |
| college admission | college catalogs | content analysis |
| hiring/firing | court cases | content analysis |
| | personnel officers | interviews, questionnaires |
| lending/borrowing | bank & credit card brochures | content analysis |
| voting | election laws & regulations | content analysis |
| **Status:** | | |
| social class | people's lifestyles | rating scales |
| citizenship | people's self-reports | content analysis |
| | census records | content analysis |
| income | people's self-reports | content analysis |

of a study's results to subjects that did not directly take part in the study is usually referred to as an *inferential* conclusion, because the pattern of scores of the 1,500 is inferred to be indicative of the pattern that would have resulted if the entire 136,000 had been tested. However, extending the conclusions about a directly studied group to a larger population always entails the danger of error, since the sample group may not truly represent the larger population. In other words, the sample may be biased.

Consequently, as you plan a survey, it is important to decide how broadly you wish to apply your findings. Will you be content to regard the results as limited to the subjects you directly studied (people, events, documents), or will you consider those subjects to be a sample of a broader population to which your conclusions can appropriately apply? If the latter, then you need to specify (a) the characteristics of the population to which you will apply your conclusions and (b) how you can select a sample of subjects that will faithfully represent those characteristics. There are various methods of drawing samples, with each accompanied by particular advantages and disadvantages. In way of illustration, consider these four approaches to sampling: *simple random, multistage, systematic,* and *convenience.*

*Simple random sampling.* The basic rule for drawing a random sample is that each member of the population should have an equal chance of being chosen. There are several ways that can be accomplished. One familiar way consists of assigning each subject in the population a number, then writing each number on a slip of paper (with all slips identical in size and texture), placing the slips in a hat or fish bowl, stirring up the slips, and drawing one slip at a time until the sample size has been reached. So, if there are 4,756 members in a college's junior class, and you plan to interview a sample of 100 juniors about their opinions of binge drinking among college students, then the first 100 numbers drawn out of the 4,756 would comprise your random sample.

Or, instead of putting 4,756 slips of paper in a hat, you could obtain a list of random numbers from a table in a statistics book or from a computer program that generates random numbers. The first 100 numbers in that list identify which students (in terms of their assigned identification numbers) would be interviewed.

The advantage of drawing a random sample is that you can now make a good estimate of the extent to which your sample of juniors probably reflects the opinions of the entire junior class (using statistical techniques described in Chapter 11). But you also may face several problems of ensuring that all 100 can be interviewed. For instance, you may have trouble getting in touch with all 100, or some of them may not agree to participate, while others may not be available at the times you need them. And if the population to which you wish to apply your conclusions is spread out geographically, the task of interviewing all respondents may be overwhelming. Such would be the case if you wanted to apply your generalizations to "college juniors in the United States." There are simply too many juniors in too many different locations to sample randomly.

*Multistage sampling.* One way to simplify the problem of drawing a random sample is to divide the selection process into stages. That is, a population can often be described in terms of a hierarchy of sampling units of different sizes and types. As an example, for our binge-drinking study we could define a hierarchy of three stages or levels: (1) regions of the nation, (2) colleges and universities, and (3) juniors in those institutions. First, we divide the United States into regions, and by random sampling we pick one region. Second, we list the names of all colleges and universities in that region, then pick four by random means. Third, we obtain the names of the juniors in those institutions and from that list we randomly select the 100 to be surveyed by telephone interviews. This procedure meets the basic requirement for random sampling (each student has had an equal chance to be chosen) and has much simplified our task of conducting the survey. Variations of multistage sampling are available to accommodate the conditions of different studies and different types of populations (Ross, 1985).

*Systematic sampling.* Within relatively small populations, a systematic sample will usually represent a population's characteristics as accurately as will a random sample. Imagine that a political-science student plans to write a thesis on the attitudes of members of local luncheon clubs (Kiwanis, Lions, Optimists, Rotary, and others) toward gun-control legislation. The membership rosters show a total of 1,379 members in the local region. Rather than soliciting the opinions of the entire population of 1,379, the student plans to conduct telephone interviews with only 50 or 3.6% of the total. To select the 50 who will be asked to participate, the student assigns each club member a number ranging from 1 to 1,379. She then writes numbers 1 to 28 on a sheet of paper (since there are about 28 fifties in 1,379) and, with her eyes closed, touches a pencil point to the sheet. The point touches number 8. That number defines the first club member to be included in the sample. The next choice will be 28 numbers beyond 8 (member 36), and the third will be 28 numbers beyond 36 (member 64), and so on until all 50 have been selected.

Because only chance errors, rather than other sources of bias, are apt to affect how closely the interview results approximate the population's opinions about gun control, the statistical techniques described in Chapter 11 for estimating sampling error (*t*-test and ANOVA) can be appropriately used with systematic sampling.

*Convenience sampling.* Many surveys in the social sciences and humanities utilize what have been called *available, convenience,* or *accidental* samples. Such is the case when teachers in a junior high school test eighth-graders' mastery of computer keyboarding, when an anthropologist describes the division of household tasks among the members of nine families, or when a social psychologist studies children's methods of settling disputes in an inner-city neighborhood. In these instances, the particular junior high school, families, and neighborhood were chosen because they were convenient to study, not because they were randomly selected representatives of a defined population. Therefore, the value of such research resides in what it tells about the people who participated directly in those investigations rather than in generalizations that might be proposed about junior high students, families, and neighborhoods in general. In short, there is no available statistical procedure for estimating how well convenience samples reflect the pertinent characteristics of whatever broad population a researcher wishes to speak about.

The best an investigator can do in such situations is to (a) identify the features of the sample that seem to be causal factors (factors that affect keyboarding, family members' roles, and means of settling disputes), then speculate about whether those same factors might be influential—and to the same degree—in other groups that could be studied and that represent the same population. For instance, the anthropologist who studied the nine families might suggest that results similar to the ones obtained in her project would likely be found in other families that displayed similar—and apparently influential—conditions, such as (a) approximately the same number of family members of about the same ages, (b) the same social-class status, (c) the same general cultural background, (d) the same general housing style, and (e) the same sort of climate. In effect, the investigator believes these five variables significantly affect family members' roles. However, generalizing from an available or convenience sample to an assumed population is a precarious venture, since there is no clear way of identifying and measuring the factors that may have biased the sample's results.

*Summary.* The four types of sampling described above represent only a few of the available options for designing samples. Other varieties, detailed methods of using them, and their advantages and disadvantages can be found in the resources listed at the end of this discussion of surveys.

***Sample projects:*** Here are titles of studies utilizing survey data:

*Voters' Predictions of Election Results* (political science)
*Welfare Recipients' Complaints* (sociology, social work)
*Teachers' Influence on Students' Perceptions* (psychology, education)
*Families' Budgeting Practices* (economics)
*Errors in Spoken Spanish* (linguistics)

***Advantages:*** Direct-data surveys offer useful information about groups by showing the dominant characteristics of a group as well as differences among members of a group. Inferences drawn from studying a sample of subjects (people, events, institutions, documents) may be applied to a larger population, thereby contributing to readers' understanding, not only of the individuals who were studied directly, but also of a wider range of similar subjects.

Surveys conducted with questionnaires distributed to respondents (by hand, by mail, by Internet) enable researchers to gather information from a large number of respondents in a short space of time with relatively little effort.

***Limitations:*** One worrisome problem with surveys that require detailed answers or touch on sensitive topics is that of ensuring that participants are diligent and truthful in answering the survey items. A further challenge is that of mounting a convincing rationale to support the extension of the findings beyond the studied sample to encompass a broader population.

Surveys conducted by means of interviews are labor intensive in that they require a large expenditure of the researcher's time. However, interviews are able to reveal nuances of meaning that cannot be obtained by means of written questionnaires.

***Resources:*** Help with survey methods and sampling is offered in


Alreck, P., & Settle, R. (2003). *Survey research handbook.* New York: McGraw-Hill.

Babbie, E. R. (1990). *Survey research methods* (2nd ed.). Belmont, CA: Wadsworth.

Barnett, V. (1991). *Sample survey principles and methods.* New York: Oxford University Press.

Bickman, L., & Rog, D. J. (Eds.). (1998). *Handbook of applied research.* Thousand Oaks, CA: Sage.

Braverman, M. T., & Slater, J. K. (Eds.). (1996). *Advances in survey research.* San Francisco: Jossey-Bass.

Chaudhuri, A., & Vos, J. W. E. (1988). *Unified theory and strategies of survey sampling.* New York: Elsevier.

Fink, A., & Kosecoff, J. (1998). *How to conduct surveys: A step-by-step guide* (2nd ed.). Thousand Oaks, CA: Sage.

Henry, G. T. (1990). *Practical sampling.* Newbury Park, CA: Sage.

Krosnick, J. A. (1999). Survey research. *Annual Review of Psychology, 50,* 537–567.

MacNeill, I. B., & Humphrey, G. J. (1987). *Applied probability, stochastic processes, and sampling theory.* Boston: Klumer.

Nardi, P. (2002). *Doing survey research: A guide to quantitative research methods.* Boston, MA: Allyn & Bacon.

Rea, L. M., & Parker, R. A. (2005). *Designing and conducting survey research.* San Francisco: Jossey-Bass.

Weisberg, H. F., Krasnick, J. A., & Bowen, B. D. (1996). *An introduction to survey research, polling, and data analysis.* Thousand Oaks, CA: Sage.


*Research-literature surveys*

***Defined:*** Frequently the information on which a graduate student's project depends is not acquired directly from people, institutions, or observed events. Instead, the information comes from previously conducted studies that bear on the project's questions.

***Purposes:*** Literature surveys can serve numerous functions, including those of (a) synthesizing studies, (b) revealing diversity, (c) exposing inconsistencies and exceptions, (d) illustrating applications, and (e) generating propositions and principles.

*Synthesizing studies.* Most research projects are very limited in scope. They focus on a specific place, time period, and restricted number of people. But, as noted above, researchers usually wish to draw conclusions that apply to a broader range of places, times, and people than they have studied. However, doing so can entail considerable risk of error. Some investigators seek to reduce this risk by collecting the results of a variety of separate studies so as to increase the places, times, and subjects on which to base generalizations. In effect, their purpose is to synthesize studies so as to show which conclusions validly apply to the entire collection and which apply to no more than one or a few of the studies.

One form of synthesizing that has become increasingly popular in recent decades bears the title meta-analysis and is founded on the following line of logic.

> The traditional process of integrating [the conclusions from] a body of research literature is essentially intuitive and the style of reporting narrative. Because the reviewer's methods are often unspecified, it is usually difficult to discern how the original research findings have contributed to the integration. A careful analysis can sometimes reveal that different reviewers use the same research reports in support of contrary conclusions. . . . The most serious problem for reviewers to cope with is the volume of relevant research literature to be integrated. Most reviewers appear to deal with this by choosing only a subset of the studies. Some take the studies they know most intimately. Others take those they value most highly, usually on the basis of methodological quality. Few, however, give any indication of the means by which they selected studies for review. (McGaw, 1985, p. 3322)

One solution proposed for the apparent shortcomings of the typical intuitive synthesizing process has been to adopt a form of meta-analysis. The term *meta-analysis* can be applied to any quantitative integration of empirical research results. Two of the most popular meta-analytic approaches to defining the domain of pertinent studies and calculating the commonalities and differences among studies are those described by Glass, McGaw, and Smith (1981) and by Hunter, Schmidt, and Jackson (1982). Three examples of studies employing meta-analysis are ones titled

*Common Themes Across Counseling Theories* (counseling psychology)
*Similarities Among Polling Systems* (political science)
*Defining "Family"—A Cross-Cultural Study* (anthropology)

*Revealing diversity.* The main intent of some research-literature surveys is not to identify characteristics shared in common by many studies but, rather, to show how various investigations of the same topic differ from each other.

Imagine, for example, that a sociology student wishes to learn how social exchanges are manifested in different cultures. As her guide, she adopts a social-exchange theory that focuses on the principles governing transactions between individuals or groups, with those transactions contributing either to the benefit or to the detriment of the participants. The assumption behind her social-exchange theory is that an individual who benefits from another person's acts is obligated to reciprocate by furnishing benefits to that person in turn. For many common types of social interaction, proper exchange is dictated by cultural tradition in the form of expectations about fairness, expectations that assume the form of *exchange norms.* Such norms are adopted in a culture as devices for coercing the parties in a social transaction to abide by what is considered fair. Members of society impose social pressure to encourage people to comply with those norms. The extent to which people abide by exchange norms influences their status in the society's hierarchy of respect, prestige, and power (Eve, 1986). The central purpose of the student's dissertation is thus to reveal and explain diverse forms in which exchange norms appear in different cultures. Here are titles of three studies focusing on diversity:

*Variations Among Conceptions of Leadership* (social psychology)
*Disparate Policies Governing Test Cheating* (education)
*Conceptions of Justice in Six Societies* (criminology, social philosophy)

*Exposing inconsistencies and exceptions.* Sometimes a reader believes that a theory, proposition, or conclusion offered by an author fails to account for all instances of the phenomenon under study. In other words, the author's proposal is valid under some circumstances (such as those situations cited in the author's account) but not in others. A student may thus seek to correct the resulting oversimplification by means of a literature survey that exposes instances that cannot be convincingly explained unless the author's proposal is revised. Hence, the student's thesis contributes to the body of knowledge by both (a) revealing inconsistencies in, and exceptions to, the original author's research and (b) suggesting the manner in which the investigated author's proposal should be revised so as to resolve the inconsistencies and accommodate the exceptions.

*When a Market Economy Explanation Does Not Suffice* (economics)
*Off Target: Melford's Theory Misapplied to Preindustrial Cultures* (anthropology)
*Problems With Voucher Systems Under Differing Versions of Democracy* (education, political science)

*Illustrating applications.* Some researchers are strong in formulating theories or methodology but weak in showing how their theories or methods can be applied to solve problems met in everyday life. A student's project may therefore be designed to illustrate practical implications of theoretical or methodological proposals.

*Skinner's Operant Behaviorism in Classrooms* (education)
*Applying Sander's Grief Theory to Distressed Children* (social work)
*Managing One's Money From Friedman's Vantage Point* (economics)

*Generating propositions and principles.* The intent of a literature survey can also be to discover features that are shared by a variety of studies, then to cast those features in the form of propositions, hypotheses, or principles that help explain the nature of the phenomenon on which the studies focus.

*Toward a Theory of Ethnic Shame* (anthropology)
*The Emergence of Sibling Rivalry* (developmental psychology)
*Principles of Reconciliation for Divorced Couples* (counseling psychology)

***Procedure:*** Here are the steps in one method of conducting a research-literature survey with the aid of a computer connected to the Internet.

1. State the issue to be investigated in the form of a guide question or a series of questions derived from your research topic.
2. To direct the hunt, select key words and phrases from the research questions, along with their synonyms and related terms.
3. Using a computer that is linked to the World Wide Web,
   (a) Locate a university library's home page.
   (b) From the array of data bases that the library offers, select one or more that you think will enumerate the kinds of studies you wish to survey. For instance, here are the names of several data bases in the University of California's Digital Library: *Anthropological literature, Chicano data base, English short-title catalog, ERIC, GeoRef, Magazine & Journal Articles, Melvyl (books), Newspaper Articles, PsychInfo.*
4. Open the data base and begin entering your key words and phrases to locate citations of studies relevant to your project.

5. Record the results of your search by means of the methods described in Chapter 3 for compiling material from the professional literature.

***Resources:*** Methods of conducting literature surveys, and examples of the results of such surveys, can be found in

Hart, C. (1999). *Doing a literary review.* Thousand Oaks, CA: Sage.

Shields, D. C. (1988). So you'd like to do a literature search: An ERIC report. *Communication Education, 37*(2), 165–172.

Stevenson, R. (1988). Black politics in the U.S.: A survey of recent literature. *Black Scholar, 19*(3), 58–61.

Stirling, K. (1989). Classical political economy: A survey of the recent literature. *Journal of Economic History, 49*(1), 252–254.

Swing, E. S. (1994). Textbooks in the kaleidoscope: A critical survey of literature and research on educational texts. *CHOICE, 31*(8), 1342.

Weaver, D. B., Baird, J. L., & Bell, W. E. (1982). *How to do a literature search in psychology.* Dallas, TX: Resource Press.

## Correlation Analyses

*Calculating positive and negative relationships*

***Defined:*** Correlation studies are guided by the generic question: What happens to one variable when another variable changes? Whenever that question is applied to particular variables, it can assume any of the following forms.

- Are females emotionally more stable than males?
- Are Germans more stubborn than the French?
- Are children from one-parent families more likely to get into trouble with the law than children from two-parent families?
- Does the incidence of illness increase with an increase in a community's population density?
- What is the relationship between the frequency of rain dances and the amount of precipitation falling in a region?
- Is the rate of divorce related to the level of married couples' formal education?

Correlations can be either positive or negative. In positive correlations, an increase in one variable parallels an increase in the other. For example, research on 14-year-olds' science achievement in 23 countries showed that pupils whose parents had more formal education scored higher on science tests than did students whose parents had less formal education (Postlethwaite & Wiley, 1992,

p. 162). In negative correlations, an increase in one variable is accompanied by a decrease in the other. A study by Barker and Gump (1964) showed that the larger the student enrollment in a high school, the fewer the number of extracurricular activities in which the average student engaged. If, when one variable changes, nothing happens to the other, then the two are not correlated.

***Procedure:*** Researchers can describe correlations in various ways, ranging from a general, imprecise statement in a historical account to a statistically precise statement in a direct-data survey.

- As more settlers moved into the Southwest, Apache resistance became increasingly violent.
- Lincoln's oratorical skill grew with each additional opportunity to speak before political gatherings.
- Eighty-three percent of Republicans and 17 percent of Democrats voted in favor of the tax bill.
- The relationship between general intelligence and extroversion was +.19 among girls and +.21 among boys.

It's apparent that not all correlated variables are related to each other in the same degree. At the highest level of correlation, the extent of change in one variable is accompanied by the same extent of change in the other variable. In contrast, at the opposite extreme of correlation, change in one variable is associated with no change at all in the other. There are many methods for expressing degrees of relationship. One popular method, applied when the variables are expressed in graduated quantities, is Pearson's product-moment correlation coefficient. In the Pearson system, the highest level of correlation is labeled 1.00, indicating that any change in one variable is always attended by the same extent of change in the other. The lowest level is labeled 0.0, meaning that change in one factor is never accompanied by any change in the other. Between these two extremes are graduated degrees of relationship. The closer the coefficient is to 1.00, the greater the relation between the variables. The closer the coefficient is to 0.0, the less the two variables are related. Thus, in the following examples, the highest level of relationship (+.82) is between fourth-graders' scores on reading and on mathematics tests (a strong tendency for skilled readers to get higher math scores than do poor readers). A considerably lower level of relationship (+.35) is obtained between students' school achievement and their self-concepts (students with high grades tend to have higher self-concepts than those with lower grades, but there are still a good many exceptions to that tendency). Only to a very slight extent (–.16) do Mexican high school applicants from smaller families have greater command of the Spanish language than do ones from larger families (the correlation is negative, because greater skill in Spanish is accompanied by smaller, rather than larger, family size). However, a coefficient as low as −.16 is so close to no correlation at all (0.0) that knowing the size of a girl's family is of almost no aid in our predicting her mastery of Spanish or predicting her family size from knowing her Spanish-language test scores.

- Fourth-graders' scores on a standardized reading test and their scores on a mathematics test = +.82 (Slavin, 1984, p. 15)
- School achievement and self-concept = +.35 (Follman, 1984)
- Family size and Spanish-language achievement of secondary-school applicants in Mexico = −.16 (Palafox, Prawda, & Velez, 1994, p. 173)

Additional ways to calculate degrees of correlation are described in Chapter 11.

***Purposes:*** Correlations are extremely important in research designed to identify the causes of events, because all statements about causation are statements about correlations among variables.

Correlations not only help people identify causes of events, but even when the relationship between two variables does not represent a causal connection, knowing the extent of relationship between two variables may help us predict the condition of Variable A by knowing the condition of Variable B. In way of illustration, by learning that a fourth-grade boy in Slavin's study has a high score on the reading test, we can predict with some confidence that the boy will have an above-average score in mathematics as well, since the relationship between the two variables is +.82. And as noted above, because the correlation between family size and Spanish-language skill among Mexican secondary-school applicants is so slight (−.16), we cannot with any confidence estimate a girl's command of Spanish by knowing the size of her family.

*Sample projects:* Correlation is the essence of such studies as:

*Causal Factors in Autism* (clinical psychology)
*Methods of Crowd Control in Public Crises* (sociology)
*Predicting Vocational Success and Failure* (counseling psychology)
*Connections Between Worldviews and Customs* (anthropology)
*Early Signs of Business Failure* (business administration)

***Advantages and limitations:*** The fact that two variables are correlated does not necessarily mean that one contributed at all to the outcome of the other. Thus, it is critical that researchers recognize the difference between *casual* or *coincidental* correlations and *causal* or *determining* correlations. For example, in a small town in Kansas they tell of an astute observer who, while spending both winter and summer hours lounging in front of the general store, noted a positive correlation between the softness of the pavement on Main Street and the speed at which milk soured. The softer the pavement, the faster milk curdled. Hence, he proposed that the town council install firmer paving (replace asphalt with concrete) to retard the souring of milk.

So, merely demonstrating a positive or negative correlation is not sufficient to support a claim of cause. What is also needed is a convincing line of logic demonstrating that one variable was at least partially the result of one or more other variables. Frequently, the supporting rationale is designed to show that one factor (the cause) preceded the other (the effect) and that the two could not have occurred in reverse order. Furthermore, constructing a persuasive argument that links two or more variables in a causal relationship often entails proposing how such a relationship is mediated by a chain of variables—a relationship involving a sequence of linkages extending from underlying causes to immediate ones.

***Resources:*** Statistical correlation procedures are provided in

Bluman, A. G. (2005). *Elementary statistics.* New York: McGraw-Hill.

Brase, C. H., & Brase, C. P. (2006). *Understanding statistics* (8th ed.). Boston, MA: Houghton Mifflin.

Dalgaard, P. (2004). *Introductory statistics.* New York: Springer.

Glass, G. V., & Hopkins, K. D. (1996). *Statistical methods in education and psychology* (3rd ed.). Boston: Allyn & Bacon.

Hays, W. L. (1994). *Statistics* (5th ed.). Fort Worth, TX: Harcourt Brace.

Kendall, M. G., & Gibbons, J. D. (1990). *Rank correlation methods* (5th ed.). New York: Oxford University Press.

Salkind, N. (2003). *Statistics for people who (think they) hate statistics.* Thousand Oaks, CA: Sage.

Siegel, S., & Castellan, N. J., Jr. (1988). *Nonparametric statistics for the behavioral sciences* (2nd ed.). New York: McGraw-Hill.

Sirkin, R. M. (1995). *Statistics for the social sciences.* Thousand Oaks, CA: Sage.

## Experiments

*General definition*

An experiment typically consists of applying a treatment to an individual, group, or institution, then describing the apparent effect of the treatment and estimating why that effect occurred. An assumption on which experiments are founded is that events are the result of one or more causal variables.

*General purpose*

The aim of an experiment is to manipulate the variables in a way that reveals (a) which ones are responsible for the outcome and (b) how much each variable has contributed to the observed result.

Designs of experiments can vary from the extremely simple to the highly complex, with each design bearing particular advantages and limitations. The simpler the design, the easier it is to carry out the research. The more complex the design, the better the experiment accounts for variables that affect the outcome and, as a result, the greater the confidence a researcher can place in the conclusions drawn from the result. Consequently, ease and feasibility are paid for by insecurity in accepting conclusions drawn about cause. On the other hand, confidence in conclusions is paid for by more difficulty in executing the experiment and by greater complexity, time, expense, and bother.

As with surveys, conclusions drawn from experiments can be applied solely to the people or events that have been directly studied, or the conclusions can be inferences applied to a population that the studied sample is thought to represent. In recognition of this distinction, patterns of experiments are often referred to as either *authentic experimental designs* or *quasi-experimental designs.* The term *authentic* refers to the practice of randomly assigning people or events to different treatments, then assuming that the results of the study can also be validly applied to the population from which the subjects were randomly drawn. A random sample is usually easier to draw in the physical sciences than in the social sciences. Researchers in chemistry, physics, and biology are typically freer to manipulate the objects they study than are researchers in the social sciences, who are obliged to accommodate their methodologies to people's everyday lives while disturbing those lives as little as possible. Thus, the great majority of experiments in the social sciences—and certainly those conducted with the limited resources available to most graduate students—render random sampling impracticable. Consequently, experiments reported in theses and dissertations typically involve convenience samples, since students usually study groups and events that are readily available. And because those people and events probably do not accurately represent the intended population, the resulting experimental schemes are referred to as quasi-experimental designs.

There are far more experimental designs available than can be described in this one chapter, so in the following pages we limit our attention to key characteristics of only four of the more common types. For more detailed descriptions of many more types, you can consult the resources at the end of this section.

*Ex post facto*

***Procedure:*** The simplest design consists of (a) applying a treatment to an entity (person, group, series of events), (b) evaluating the entity's performance following the treatment, and (c) estimating how much that treatment contributed to the outcome of the event. For example, a political candidate's advertisement is aired on a television station (the treatment); then a researcher questions a number of viewers to discover their opinions of the candidate (the evaluation). If the interviewees' opinions of the candidate are favorable, then the researcher may conclude that the TV ad has been responsible for that outcome.

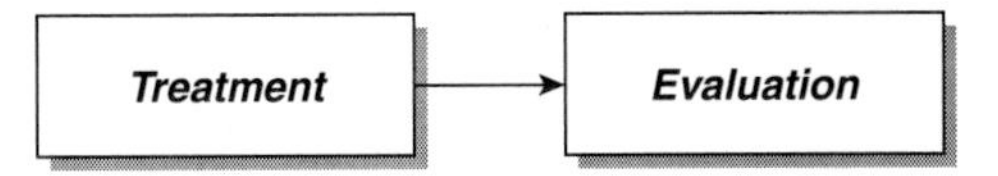


This is an ex-post-facto or after-the-fact design, because the researcher has drawn conclusions about the apparent effect of the treatment—the TV ad—solely on the basis of evaluating viewers' opinions after they experienced the treatment.

***Advantages:*** The main advantage of the ex-post-facto model is that it's easy to use. It requires minimal time and bother for the researcher and for the participants in the experiment.

***Limitations:*** The most obvious shortcoming is that the design fails to answer questions about the viewers' beliefs before they saw the TV program. Possibly the advertisement had no effect on their attitudes, or it may have damaged the politician's image in some viewers' eyes while enhancing it in others.' Hence, an ex-post-facto plan leaves the researcher in an indeterminate position when trying to explain the effect of treatments.

***Sample projects:*** Using an ex-post-facto design is most defensible when the ability of the subjects (such as individuals or groups) to display the evaluated knowledge, skills, or attitudes could not have been acquired prior to the treatment. For instance, it seems highly unlikely that students in a typical North American college would have any ability to read, write, or speak the Javanese language before they enrolled in a course in Javanese. Thus, after six weeks in the course, their performance on a test of Javanese probably reflects the effect of the course (the treatment) and not the effect of prior knowledge.

Sample projects: An ex-post-facto design could appropriately be applied in projects bearing such titles as

*Mastering Micronesian Ocean Navigation Skills* (education)
*Learning to Identify Islamic Art Influences* (religious studies, history)
*Applying Jungian Dream Symbolism* (psychology)
*Identifying Key Elements of Voodoo Belief* (anthropology, religion)
*Critiquing Piaget's Theory of Child Development* (psychology)

*Pretest-treatment-posttest*

***Procedure:*** To furnish a more convincing answer to the question about the effect of the politician's TV commercial, the researcher could adopt a pretest-treatment-posttest design. In this case, at the outset of the study the investigator would have the viewers take a pretest in the form of an interview or a printed questionnaire focusing on the respondents' present knowledge and opinions about the politician before they saw his TV ad (treatment). After viewing the advertisement, the respondents would once again express their opinions of the politician by means of interviews or questionnaires (posttest). To determine the apparent influence of the treatment, the researcher subtracts each participant's pretest results from his or her posttest results, then computes the average of those differences to obtain an overall assessment of the effect of the ad for the group as a whole. Consequently, the investigator's judgment of the advertisement would be based not on the final posttest scores, but on the extent of change from pretest to posttest.

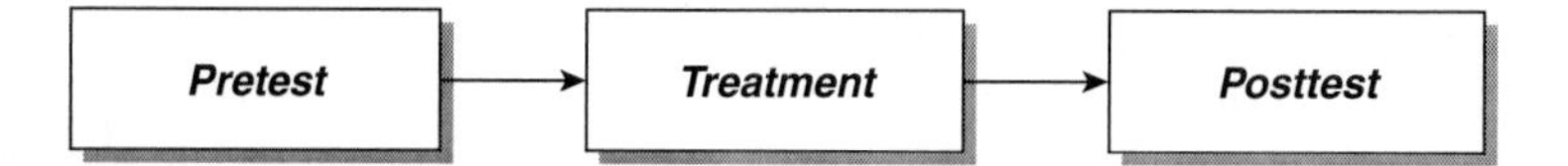


***Advantage:*** Compared to the ex-post-facto design, a pretest-treatment-posttest (p-t-p) experiment enables a researcher to estimate with greater confidence and precision the apparent influence of the treatment.

***Limitations:*** The p-t-p design can still leave the investigator in doubt about (a) possible reactive effects and (b) the comparative worth of alternative treatments.

As Ball (1985, p. 4200) has explained,

> Reactive effects in measurement occur when the behavior elicited by a measurement procedure is not characteristic of the behavior that would have occurred in the absence of the measurement procedure.

One type of reactive effect is the influence that a pretest may exert on a posttest result. In the case of the political-ad experiment, the pretest interview may, in itself, have altered participants' attitudes toward the politician and thereby served as a kind of treatment that influenced their posttest results. For example, the questions posed in the pretest could have alerted participants to think about the politician in a manner that would have shown up on their posttest, even if they never saw the TV advertisement. Thus, the posttest scores might derive from a combination of both the pretest and intended treatment, leaving the researcher in doubt as to how much the TV ad itself influenced viewers' opinions.

Our illustrative version of the p-t-p design also fails to reveal how the lone treatment option—the single TV ad—influences people's judgments in comparison with other potential treatments, such as a series of TV ads, a televised debate between the candidate and other candidates, a newspaper article, or a radio talk show.

Sample projects: Titles of studies using a pretest-treatment-posttest model can include

*The Influence of Movies on Empathic Responses* (psychology)
*The Effect of Humorous Anecdotes in Public Lectures* (psychology)
*Memorizing the Succession of British Monarchs* (education)
*Increasing the Speed and Accuracy of Mathematics Calculations* (education)

*Multiple treatments*

***Procedure:*** A design intended to compensate for the above-mentioned limitations of the p-t-p form (the reactive effect of pretesting and the lack of comparative treatments) is one that requires multiple sets of participants. In our hypothetical experiment, we will attempt to determine the comparative effectiveness of two contrasting treatments—a TV commercial prepared by the political candidate's staff and a radio talk show on which the candidate appears. As shown in the diagram on the next page, the first step in conducting the experiment consists of randomly assigning participants (TV viewers or radio listeners) to four groups of equal size—groups A, B, C, and D.

The practice of randomly assigning subjects to different treatments is based on the assumption that the four groups will be equal in regard to the attitudes and knowledge of the candidate that they bring to our experiment. In other words, the number of people who already have a favorable opinion of the candidate will be about the same in each group, the number who bring an unfavorable opinion of him will be about the same in each, and the number who will know nothing of the candidate will be about the same. Therefore, any differences we find in the groups' opinions in the posttest will be the result of what goes on within the experiment.

We plan to have two of the groups (A and B) view the TV advertisement and the other two (C and D) listen to the radio talk show. The results on the posttest are expected to tell us whether the TV commercial or the talk show had the greater effect on participants' opinions of the candidate and whether that effect was positive or negative. To determine what influence, if any, pretesting exerted on the ultimate outcome, we will pretest members of Groups A and C, but not pretest members of B and D. The information derived from the pretesting and final testing should equip us to judge (a) the comparative effectiveness of the four types of experience and (b) whether pretesting affected posttest results. In way of illustration, let's assume that 600 university students took part in the experiment, with 150 students randomly assigned to each group. On the final 100-item posttest questionnaire, the groups' average scores were:

Group A = 82  Group B = 72  Group C = 90  Group D = 81

These results suggest that the pretest did indeed function as a kind of treatment, because the students who took the pretest in either a TV-ad or a radio-program group scored about 10 points higher than students who were not pretested. It would also appear that the TV advertisement had more influence than the radio broadcast, since the scores under group C and D conditions were higher than those under group A and B conditions.

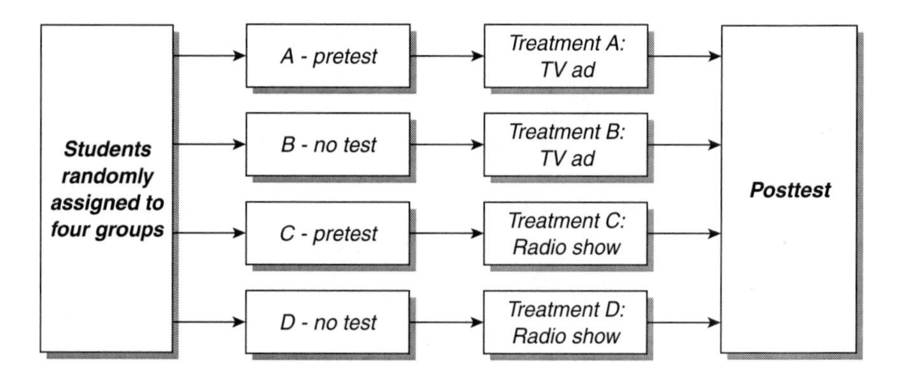


***Sample projects:*** Projects employing such a multiple-treatments design can bear such titles as

*Textbook Versus Lecturing in Teaching American History* (education)
*Reducing Race Prejudice—A Comparison of Role Playing and Pen Pals* (social psychology)
*Cost-Accounting Methods: Markinson's and Carswell's Approaches* (economics)
*Effects of Three Incentives on Welfare Recipients' Attitudes* (social work)

***Advantages:*** The multiple-treatments design, when it includes the pretest/no-test feature, enables a researcher to compare two or more treatments and to identify the possible influence of pretesting on the final outcome.

***Limitations:*** The problems of finding enough subjects to participate and of administering the experiment mount with each increase in the number of conditions and groups in the design. Such tasks as scheduling testing and treatment sessions, ensuring that participants follow directions, and compiling test results become increasingly complicated when many participants are involved. But if the total number of participants is much reduced, such as to a total of 24 or 36, each group will contain only 6 or 9 individuals. Then any attempt to apply the results of the study to a larger population becomes very hazardous since the conclusions have been based on evidence from so few subjects.

Something else that we would like to learn in our study of ways to publicize political candidates is how lasting a given treatment will be as an influence on people's opinions. Our multiple-treatments design, in the above form, does not give us that information; but, as illustrated below, changing the design into a time series can help answer our query.

*Time series*

***Procedure and advantage:*** Information about how the result of a treatment may diminish or may increase with the passing of time can be obtained by adding posttesting at various junctures following the end of the treatment.

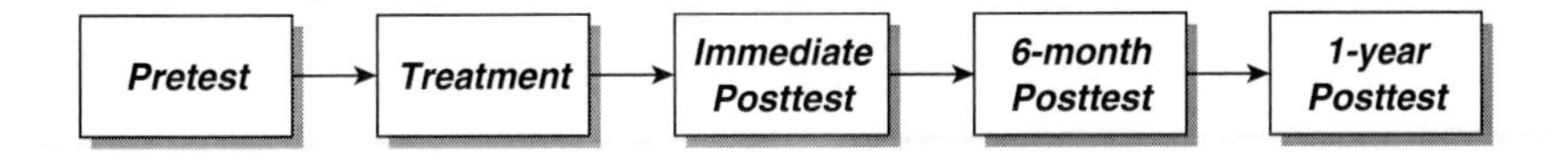


***Limitations:*** If the experiment has been conducted with subjects who are not readily available for a considerable time after the treatment ended, then a time-series design can be difficult to implement, because participants can be lost before the later phases of posttesting are administered. Furthermore, such a design does not provide information about what factors following the end of the treatment have caused any decrease or increase in participants' test scores, opinions, or skills that appear in the later stages of posttesting.

### *Additional models*

The four experimental designs described above represent only a small number of the forms that experiments can assume. Numerous other types are available to suit the demands of different research agenda. The nature of diverse designs, the situations for which they are suited, and the steps to be followed in applying those models are described in such publications as the following:

Campbell, D. T., & Stanley, J. C. (2005). *Experimental and quasi-experimental designs for research.* Chicago: Rand McNally.

Glass, G. V., McGaw, B., & Smith, M. L. (1981). *Meta-analysis in social research.* Thousand Oaks, CA: Sage.

Miles, M. B., & Huberman, A. M. (1994). *Qualitative data analysis* (2nd ed.). Thousand Oaks, CA: Sage.

Pereceman, E., & Curran, S. (Eds.). (2006). *A handbook for social science field research.* Thousand Oaks, CA: Sage.

### *Selecting an appropriate design*

The task of choosing a suitable design can entail three principal steps: (1) considering the characteristics of different experimental designs, (2) deciding whether one of those designs will be the most appropriate method for answering your research question (or will some other approach—historical, case-study, survey—be more relevant?), and (3) choosing a design that will furnish the most convincing evidence about the problem you are investigating within your research context.

The phrase "convincing evidence about the problem you are investigating within your research context" refers to such variables as (a) the magnitude of the consequences that could potentially result from your study and (b) the availability of the time, funds, facilities, and participants that the experiment would require.

***Magnitude of consequences:*** When estimating the magnitude of potential consequences, you can properly consider how greatly decisions derived from an experiment could influence people's welfare and how many people might be affected. The influence of this estimate on your choice of an experimental design can be illustrated with the following examples.

Imagine that a high school teacher wishes to assess the comparative effectiveness of two videotapes of the Civil War so as to decide which one the school should purchase for use in American history classes. She intends to derive her assessment from an experiment in which one group of students views Tape A and the other group views Tape B. In terms of the welfare of students, it likely makes little difference which tape is judged more effective. One tape is not apt to affect students' overall academic progress much more than the other. Furthermore, a relatively small number of people will be influenced by whichever tape is judged the better, since the number will be limited to students who enroll in that one school's American history classes over the next few years. Thus, the teacher is not risking students' lives if she adopts a simple, rather than a complex, experimental design. Probably a two-group pretest-treatment-posttest form will be sufficient as a guide to choosing the tape to purchase. It's true that such a design will fail to account for a number of variables that might affect students' test scores—such variables as sample size (the two groups will be rather small), distractions during the videotape viewing, the reactive effect of pretesting, and memory loss over the coming months. However, adopting a design that would accommodate all such variables would entail more bother and expense than the choice between tapes is worth. The simple pretest-treatment-posttest seems to represent an acceptable compromise between feasibility and precision. Although the results of this quasi-experiment will not be foolproof, they should be sufficient for the teacher's rather modest aim.

Now imagine that a doctoral candidate in the field of clinical psychology is cooperating with a large city's schools in studying the effects of three drugs for the treatment of hyperactive elementary-school pupils. The aim of the study is to determine which of the drugs reduces distractibility in pupils, enabling them to concentrate on their school work without suffering such undesirable side effects as drug addiction, lethargy, depression, and long-term memory loss. The doctoral student, aided by school counselors, intends to conduct an experiment that will reveal which of the drugs is best. In this case, the choice of a research design is far more crucial than in the case of the Civil War videotapes. The final decision about which drug, if any, should be administered to hyperactive pupils could critically affect the academic success and general health of large numbers of children—not only children in this one city's school, but hyperactive pupils throughout the nation if the experiment's results are widely disseminated. Therefore, it will not suffice to employ a simple pretest-treatment-posttest design that includes four groups of hyperactive pupils (one group taking no medication and each of the other groups taking one of the three drugs). It will be more appropriate to adopt a time-series design that includes large numbers of participants who are randomly assigned to the treatments. Adequately assessing the outcome of the experiment will also require a far more complex evaluation scheme than the one called for in the videotape study. Whereas the American history teacher's pretesting and posttesting could reasonably consist of paper-and-pencil tests of the content of the videotapes, the psychology student's drug study requires a variety of measures, including appraisals of hyperactivity (type, magnitude, frequency), pupils' concentration skills, environmental distracters, mood (depression, optimism, self-confidence), speed and accuracy of learning, study habits, and length of memory.

***Available time, funds, facilities, participants:*** Apparently, most master's and doctoral students wish to earn their degree within a few years. Hence, the time that an experiment will require becomes a serious concern. An experimental design that provides for the collection of data within a few weeks or few months is therefore better suited to the researcher's time constraints than one that requires several years, as can be the case with a time-series study.

The choice of an experimental design is often influenced as well by the expense it will involve. If the cost of a preferred design will be excessive, the researcher must settle for a design that is less sophisticated but affordable. The same is true of the instrumentation, personnel, and facilities required by different experimental designs. A design that will yield results short of the ideal may be necessary if the needed facilities are beyond a graduate student's means.

In studies that involve people as the objects of interest, large numbers of participants are usually desirable so that conclusions drawn from the results will represent a wide range of conditions and types of people. However, the necessary kinds of participants may be difficult to find, or the manner of studying them may be so complex and time-consuming that a graduate student finds it feasible to study no more than a few individuals.

In summary, there is no experimental design that is superior to all others for all research situations. The choice of a design requires achieving a reasonable balance among costs (time, energy, funds, facilities, number of participants, bother, undesirable side effects), the gravity of actions that could result from the study's findings, and the benefits that could derive from the research results.

With our overview of popular research methods now complete, we return to the four hypothetical projects described at the beginning of this chapter.

## MATCHING METHODS TO RESEARCH QUESTIONS

You may recall that earlier in this chapter we identified four research projects along with questions the projects were expected to answer. We suggested that you might find it useful, as you read the chapter, to estimate which of the chapter's types of research methods would be most suitable for answering the questions. To close the chapter, we now propose what we believe would be appropriate matches. Our choices are displayed within brackets following each question.

Project title 1: *One Size Fits All: State and Federal Legislators' Solutions for Students' Unsatisfactory School Achievement*

Guide questions:

- How do educational experts (teachers, school psychologists, researchers) diagnose and treat students' problems of unsatisfactory achievement? [*direct-data survey of experts, published-studies survey*]
- How do legislators, as reflected in laws they pass, propose that students' unsatisfactory achievement be diagnosed and treated? [*direct-data survey of legislation*]
- How well do the solutions proposed by educational experts match the solutions proposed by legislators? [*researcher's own analysis*]

Project title 2: *Destined to Preach the Gospel: A Social-Psychological Study*

Guide questions:

- What factors in the life of the Reverend Delevon Johnson determined that he would become a lifelong missionary in Africa? [*interpretive biography based on a literature survey*]
- How did the causal factors in the Reverend Johnson's life compare with those in other African missionaries' lives? [*interpretive biography based on a literature survey*]

Project title 3: *The Comparative Effectiveness of Same-Sex Therapists Versus Opposite-Sex Therapists With Teenage Drug Users*

Guide question:

- In counseling teenage drug users to stop using illicit drugs, is greater success achieved when the counselor is of the same sex as the client than when the counselor is of the opposite sex? [*multiple-treatments experiment*]

Project title 4: *The Dynamics of Choosing Candidates to Run for Political Office in Adams County*

Guide questions:

- Who are the candidates that have run for political office in Adams County over the past 12 years? [*direct-data survey of public documents*]
- What other individuals were potential candidates but were not selected to run? [*direct-data survey via interviews with political party leaders*]
- By what processes were candidates selected to run for different offices? [*direct-data survey of public documents and direct-data survey via interviews with political party leaders*]
- What inferences can be drawn about those processes' effect on the quality of political officeholders in Adams County? [*researcher's own analysis*]

## PLANNING CHECKLIST

As an aid in applying the contents of this chapter to your own thesis or dissertation, you may find it helpful to carry out the following activities.

1. What is the target question or series of questions that my research is intended to answer?______________________________________

2. Which approach or combination of approaches will I employ in my research?

   ___ 2.1 Historical

   - ___2.1.1 Descriptive chronicle
   - ___2.1.2 Interpretive history
   - ___2.1.3 Biography—descriptive
   - ___2.1.4 Biography—interpretive
   - ___2.1.5 Autobiography—traditional
   - ___2.1.6 Autobiography—mediated
   - ___2.1.7 Other (describe)____________________________

   ___ 2.2 Case Study—Ethnography

   - ___2.2.1 Single person, from outside
   - ___2.2.2 Single person, from inside
   - ___2.2.3 Group or institution—from outside
   - ___2.2.4 Group or institution—from inside
   - ___2.2.5 Other (describe)____________________________

   ___ 2.3 Survey

   - ____2.3.1 Direct data
   - ____2.3.2 Research literature
   - ____2.3.3 Other (describe)____________________________

   ___ 2.4 Correlation Analysis

   ___ 2.5 Experiment

   - ___2.5.1 Ex post facto
   - ___2.5.2 Pretest-treatment-posttest
   - ___2.5.3 Multiple treatments
   - ___2.5.4 Time series
   - ___2.5.5 Other (describe)____________________________

   ____ 2.6 Other (describe)___________________________________

EIGHT

# DATA-COLLECTION TECHNIQUES AND INSTRUMENTS

*"I need a test for evaluating the level of people's tolerance for ethnic diversity. Is such a test available? If not, how do I go about creating one?"*

This chapter describes five procedures and instruments useful for collecting data in research projects. The five are observations, content analyses, interviews, questionnaires, and tests. Each is portrayed in terms of its definition, types, advantages, limitations, and sources of additional information.

## OBSERVATIONS

Gathering information by observing involves watching and/or listening to people and events, then recording what has been discovered.

### Ways of Observing

As noted in the discussion of case studies in Chapter 7, an important feature of observation procedures is the relationship that different procedures represent between the observer and the observed. This observer/observed association can range from the very remote to the very intimate. The following five examples of observation types progress from the most removed association to the most immediate.

> Inconspicuous television cameras at four locations in a conference room were used for videotaping the activities of 12 members of a political candidate's support group as they planned campaign strategies. The researcher later scrutinized the tapes (a) to discover dominant and submissive roles displayed by the participants in their interactions and (b) to estimate the characteristics of individuals that determined the roles they adopted.
>
> A PhD candidate in sociology used a videotape camera to photograph confrontations between labor-union strikers and nonunion workers who were crossing picket lines in an effort to enter an automobile assembly plant that was being blockaded. The videotapes were later analyzed by three graduate students—each working alone—to identify (a) tactics used by strikers to dissuade workers from entering the plant and (b) types of responses of nonunion workers. Following the viewing sessions, the students compared their records to determine how closely their analyses agreed.
>
> A graduate student seated at the rear of a third-grade classroom on three successive days observed the types of pupil responses that were elicited by the different style the teacher used in leading class discussion each of those days. On each occasion, the observer recorded the particular day's leadership style in the form of code letters symbolizing the relationship between the teacher's mode of questioning and the quality and amount of pupils' responses.
>
> For his thesis titled *Group-Think Patterns,* a student received permission to witness how a recruiting committee in each of four college groups (two fraternities, two sororities) planned to attract new members to their organization. The aim of the research was to chart the patterns of interaction among participants that produced group decisions. To help ensure the accuracy of his data, the student used an audiotape recorder to capture the conversation of committee members.
>
> To gather data about the personality traits and life experiences of people who seek help in becoming more outspoken in their social relationships, a master's degree candidate joined an eight-member assertiveness-training group led by a counseling psychologist. Immediately following each of the group's weekly sessions, the student retired to an adjacent room to fill out a personality-profile rating scale for each participant. She also wrote brief descriptions of what the participants had said and done during the session that determined the ratings she assigned them.

Three noteworthy features of the five cases are (a) the consequences of remote versus intimate methods of observing, (b) ways of recording observations, and (c) the protection of subjects' welfare.

### *Remote versus intimate*

The more remote the connection between observers and the people they observe (cases 1 and 2), the less likely the observers will influence the incidents they witness. Remoteness increases the probability that participants in the incident will act in their typical manner. Thus, the observed events will be an accurate sample of the participants' usual behavior. However, in being remote, an observer is apt to miss subtle aspects of events or to misinterpret what occurs. This is where intimacy makes its chief contribution. The closer the observer's relationship with the observed (cases 4 and 5), the more likely the observer will see, hear, and feel the inconspicuous but significant features of an event and will have the background knowledge required for deriving an insightful interpretation of what those features mean. But too much intimacy—too close an emotional identification of the observer with the observed—can damage the objectivity of the investigation.

### *Recording techniques*

Four means of recording observations have been illustrated in the five cases: (a) videotapes, (b) audiotapes, (c) handwritten notes taken at the time of the observation, and (d) rating scales marked and notes taken after the observation session. Videotapes and audiotapes have the advantage of recording exactly what occurred, so a researcher can review the original events as often as necessary when preparing an interpretation. However, if participants are aware that their actions are being taped, they may not behave in their usual ways. Participants may also be intimidated by an observer who takes handwritten notes in their presence. Yet, if the observer does not record events as they occur, but waits until later to register what happened, the accuracy and completeness of the report may suffer.

### *Subjects' welfare*

Recent decades have witnessed increasing sensitivity to the safety and rights of the people or animals that are observed, tested, or subjected to experiments. As a result, in order to foster humane and nonexploitative treatment of participants in research, higher-education institutions today maintain committees (*human-subjects committees, experimental-subjects review boards*) responsible for approving and monitoring the research plans of students and faculty members. The general rule governing the decisions of such committees is that any stress, inconvenience, or harm that might be suffered by the subjects of research must be far outweighed by the value of the research results—value in terms of the contribution the research makes to the world's knowledge and to the welfare of humans, animals, and the environment. Thus, students who are planning research for their graduate degree are advised, when designing their projects, to obtain a copy of their college's human-subjects standards so that their data-gathering methods will comply with the standards. For example, in case 1 above, it is likely that a human-subjects committee would require the student (who intends to videotape the political candidate's support group) to inform the group members ahead of time that their activities are going to be recorded.

### Observation Resources

Suggestions for conducting observations can be found in

Archer, J. (1992). *Ethology and human development.* New York: Harvester Wheatsheaf.

Bentzen, W. R. (2006). *Seeing young children: A guide to observing and recording behavior* (3rd ed.). Albany, NY: Delmar.

Denzin, N. K. (2001). *Interpretive interactionism.* Newbury Park, CA: Sage.

Fenno, R. F. (1990). *Watching politicians: Essays on participant observation.* Berkeley, CA: Institute of Governmental Studies, University of California.

Hinde, R. A. (1983). Ethology and child development. In M. M. Haith & J. J. Campos (Eds.), *Handbook of Child Psychology. Vol. 11: Infancy and developmental psychobiology* (pp. 37–38). New York: Wiley.

Jorgensen, D. L. (1989). *Participant observation: A methodology for human studies.* Newbury Park, CA: Sage.

Shaffir, W. B., Stebbins, R. A., & Turowetz, A. (Eds.). (1980). *Fieldwork experience: Qualitative approaches to social research.* New York: St. Martin's.

Smith, C. D., & Kornblum, W. (Eds.). (1996). *In the field: Readings on the field research experience* (2nd ed.). Westport, CT: Praeger.

Stewart, A. (1998). *The ethnographer's method.* Thousand Oaks, CA: Sage.

Stocking, G. W., Jr. (Ed.). (1983). *Observers observed: Essays on ethnographic fieldwork.* Madison: University of Wisconsin Press.

## CONTENT ANALYSES

The process of content analysis entails searching through one or more communications to answer questions that an investigator brings to the search. Content analyses are not limited to written or printed documents but extend as well to audio recordings, still photographs, motion picture films, video recordings, Internet websites, and the like. Comparisons can involve documents from different times, different places, different authors, and more.

Investigators typically analyze communications in order to answer two levels of questions—the descriptive and the interpretive. Descriptive questions focus on what a communication contains. Interpretative questions focus on what those contents are likely to mean. Our concern in the present chapters is limited to techniques of descriptive analysis. Ways of interpreting the content of communications are addressed in Chapter 12.

### Typical Kinds of Descriptive Analyses

Three key descriptive-analysis questions concern qualities, quantities, and patterning. The qualitative question is: Does this document contain the characteristic for which I am searching? The quantitative question is: In what amounts does the intended characteristic appear? The patterning question is: Which relationships among the characteristics interest me?

#### *The qualitative*

Among the diverse aspects of quality that you can study are field-of-focus, reflected attitude, and discursive style.

The field-of-focus of a communication is the facet of life it discusses—political-party policies, social-class structures, sexual harassment, macroeconomic theories, forms of government, comprehensive schools, mental disorders, welfare systems, business ethics, and thousands more. In a comparative study, the analyst's task can involve inspecting two or more documents to determine how they treat the field of interest. The documents may represent different times, different places, or different authors.

- *Different Times:* Women's Rights in Finland From 1600 to 2000
- *Different Places:* Hiring Policies in Five Fortune-500 Companies
- *Different Authors:* Thatcher and Blair on Northern Ireland and the IRA

The term *reflected attitude* refers to a communication's general emotional or judgmental tone. An analyst's purpose is to reveal attitude similarities and differences among the documents being compared. Kinds of attitudes on which the researcher's attention centers can be reflected in such contrasting terms as optimistic/pessimistic, critical/noncritical, antagonistic/ supportive, prejudicial/ nonjudgmental, positive/negative, and the like.

- The Role of Government Regulation à la Nader, Friedman, and Greenspan
- Decentralizing School Management: New Life or Suicide?

The phrase *discursive style* means the pattern of logic by which an author seeks to convey his or her message. The content analyst's task can involve comparing the communication modes of two or more documents.

- Speeches About Taxes: Politicians' Tricks of the Trade
- The Writing Styles of History Textbooks in Peru, Morocco, and Spain
- Ethnic Rhetoric: Rationales Supporting Immigration Controls, 1920–2000

*The quantitative*

We do not believe that quantitative methods are in conflict with qualitative approaches. Instead, the quantitative are merely extensions of the qualitative, representing an effort to determine with some precision (1) the amount or frequency of existing characteristics (incidence) or (2) the degree of relationship among characteristics (correlation).

In way of illustration, the amount of a characteristic could be the aim of a study about the treatment by different newsmagazines of different religious groups. A researcher wishing to derive a picture of a possible link between news media and religious denominations could do so by analyzing the contents of five weekly newsmagazines that are thought to represent political preferences. The analysis, conducted over a period of months, would be designed to reveal (a) the number of articles in which a given religion is mentioned, (b) the total amount of space devoted to each religion, and (c) the articles' evaluative remarks or implications about each denomination (neutral, favorable, unfavorable). These quantitative data could then be manipulated statistically to provide a numerical appraisal of the relationship between each magazine's political stance and its treatment of news in which people's religious affiliation is identified.

*Patterning*

Sometimes investigators are interested in discovering patterns of relationships among characteristics found in a communication. A historian may study the minutes of city-council meetings in order to establish the chronology of events in a city government's treatment of sexual harassment of its employees. A sociologist may peruse students' cumulative folders to learn the extent of correlation between students' academic success and such home background features as parents' education, housing, family size, and available reading matter in the home. A political scientist may compare a ministry of the interior's administrative-organization chart with a collection of memoranda from different offices in the ministry in order to trace the flow of ideas about a zoning plan. A social psychologist may inspect biographies published in *Who's Who* to find the sorts of postsecondary institutions that had been attended by prominent business executives as compared to ones attended by eminent artists, authors, and scientists.

## Conducting Content Analyses

One typical process of content analysis consists of five steps: (1) stating the general question that the research project is intended to answer, (2) decomposing the general question into constituent subquestions, (3) finding communications that will likely answer the subquestions, (4) inspecting communications to locate passages pertinent to the subquestions, and (5) recording and organizing the results of the inspection.

The following examples demonstrate two approaches to the content analysis task. The first example illustrates a qualitative analysis in which the researcher studies documents and takes notes by hand. The second describes a combined qualitative-quantitative analysis employing a personal computer equipped with a scanner and optical-character-recognition program.

*A qualitative analysis of a science-versus-religion dispute*

Consider the steps to be taken by a political science doctoral candidate who is planning a dissertation titled *Darwin in the Classroom Revisited: Political Strategies and Consequences—1925 and 2005*. The student's stimulus for choosing such a topic was the Kansas state board of education's decision in 1999 to outlaw from school achievement tests any mention of Charles Darwin's theory of evolution. News of the decision was widely debated in the public press, with the 1999 event reminding readers of the 1925 Tennessee court case in which a substitute teacher, John Scopes, was convicted of teaching Darwinism in a public school. The doctoral candidate plans to compare the two events' political ramifications in terms of (a) the strategies attempted by the advocates on each side of the pro-Darwin/anti-Darwin controversy and (b) the resulting political consequences.

***Step 1:*** *State the general question to be answered by the study.* The general question delineates the principal domain of communications that can profitably be analyzed.

> In the Scopes trial of 1925 and the Kansas state board of education decision of 1999, (a) what strategies did anti-evolution advocates and pro-evolution advocates attempt in support of their causes and (b) what political consequences resulted from those two events?

Hence, the relevant communications will be ones mentioning the two events. The communications bearing on the Scopes trial can extend from 1925 through 1999. Communications relating to the Kansas decision begin during the month the decision was issued, August 1999.

Sometimes the initial question is sufficiently specific to serve as the complete guide to the precise information sought during the inspection of communications. Frequently, however, the initial question is too broad to suggest the exact information that should be extracted from documents. In such instances, a second step is recommended.

***Step 2:*** *State subquestions that identify components of the general question.* The subquestions not only indicate the precise information to be sought during the process of inspecting documents, but also clarify the investigator's conception of which topics should make up the final research report.

- How are the terms *strategies* and *political consequences* best defined for the purposes of the present investigation?
- What were the points of disagreement between the anti-Darwin and pro-Darwin forces?
- What kinds of evidence did each side adopt in support of its position, and what were the sources of such evidence? What line of argument did the proponents on each side adduce in support of their position?

- What individuals and organizations were aligned with each side?
- What consequences resulted from the Scopes trial in terms of school practices in Tennessee and in other states over the following three-quarters of a century? What court cases after 1925 addressed the same issues as those of the Scopes trial? How did those cases turn out?
- What groups and individuals were the apparent winners and apparent losers in the evolutionism-versus-creationism controversy?

This list will guide the choice of which contents of communications will be included in the final research report. However, it is also the case that, in the process of inspecting documents, the documents' contents might suggest additional subquestions that can help answer the researcher's initial general query. Those new questions will then be added to the list.

***Step 3:*** *Identify communications that likely contain answers to the subquestions.* Guided by the key words Darwin, Darwinism, Scopes, evolution, and creationism, the investigator searches libraries' and the Internet's listings of books, journal articles, magazine articles, and newspaper reports to locate resources pertinent to the research questions. The bibliographies and references at the end of relevant books also provide titles of additional useful resources. The ultimate collection of communications to be inspected includes speeches, articles, books, and conference deliberations focusing on the two events—1925 and 1999—and their apparent aftermath. Newspaper archives from 1925 to 1926 and from 1999 to 2003 are included in the search.

Here, then, are examples of relevant books about the Scopes trial and its consequences:

Caudill, E. (1989). *The roots of bias: An empiricist press and coverage of the Scopes trial.* Columbia, SC: Association for Education in Journalism and Mass Communication.

DeCamp, L. S. (1968). *The great monkey trial.* Garden City, NY: Doubleday.

Ginger, R. (1969). *Six days or forever?* Tennessee v. John Thomas Scopes. New York: Oxford University Press.

Larson, E. J. (1997). *Summer for the gods: The Scopes trial and America's continuing debate over science and religion.* New York: Basic Books.

Scopes, J. T., & Presley, U. (1967). *Center of the storm: Memoirs of John T. Scopes.* New York: Holt, Rinehart, and Winston.

Thomas, R. M. (2006). *Religion in schools: Controversies around the world* (Chapter 12). Westport, CT: Praeger.

Thomas, R. M. (2007). *God in the classroom—religion and America's public schools* (Chapter 3). Westport, CT: Praeger.

Useful journal and magazine articles include

Donohue, J. W. (1996). Of many things (Catholicism and evolution). *America, 175*(20), 2.
Iannone, C. (1997). The truth about *Inherit the Wind* [play and motion picture about debate between evolution and creationism]. *First Things: A Monthly Journal of Religion and Public Life, 70*, 28–35.
Moore, R. (1998). Creationism in the United States; II. The aftermath of the Scopes trial. *American Biology Teacher, 60*(8), 568–577.
Paterson, F. R. A., & Rossow, L. F. (1999). "Chained to the Devil's throne": Evolution and creation science as a religio-political issue. *American Biology Teacher, 61*(5), 358–364.

Typical newspaper articles about the Kansas affair are

Belluck, P. (1999, August 12). Board for Kansas deletes evolution from curriculum; a creationist victory; new strategy of Darwin foes after court setbacks is to discourage teachings. *New York Times,* p. A1.
God and man in Kansas. (1999, August 13). *Wall Street Journal,* p. W11.

***Step 4:*** *Analyze the contents of the chosen communications.* Analyzing the collected documents involves keeping a list of the subquestions at hand to guide the process of scanning the pages of a book chapter or an article in order to locate passages bearing on any of the subquestions.

***Step 5:*** *Record and organize the findings.* The researcher prepares five-by-eight-inch cards on which to write notes about relevant passages of each document inspected. To facilitate the task of later organizing the cards in a useful sequence, the investigator assigns a code to each question. For example, *Dis* refers to the question: What were the points of disagreement between the anti-Darwin and pro-Darwin forces? The codes *AntiDar* and *ProDar* refer to the question: What kinds of evidence did each side cite in support of its position, and what were the sources of such evidence? *AntiDarArg* and *ProDarArg* refer to: What line of argument did the proponents on each side employ to support their position? As these examples suggest, codes are typically easier for the researcher to recall if they are cast as concise mnemonic reflections of the essence of the subquestions to which they refer. To illustrate, the connection between a code number such as *4* or *9* and the intended subquestion is more difficult to remember than is the code word *CrtCase* (What court cases after 1925 addressed the same issues as those of the Scopes trial?).

At the top of a note card, the analyst writes the code that identifies the type of material treated on that card's notes. The code letters are followed by the bibliographic source of that card's material. Usually the name of the author, the publication year, and the page numbers of the selected passage will be sufficient, since a separate card will be prepared with the complete bibliographic reference that will appear in the list of references at the end of the final research report. Beneath the identifying information, the researcher either (a) summarizes the essence of the relevant passage in her or his own words and/or (b) directly quotes an entire passage or a segment of it. Here is a sample note card:

> CrtCase Marcus, 1999, p. 32
>
> "In the past four years, legislators in Texas, Ohio, New Hampshire, Washington, and Tennessee have sought, but failed, to challenge the primacy of teaching evolution." Current Alabama law requires that a sticker be attached to biology textbooks labeling Darwin's proposal a "controversial theory."

The bibliography card relating to this note card reads:

> Marcus, David L. (1999, August 30). Charles Darwin gets thrown out of school. (A Kansas ban on the mention of evolution). *U.S. News & World Report,* p. 32.

Note cards prepared in such a manner can later be organized in a sequence that facilitates the researcher's writing about each of the subquestions. In effect, all cards bearing the same code can be organized in a chronological sequence to reflect the way the Darwinism-versus-creationism controversy advanced over the period 1925–1999.

There are several variations of the above procedure. For instance, some authors prefer to take notes on a lined tablet rather than on cards and to place the code words and each passage's page numbers in the left margin adjacent to the notes and quotations.

*A qualitative/quantitative comparison of textbooks*

The Darwinism study was concerned entirely with qualitative matters—the strategies adopted by opponents of Darwinian theory to replace the teaching of evolution in schools with a biblical version of creation. However, some content analyses center attention on both qualitative and quantitative aspects. Such is the case in a study of textbooks' characterizations of combatants in World War II.

The five steps in content analysis described for the Darwinism study are the same as those adopted for the textbook investigation. But while none of the steps in the Darwinism example involved the use of computers, the procedures adopted for the textbook project make heavy use of computer technology. As noted at the end of this section, numbers of software programs have been designed specifically for content analysis, each with its own special features. However, the following history textbook example illustrates a computer application that requires no more than an up-to-date word processing program, a scanner, and optical-character-recognition software.

***Step 1:*** *State the general questions to be answered by the study.*

> Which nations' military forces were mentioned in successive editions of popular secondary-school history textbooks published in Australia, Great Britain, India, and the United States in the 1950s and 1990s? How much attention was accorded each nation's forces, and what was the tenor of the attention?

***Step 2:*** *State subquestions that identify components of the general questions.*

In each edition of the selected textbooks:

(1) How much space (in terms of words and pictures) is dedicated to each of the following nations' military forces: Australia, China, France, Great Britain, India, Soviet Union, United States, Germany, Italy, Japan.

(2) To what extent is the mention of a nation's forces solely descriptive, with no negative or positive implications regarding the forces' intentions, tactics, efficiency, and treatment of prisoners?

(3) To what extent does the attention to a nation's forces include negative, condemnatory evaluations of their roles in the war?

(4) To what extent does the attention to nation's forces include positive, complimentary evaluations of their roles in the war?

In comparisons between each nation's (Australia, Great Britain, India, United States) 1950s and 1990s textbooks, to what extent did the answers to questions (1) through (4) change? If they did change, then in what manner?

In comparisons across the four nations' 1950s textbooks (Australia, Great Britain, India, United States) and across the 1980s textbooks, to what extent did the answers to questions (1) through (4) differ from one nation's texts to another's? If they did differ, then in what manner?

***Step 3:*** *Identify communications that likely contain answers to the guide questions.* The investigator writes to education officials in the four target countries to (a) learn the titles of popular secondary-school world history texts from the 1950s and from the 1990s and (b) learn the sources from which copies of the texts can be purchased. Representative textbooks from each country are then obtained.

***Step 4:*** *Analyze the contents of the chosen communications.* To implement the process of analysis, the researcher first enters representative chapters of each book into a personal computer by means of a scanner and optical-character-recognition (OCR) software. The scanner photographs one page at a time as the OCR translates the page's words into the same form that would result if the words had been typed into the computer from the keyboard. Even though this procedure uses a large quantity of computer memory, as personal computers provide increasingly large amounts of storage (large quantities of gigabytes on the hard disk), the length of a scanned document becomes less an impediment to recording multiple pages. (If a scanner and OCR program were not available, the researcher could still copy the book's contents into the computer by typing from the keyboard, but that would be a laborious and time-consuming task, susceptible to typing errors.) The textbooks' contents can now be read from the computer screen rather than from the books themselves.

Analyzing a textbook chapter involves keeping a list of the subquestions at hand to guide the process of examining the pages to locate passages bearing on subquestions (1) through (4).

***Step 5:*** *Record and organize the findings.* There are several ways that the textbook contents, as viewed on the computer screen, can be analyzed and recorded. Which method is best depends on such considerations as the amount of the computer's available random-access memory (RAM), the types of research questions to be answered, and the researcher's preferred way of working. One of these possibilities is presented here. It consists of five phases:

*Phase 1:* For each nation, subquestions (2), (3), and (4) are assigned code identifications. For instance, the codes for Italy are:

I-0 refers to passages mentioning Italian forces with no negative or positive implications regarding the forces' intentions, tactics, efficiency, and treatment of prisoners. [Subquestion (2)]

I-neg refers to passages mentioning Italian forces that include negative, condemnatory evaluations of the forces' intentions, tactics, efficiency, and treatment of prisoners. [Subquestion (3)]

I-pos refers to passages mentioning Italian forces that include positive, complimentary evaluations of the forces' intentions, tactics, efficiency, and treatment of prisoners. [Subquestion (4)]

The same three types of codes are assigned for the other nations, so there are US-0, US-neg, US-pos, GB-0, GB-neg, GB-pos, and the like for each group.

*Phase 2:* The book chapter that has been entered into the computer will be analyzed for each nation in turn. First, following the end of the computer's version of a chapter, the researcher places the three codes for the particular nation that is currently the focus of attention. Then the investigator begins perusing the chapter contents. A quick way to locate each mention of the ethnic group consists of using the "find" function from the word-processing program's "edit" menu. When the "find" rectangle is brought onto the screen, the name of the desired ethnic group is typed in, so that each time the "return" key is pressed, the computer will find the next use of that name. The researcher can then read the passage containing that nation designator in order to discover how much space is dedicated to that country and whether the contents are solely descriptive [subquestion (2)], negative [subquestion (3)], or positive [subquestion (4)].

*Phase 3:* After evaluating the nature of a passage [in terms of questions (2), (3), and (4)], the researcher employs the "copy" function from the "edit" menu to copy the words, phrases, or sentences that comprise the reference. Once again the "find" function is brought onto the screen, and the code appropriate for the copied passage is entered. For example, when the Japanese passage is complimentary, the code *J-pos* is entered, and the computer cursor jumps to the *J-pos* location at the end of the textbook chapter. At that location, the researcher places the copied passage.

By repeating phases 2 and 3 throughout the chapter, the researcher accumulates under each code all of the passages that allude to the particular nation's forces, with the passages organized according to whether they are descriptive, negative, or positive. To make space in the file containing the chapter for the next ethnic group, all of the material under the codes can be copied and transferred to a separate file designated for the group that has just been analyzed. The coded material following the chapter is then erased, leaving room for new codes that refer to the next nation whose passages will be extracted and placed under that new set of codes. This same process is repeated for all nations' categories, so each country ends up with its separate file containing all references to it in the textbook chapter.

*Phase 4:* When phase 3 has been completed for all nations, the researcher has a series of separate files, each containing all of the chapter material referring to that file's particular country. It is now a simple matter to compute the quantity of chapter space dedicated to each nation. For instance, opening the German file, the investigator selects (highlights or blackens) all of the material under the code *G-0* and activates the "word count" function, which yields the total number of words describing Germany's armed forces. The same procedure furnishes an instantaneous word count for any other set of material under a given code. By this means, the researcher promptly and accurately answers subquestions (1) through (4). And when phases 1 through 4 have been completed for each of the textbooks under review, the material is available for answering the questions regarding (a) trends in the treatment of a nation's armed forces over time and (b) comparisons of one textbook series with another.

*Phase 5:* When writing the final interpretation of the study's findings, the author selects illustrative passages from the separate nations' files to demonstrate the qualitative differences in the treatment of military forces that appeared at different time periods (1950s, 1990s) in a particular nation's history books.

## Specialized Content Analysis Programs

As noted earlier, a variety of computer software programs have been developed to facilitate the process of content analysis (Weitzman & Miles, 1994). Examples of ones that systematically organize text for search and retrieval are *askSam, FolioVIEWS,* and *Orbis.* Such programs facilitate searching for and retrieving various combinations of words, phrases, coded segments, and memos. Other programs not only include code-and-retrieve capabilities, but also permit analysts

> to make connections between codes (categories of information); to develop higher-order classifications and categories; to formulate propositions or assertions, implying a conceptual structure that fits the data; and/or to test such propositions to determine whether they apply. They're often organized around a

system of rules, or are based on formal logic. Examples are *AQUAD, ATLAS/ti, HyperRESEARCH, NUDIST,* and *QCA*. (Miles & Weitzman, 1994, p. 312)

In the following list of content-analysis computer programs, the title of the software is followed by the name and address of the creator and/or distributor of the program.

AQUAD: Günter Huber, University of Tübingen, Department of Pedagogical Psychology, Munzgasse 22–30, D-72070 Tübingen, Germany.

askSam: P.O. Box 1428, 119 S. Washington Street, Perry, FL 32347.

ATLAS/ti: Thomas Muhr, Trautenaustrasse 12, D-10717 Berlin, Germany.

FolioVIEWS: Folio Corporation, 2155 N. Freedom Blvd., Suite 150, Provo, UT 84604.

HyperRESEARCH: Researchware, Inc., 20 Soren St., Randolph, MA 01268-1945.

NUDIST: Tom and Lyn Richards, Qualitative Solutions and Research Pty. Ltd., 2 Research Drive, La Trobe University, Melbourne, Victoria 3083, Australia.

Orbis: XYQuest, The Technology Group, Inc., 36 S. Charles St., Baltimore, MD 21201.

QCA: Kriss Drass and Charles Ragin, Center for Urban Affairs and Policy Research, Northwestern University, Evanston, IL 60208.

## INTERVIEWS

Interviews and questionnaires enable people to report information about themselves—about their life condition, beliefs, or attitudes. In interviews, questions eliciting people's reports are asked orally. In questionnaires, the queries are printed and require written responses. Observations, in contrast to interviews and questionnaires, are people's reports about other individuals, whereas tests are reports of people's intellectual or physical performances.

The term *life condition,* in relation to interviews and questionnaires, refers to characteristics of individuals that identify their status in terms of gender, age, place of residence, vocation, income, education, religious affiliation, ethnic background, and the like. Such information is typically used to place respondents in categories that are easily compared, on the assumption that the categories may be associated with the study's target variables. In a project focusing on attitudes toward birth control methods, the investigator may estimate that females' and males' attitudes could differ significantly. Thus, it is important to know the gender of each respondent. But if there is no reason to suspect that a particular aspect of the respondents' status—gender, age, level of formal education, or such—might be correlated with a target variable, there is no good reason to include information about that aspect in an interview or a questionnaire.

The word *beliefs* refers to respondents' knowledge and convictions about a topic—what occurred during a city council meeting, typical child-rearing practices of an ethnic group, children's rights, immigration laws, religious doctrine, or the average cost of attending college.

*Attitude*s are underlying tendencies for people to act in certain ways. The tendencies derive from the individuals' collection of values, which can be of various kinds, including those bearing on moral behavior, etiquette, fair play, human rights, financial responsibility, job efficiency, artistic taste, protecting the environment, and more. A researcher asks for opinions on the assumption that information about people's preferences can help explain and predict their behavior in decision-making situations.

Despite the similar aims of interviews and questionnaires, the two approaches are sufficiently different to warrant our discussing them separately. This section treats only interviews; the next section treats questionnaires.

### Alternative Interview Strategies

Interviews are often employed in case studies, ethnographic research, biographies, and surveys. Their use in historical studies and experiments is less frequent.

Researchers with little experience planning interviews are often prone to devise their interview questions in a rather haphazard fashion, when they would be better advised to design the questions to fit an intentional strategy. The forms and purposes of different strategies can be illustrated with examples of four types labeled *loose, tight, converging,* and *response-guided.*

#### *Loose-question strategy*

The aim of a loose or broad question approach is to reveal the various ways respondents interpret a general question. Consider, for instance, a proposed study of religious beliefs that includes this query:

> What diverse meanings do people attach to words and phrases that relate to religions; and what implications does such diversity hold for people's behavior

toward others (with "others" possibly including both humans and supernatural beings or spirits)?

Because the purpose of the study is to expose the extent of variability among individuals' interpretations, the interviewer plans to pose questions in a very general form, offering interviewees unrestricted freedom to tell their interpretation of a particular word or phrase.

What does the word *karma* mean to you?
What do you think about the statement in the Bible that God created the earth and all the earth's contents in a period of six days?
For you, what is the meaning of the phrase *the true religion?*
When you hear the expression *God-given rights,* what does that mean? Could you give examples of God-given rights?

In pursuing a loose strategy, interviewers resist respondents' attempts to have questions rephrased in greater detail, since the intent of the approach is to expose the variety of interpretations to which different respondents subscribe.

*Tight-question strategy*

The purpose of a tight or restricted strategy is to discover which selections respondents prefer among several limited options. Thus, while a loose strategy features open-ended queries, a tight strategy usually involves multiple-choice questions. This type is typical of public opinion surveys, such as the Gallup poll.

Questions sometimes focus on people's activities, traits, or habits. For instance, a survey of people's drinking habits may include such items as

How often do you have at least one drink of an alcoholic beverage? Daily? Two or three times a week? Two or three times a month? Never?
What form of alcohol do you most often drink? Beer or ale? Wine? Hard liquor?
Have you ever driven a car after drinking?

In other studies, the questions concern respondents' opinions.

Which political party's agenda do you find most appealing? Democratic? Republican? Reform? Libertarian?
Do you approve of affirmative action policies that provide special employment opportunities for people from disadvantaged minority groups?

A tight-question approach is sometimes enriched by the interviewer asking respondents to support their decisions with reasons for selecting the answer they chose.

Why do you think the Libertarians have the best policies?
Why do you feel affirmative-action college-admission policies should be continued?

One of the appealing advantages of a tight-question approach is the ease with which the results of the study can be compiled. The researcher's job of organizing the answers merely requires that the percentage of people selecting each option be reported. In contrast, organizing the answers to open-ended questions (including respondents' rationales) is often a complex, demanding task.

*Converging-question strategy*

A converging approach is intended to incorporate the advantages of both the loose and tight strategies. The interviewer first asks broad, open-ended questions to discover what seems uppermost in the respondent's mind in relation to the topic at hand. Then, following the respondent's answer, the interviewer asks one or more limited-choice questions. The label *converging-question strategy* refers to a funnel-like approach with broad queries followed by one or more sharply focused questions.

*Broad question:* What's your opinion about people being able to own and carry guns?
*Narrow-focus questions:* Do you think that people younger than age 21 should be allowed to own guns? What should school authorities do if a student brings a gun to school?

By starting with broad questions, the interviewer optimizes the likelihood of eliciting diverse opinions. If the process were conducted in reverse, with specific multiple-choice options (*yes/no* on the death penalty or on affirmative-action policies) posed first, followed by general open-ended questions, respondents' answers to the open-ended queries might be influenced by the options suggested in the multiple-choice phase.

*Response-guided strategy*

A response-guided approach consists of the interviewer beginning with a prepared question, then spontaneously creating follow-up queries relating to the interviewee's answer to the opening question. This technique enables the researcher to investigate in some depth the respondent's detailed comprehension of issues related to the initial question. Perhaps the best known version of such a strategy is the *clinical method* popularized by the Swiss child psychologist, Jean Piaget (Inhelder & Piaget, 1964). Piaget defended his deviation from using a single, standard set of questions by explaining that all children do not interpret a given question in the same way. Thus, the experimenter probes the child's understanding and may then cast the problem in a different form to help ensure that the problem situation is the same for each child, even though the wording may not be identical each time. In effect, the child's initial answer guides the interviewer in devising additional questions to pose.

A typical interview of this type is illustrated in the following passage in which eight-year-old Per was asked about some flowers—primulas (primroses) and other varieties—that the interviewer placed before the child. The interviewer's purpose was to discover how Per classified objects into a general set (flowers) and into subsets within the general set (primulas, violets, tulips). At the point we enter the discussion, Per has already responded to the initial question that asked her to order the flowers into three levels of classes: yellow primulas, primulas, and flowers (adapted from Inhelder & Piaget, 1964, p. 107).

*Interviewer:* Can one put a primula in the box of flowers (without changing the label)?

*Per:* Yes, a primula is also a flower.

*Interviewer:* Can I put one of these flowers (a tulip) in the box of primulas?

*Per:* Yes, it's a flower like the primula. . . .

*Interviewer:* Suppose I remove all the primulas, will there be any flowers left?

*Per:* Oh, yes, there will still be violets, tulips, and other flowers.

*Interviewer:* Well, suppose I pick all the flowers, will there be any primulas left?

*Per:* No, primulas are flowers. You're picking them, too.

*Interviewer:* Are there more flowers or more primulas?

*Per:* The same number. Primulas are flowers.

*Interviewer:* Count the primulas.

*Per:* Four.

*Interviewer:* And the flowers?

*Per:* Seven.

*Interviewer:* Are they the same number?

*Per (astonished):* The flowers are more.

It's apparent that the experimenter in this example not only was interested in gathering information about Per's reasoning processes, but also had a didactic aim in mind—that of advancing Per's command of logic by confronting her with inconsistencies resulting from her initial mode of classifying the flowers.

As the foregoing examples of strategies have suggested, it is important for researchers to design their interview techniques carefully to suit the particular aims of the research project at hand.

### Advantages of Interviews

It should be apparent that many interview questions could be presented to respondents in questionnaire form rather than as part of a personal conversation. Distributing questionnaires to a group enables a researcher to save the time that interviewing would require. In addition, a far larger number of people can participate in a questionnaire survey than would be possible through individual interviews. Nevertheless, substantial advantages that interviews provide make interviewing the preferred data-gathering technique for certain kinds of research.

An investigator's taking the time and trouble to conduct personal interviews rather than simply passing out questionnaires to a classroom of students or sending forms through the mail suggests to respondents that the researcher particularly values their opinions. This display of sincere interest in respondents' views can enhance the diligence and care with which interviewees answer questions. Furthermore, the interview setting enables a researcher to clarify items that participants may find confusing. Interviews also make it easy for participants to amplify their answers or to digress from the central topic in ways that prove useful to the investigator. Furthermore, interviews can provide an in-depth understanding of a respondent's motives, pattern of reasoning, and emotional reactions that is not possible with questionnaires.

### Interview Resources

Aubel, J. (1994). *Guidelines for studies using the group interview technique.* Geneva: International Labour Office.

Banaka, W. H. (1971). *Training in depth interviewing.* New York: Harper & Row.
Bedarf, E. W. (1986). *Using structured interviewing techniques.* Washington, DC: U.S. General Accounting Office.
Belson, W. A. (1981). *The design and understanding of survey questions.* Aldershot, England: Gower.
Bradburn, N. M. (1979). *Improving interview method and questionnaire design.* San Francisco: Jossey-Bass.
Brady, J. J. (1976). *The craft of interviewing.* New York: Vintage.
Cannell, C. F. (1977). *A summary of research studies of interviewing methodology.* Rockville, MD: U.S. Government Printing Office.
Chirban, J. T. (1996). *Interviewing in depth: The interactive-relational approach.* Thousand Oaks, CA: Sage.
Douglas, J. D. (1985). *Creative interviewing.* Beverly Hills: Sage.
Fowler, F. J. (1990). *Standardized survey interviewing: Minimizing interview-related errors.* Newbury Park, CA: Sage.
Groves, R. M., & Khan, R. L. (1979). *Surveys by telephone: A national comparison with personal interviews.* New York: Academic.
Gubrium, A., & Joyner, R. (2005). *Postmodern interviewing.* Thousand Oaks, CA: Sage.
Guenzel, P. J. (1983). *General interview techniques: A self-instructional workbook for telephone and personal interviews training.* Ann Arbor, MI: Institute for Social Research, University of Michigan.
McMahan, E. M., & Rogers, K. L. (Eds.). (1994). *Interactive oral history interviewing.* Hillsdale, NJ: Erlbaum.
Rubin, H. J., & Rubin, I. S. (2004). *Qualitative interviewing: The art of hearing data.* Thousand Oaks, CA: Sage.

## QUESTIONNAIRES

As already mentioned, a questionnaire is a research instrument consisting of a series of questions people answer about their life condition, beliefs, or attitudes. A questionnaire can be administered either as a printed document that respondents fill out or as a list of queries posed by an interviewer, who then compiles interviewees' answers either by writing on a printed form or by recording the replies on audiotape or videotape.

### Types of Questionnaire Items

Questionnaires typically contain one or more item types: (a) dual-choice, (b) multiple-choice, (c) short-answer, or (d) narrative or essay.

### *Dual-choice items*

Dual-choice items offer respondents two options from which to select—yes/no, agree/disagree, like/dislike, approve/disapprove, ever/never. Two advantages of the dual-choice questions are that the items can be quickly answered and the results easily compiled. In research reports, the results are typically reported as percentages—"53% of Democrats favored the welfare proposal" or "19% of students reported that they had never tried any form of alcohol." A further advantage is that researchers can include more items on a two-choice questionnaire than is generally the case with instruments that require more complex responses, as do open-ended questions that call for a narrative answer.

One limitation of dual-choice items is that they fail to reveal graduated levels of belief that would be discovered if respondents were able to show where their opinions belonged on a scale ranging from extremely high to extremely low. A second potential disadvantage is that the very ease with which two-level items can be marked may encourage a hasty person to check off answers carelessly without thoroughly considering each item's implications.

### *Multiple choices*

Respondents can be offered multiple options either as a list of discrete answers from which to choose or as a dimension or scale extending from one extreme to the other. The following are two sorts of discrete answers:

Directions: Place an X on the line before the one candidate you would prefer as president of the Rotary Club.

____ Martin Benson
____ Elizabeth Clark
____ Michael Scolari
____ Fabian Tracy

Seven uses have been suggested for spending the money collected in the Kiwanis lottery. Place a *1* beside the item you think is the best way to use the money, a *2* beside the way you consider second best, and a *3* beside the way you think is third best.

____ Cheerleader uniforms for the high school
____ Computers for the junior high
____ High school football uniforms
____ The county blood bank
____ The annual club picnic
____ Expanding the club newsletter

Frequently people's opinions are most accurately reported as positions along a dimension whose divisions represent sequential qualities, frequencies, or amounts. The choice alternatives can be represented as degrees along a scale line, as proportions, or as successive discrete items.

Figure 8.1 illustrates one popular form of a researcher-constructed rating scale, a semantic-differential type featuring diametrically contrasting adjectives at the opposite ends of each scale line. This example displays the first four lines of an assessment instrument designed to elicit observers' judgments of trial lawyers' questioning styles as shown in scenes recorded on videotape. The "favorable" end of scales is randomly changed from left to right on successive lines so as to combat any tendency of participants to carelessly mark the same end of all scales on the basis of the response-set they bring to the task, such as a tendency to generally approve or disapprove of the lawyer in the scene. Thus, raters must study every scale line individually in order to produce a coherent overall judgment of the lawyers' styles.

A researcher can later convert the raters' judgments into numerical form for purposes of analysis by weighting the seven spaces from 1 (least favorable rating) to 7 (most favorable rating).

*Short-answer items*

This approach requires respondents to offer a word or phrase in reply to a question. One advantage of such items is that they do not restrict people's

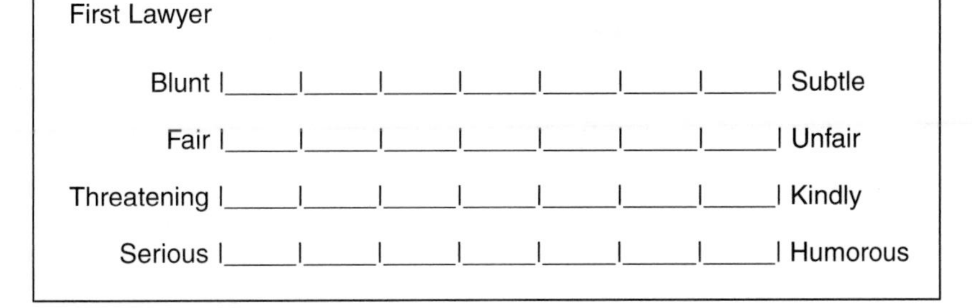

Instructions: As you watch the videotape, use a copy of this rating sheet to record your impression of the questioning style of each of the four lawyers portrayed in the court scenes. Place an X in the space on each line that you believe best represents the lawyer's style.

First Lawyer

Blunt I_____I_____I_____I_____I_____I_____I_____I Subtle

Fair I_____I_____I_____I_____I_____I_____I_____I Unfair

Threatening I_____I_____I_____I_____I_____I_____I_____I Kindly

Serious I_____I_____I_____I_____I_____I_____I_____I Humorous

**Figure 8.1** Trial Lawyers' Questioning Styles

answers to a set of options presented by the researcher but, rather, they allow people to reply in any way they wish. A disadvantage is that the range of answers may be so diverse that the responses are difficult to classify into categories that are easy to compile and interpret. Yet such diversity may be necessary if people's answers are to accurately represent their opinions and knowledge.

Here are two short-answer questions from a study of prison inmates' interests.

- How do you spend your recreation time?
- Which kinds of television programs do you like best? Which don't you like?

Some questions require replies in the form of extended descriptions or explanations. Such items often concern past experiences in respondents' lives or their predictions about the future. The first of the following examples is designed for a survey of restaurant managers' perceptions of their jobs. The second is intended for a study of the problems nurses see in a proposed hospital policy governing the rights and privileges of drug-abuse patients.

- Describe two difficult decisions and two easy decisions that you were obliged to make during the past year.
- What do you see as disadvantages or dangers in the suggested rules about drug-abuse patients' rights and privileges? What do you see as advantages?

Items calling for explanation are of the "why" variety, aimed at discovering the line of reasoning behind respondents' preferences and actions. Such questions are typically asked as follow-ups to another kind of item, as in a study of physicians' analyses of medical books intended for families' home use.

(A) Of the four medical-help books that you inspected, which one do you prefer?

____ The American Medical Association's Encyclopedia of Medicine

____ Mayo Clinic Family Health Book

____ Medical Treatment Quick Reference

____ Guide to Prescription and Over-the-Counter Drugs

(B) Why do you prefer that book over the others?

*Narrative items*

In contrast to multiple-choice and short-answer questions, narrative items enable respondents to identify in detail a variety of factors that have influenced their experiences and opinions. As a result, narrative responses can reveal the unique patterning of different people's knowledge and attitudes. However, the individualistic nature of narrative answers increases the difficulty of classifying responses into categories that are readily compared.

### Questionnaire Resources

Aiken, L. R. (1997). *Questionnaires and inventories: Surveying opinions and assessing personality.* New York: Wiley.

Angleitner, J. S., & Wiggins, J. S. (Eds.). (1986). *Personality assessment via questionnaires: Current issues in theory and measurement.* New York: Springer-Verlag.

Berdie, D. F., Anderson, J. F., & Niebuhr, M. A. (1986). *Questionnaires: Design and use* (2nd ed.). Metuchen, NJ: Scarecrow Press.

Cox, J. (1996). *Your opinion, please! How to build the best questionnaires in the field of education.* Thousand Oaks, CA: Corwin Press.

Dillman, D. A. (2006). *Mail and Internet surveys: The tailored design method.* New York: Wiley.

Foddy, W. H. (1993). *Constructing questions for interviews and questionnaires.* New York: Cambridge University Press.

Labaw, P. J. (1981). *Advanced questionnaire design.* Cambridge, MA: Abt.

Oppenheim, A. N. (1992). *Questionnaire design, interviewing, and attitude measurement.* New York: St. Martin's.

Willis, G. B. (2004). *Cognitive interviewing: A tool for improving questionnaire design.* Thousand Oaks, CA: Sage.

## TESTS

Tests can be divided into categories according to their intended functions and their sources.

### Tests' Functions

One way to classify a test in terms of its functions is by locating it in one of five categories—achievement, aptitude, attitude (opinion), interest, and personality.

Achievement tests are designed to determine how well a person has learned to do something, such as read, spell, calculate, recall historical facts, conduct scientific experiments, analyze social problems, repair automobiles, and more.

Aptitude tests aim at measuring individuals' potential ability to develop a type of skill or knowledge. Such tests are often used to predict people's academic achievement in college, their likely success as a police officer, how suitable individuals are for pilot training, and the like. Measures of intelligence qualify as one variety of aptitude test.

The purpose of attitude or opinion inventories is to estimate how favorably disposed people are toward selected individuals, groups, institutions, values, doctrines, or events. Interest tests—a subclass of attitude inventories—are used to identify people's likes and dislikes regarding kinds of activities and styles of life, such as vocations, fields of academic study, or recreational pursuits.

The term *personality tests* designates a catch-all class of instruments for appraising such things as people's character traits, personal adjustment, values, sociability, emotional stability, adaptability, or personality structure.

## Sources of Tests

The two chief sources of tests are formal test publishers and researchers themselves. Tests issued by publishers are typically of a standardized variety, designed to assess aptitudes or knowledge that people wish to measure. However, when no available published instruments are deemed suitable for a given study, researchers create tests that precisely fit their needs.

### *Published tests*

A great many tests and related assessment instruments have been developed to perform a variety of functions. For example, the Educational Testing Service's test collection library contains well over 16,000 tests and measurement devices gathered from a wide range of sources (Educational Testing Service, 1990).

The most useful descriptions of tests are found in compilations of testing instruments, test publishers' catalogs, library holdings, and journal articles relevant to the aims of the researcher's proposed study.

Probably the two most valuable compilations of test descriptions are those found in the periodic editions of the *Mental Measurements Yearbook* and *The ETS Test Collection Catalog.*

For several decades the most helpful guide to standardized tests has been the series of *Mental Measurements Yearbooks* initiated by Oscar Buros and, since his demise, continued by the Buros Mental Measurements Institute at the University of Nebraska (Conoley & Impara, 1994, 1995; Conoley & Kramer, 1989, 1992; Kramer & Conoley, 1990; Mitchell, 1985). The yearbooks, which are not necessarily issued annually, contain reviews of achievement, aptitude, intelligence, and personality tests written by analysts who have no connection with the publishers of the tests. Thus, the descriptions and appraisals are likely to be more objective than are the contents of publishers' catalogs, advertising brochures, and manuals that accompany tests. Each new edition of the Buros publications does not repeat reports of tests in earlier editions but describes only the most recent versions of tests. Therefore, if you wish to survey all types of tests from all times, it is necessary to consult all editions.

An even more extensive survey of published tests and related measuring devices is provided in descriptions compiled by the Educational Testing Service's test-collection staff. The first *ETS Test Collection Catalog* (Educational Testing Service, 1990) consists of six volumes (achievement tests and measurement devices; vocational tests and measurement devices; tests for special populations; cognitive aptitude and intelligence tests; attitude tests; and affective measures and personality tests). The second edition (1993–1995) is in two volumes (updated achievement tests and measurement devices; vocational tests and measurement devices). Unlike the *Mental Measurements Yearbook*s, the ETS volumes include no assessments of the strengths and limitations of the listed tests but, rather, confine their treatment to each measuring instrument's name, purpose, contents, types of people for whom the test is intended, and its source. The breadth of coverage is impressive, as suggested by the fact that the volume treating cognitive aptitude and intelligence measures contains descriptions of over 1,300 assessment instruments.

Further sources of test descriptions are the catalogs issued by such publishers as the Educational Testing Service (Princeton, NJ), Psychological Corporation (555 Academic Court, San Antonio, TX 78204), and Psychological Assessment Resources (P. O. Box 998, Odessa, FL 33556). Catalogs frequently offer more detailed information than that found in the Buros yearbooks and ETS volumes. Publishers' materials also include information about new tests or recent revisions of established instruments that does not appear in the above-mentioned compilations of tests.

The appearance of computerized university library catalogs has greatly facilitated the hunt for information about tests. A computer search for names and descriptions of tests can be conducted by the investigator's bringing the library's catalog onto the computer screen, then entering key words to locate pertinent books and journal articles that likely offer assessments of tests or contain descriptions of studies in which standardized tests have been used. Key terms that serve this purpose can combine (a) the field knowledge, the behavior, or the personal traits that the researcher wishes to assess and (b) a word that either refers to the act of assessing or identifies the time-focus of the assessment.

*Researcher-created tests*

When none of the available published tests precisely evaluate for the skills or knowledge that a researcher wishes to assess, the researcher is obliged to create a suitable instrument. The following resources are helpful guides to test construction.

Byrne, B. M. (1996). *Measuring self-concept across the life span: Issues and instrumentation.* Washington, DC: American Psychological Association.

Fischer, C. T. (1994). *Individualizing psychological assessment.* Hillsdale, NJ: Erlbaum.

Goldman, B., & Mitchell, D. (Eds.). (2002). *Directory of unpublished experimental mental measures.* Washington, DC: American Psychological Association.

Graham, J. R. (1984). *Psychological testing.* Englewood Cliffs, NJ: Prentice Hall.

Gronlund, N. E. (2005). *Assessment of student achievement* (8th ed.). Boston: Allyn & Bacon.

Hambleton, R. K., & Zaal, J. N. (Eds.). (1991). *Advances in educational and psychological testing.* Boston: Kluwer.

Heaton, J. B. (1990). *Classroom testing.* New York: Longman.

Loevinger, J. (Ed.). (1998). *Technical foundations for measuring ego development.* Mahwah, NJ: Erlbaum.

McArthur, D. L. (Ed.). (1987). *Alternative approaches to the assessment of achievement.* Boston: Kluwer.

Roid, G. H., & Haladyna, T. H. (1982). *A technology for test-item writing.* New York: Academic.

## PLANNING CHECKLIST

Filling out the following checklist may help you identify which of the techniques described in this chapter you intend to employ in your research.

Place an X on the line in front of each technique that you plan to use for gathering information.

1. Observation

   1.1 Observer's relationship to the observed

   ____ 1.1.1 Participant observer

   ____ 1.1.2 Remote observer

   1.2 Recording method

   ____ 1.2.1 Videotape

   ____ 1.2.2 Audiotape

   ____ 1.2.3 Handwritten notes

   ____ 1.2.4 Rating scale or checklist

   ____ 1.2.5 Other (describe) ____________________

2. Content Analysis

   ____ 2.1 Qualitative

   ____ 2.2 Quantitative

   ____ 2.3 Patterning

3. Interview

   3.1 Question strategy

   ____ 3.1.1 Loose question

   ____ 3.1.2 Tight question

   ____ 3.1.3 Converging

   ____ 3.1.4 Response guided

   3.2 Contact method

   ____ 3.2.1 Direct face-to-face

   ____ 3.2.2 Telephone

4. Questionnaire

   ____ 4.1 Dual choice

   ____ 4.2 Three or more discrete choices

*(Continued)*

(Continued)

____ 4.3 Scaled choices

____ 4.4 Short answers

____ 4.5 Narrative answers

5. Test

____ 5.1 Published test (identify title): ______________________

____ 5.2 Researcher-created test

# NINE

# THINGS THAT GO WRONG

*"I'm afraid I'm sunk. It's not working out at all the way I'd planned. So what's to be done?"*

Troubles can crop up at any point in the process of doing theses and dissertations. However, the data-collection stage seems particularly vulnerable to problems, so we've chosen this place in the book to identify a series of familiar difficulties and to propose ways of managing them. Throughout the chapter the presentation is cast as conversations between a succession of distressed graduate students and their academic advisors, with the students describing their troubles and the advisors suggesting potential solutions. It should be apparent that the suggestions offered by the advisors in these anecdotes are not ones that all advisors would give. In effect, these examples illustrate no more than a few of the potential solutions that can be attempted to cope with things that go wrong.

The issues inspected in the five cases concern projects that (a) failed to achieve the authors' desired outcomes, (b) included uncooperative participants, (c) yielded statistically insignificant results, (d) failed to meet a professor's concept of an adequate number of subjects, and (e) the author feared would be less than perfect.

## SHATTERED EXPECTATIONS

*Student:* "As I've collected more and more interviews, I realize my project's turning out all wrong. A lot of the kids aren't answering the way they should."

*Advisor:* "What do you mean by *should?*"

*Student:* "I asked them what consequence they would recommend for the main character in each of eight cases of wrongdoing. So I expected kids at the juvenile detention facility to give different answers than the ones in the church school. But while there's lots of variety among the consequences suggested within each of the groups, there doesn't seem to be any significant difference between the pattern of answers of the two groups as a whole. Something's wrong."

*Advisor:* "Obviously. But maybe what's wrong is that you've been hunting for evidence to support your preconception rather than accepting reality as revealed by your interviews. Why not follow your data instead of trying to force your hypothesis onto the data? The fact that your interview answers surprise you should be good news—you've learned something new; and the readers of your thesis will also learn something worthwhile if you interpret the outcome insightfully. If you accept the interview results as accurately showing diversity within each of the two groups rather than showing a significant difference between the groups as a whole, then you have valuable evidence about the danger of stereotyping people who are members of each group. Your interpretation task can now be one of investigating likely reasons behind such an outcome. Your project hasn't gone wrong. For me, your actual results are more interesting than the results you'd hoped for. Follow your data."

## UNCOOPERATIVE PARTICIPANTS

*Student:* "I was trying to learn what changes in teachers' treatment of students result from teacher-parent conferences. A study like this had been conducted in a small California community and I wanted to see if similar changes would occur in schools in a South Sea Islands community as well. I wanted to compare the results from California with ones I collected in American Samoa. The Department of Education in American Samoa was fully behind the plan, so we had successful training sessions for teachers in how to conduct parent conferences. Then we had the teachers set schedules for their meetings with each child's parents. But at the end of the six weeks during which the conferences were to be completed, we discovered that hardly any teachers had followed the plan. They didn't object to the plan; they just didn't have any conferences. It was passive resistance, simple stonewalling. So I ended up with no results to report. I'm ruined."

*Advisor:* "Not necessarily. The interesting question here is: Why did the California teachers carry out the plan whereas the Samoan teachers did not? What you might do to save your project is to change the question you were trying to answer."

*Student:* "But in the middle of your project, you can't change your topic. I'm told that's not acceptable scientific procedure."

*Advisor:* "The purpose of research is to discover something that's a worthwhile contribution to knowledge. Why can't you change horses in the middle of the stream if it can save you from disaster and produce a desirable result? Finding that your plan succeeded in California and failed in Samoa is worth explaining and can provide guidance for other researchers who pursue studies in diverse social settings. Your new task can be that of identifying the factors in the two cultures—those of a California community and American Samoa villages—that account for the conflicting outcomes of teacher-parent conferencing in the two settings. This likely means conducting interviews with teachers and parents in each setting to learn their views of the proper roles of teachers and parents. Or, since you aren't Samoan, the interviews with the islanders might well elicit more candid responses if one of your Samoan colleagues did the interviewing. In any case, it seems to me that you can produce a first-rate contribution by setting aside the original question—'What changes in teachers' treatment of students result from teacher-parent conferences?'—in favor of a new one—'What cultural factors influence the conduct of research in diverse social settings?' Your original plan and the way you implemented it are still important elements of your study. The aim, however, becomes that of explaining why the plan didn't work as you'd hoped."

## NEGATIVE RESULTS

*Student:* "As I'd intended, I divided the philosophy class that I teach into two groups. I taught the unit on forms of logic to one group by my traditional lecture and discussion method. Then I had the other group study the same material individually on computers, using the program I wrote about forms of logic. Finally, I tested both groups, but I got negative results. It didn't work out."

*Advisor:* "What do you mean by *negative results?*"

*Student:* "There was no significant difference between the two groups' average test scores. The averages were nearly the same."

Advisor: "So that means your experiment failed?"

*Student:* "I figured one group would do better than the other, so I'd know which teaching method was better. That would be something worth reporting."

*Advisor:* "It seems to me you have plenty that's worth reporting. Let's imagine that a student misses your lectures about logic. So you can have her try the computer program on her own, being rather confident that she'll master the material as well as if she had attended the lectures. Discovering that on the average the two methods work equally well is good news. Your experiment wasn't a failure. You revealed something useful, and your readers can profit from that.

"Of course, what you don't know is which method might work better with some students than with others. It's the *aptitude-treatment-interaction* issue—the notion that some learners' characteristics equip them to succeed better with some instructional methods than with other methods. That's something you might want to investigate in the future by adopting a different experimental design than the one you used.

"The real danger in getting negative results comes from having chosen a noncontroversial topic for your experiment or survey in the first place. Let's say you chose to investigate the question 'Can individual differences among students in learning to play tennis be erased (so all succeed equally well) by their eating the same diet for three weeks?' This is a noncontroversial matter, because essentially no one beyond the years of childhood will imagine that diet is the sole determining factor differentiating one player's skills from another's. Thus, in order to produce a study of such a question that anyone takes seriously, you will have to get positive results. Your study will have to show that, within a heterogeneous group of tennis students, all of them demonstrated the same skills by the end of the three-week diet. Such a result would be dramatic, indeed, and warrant a lot of attention in both academia and the public press. But if you get negative results, showing that after three weeks there were still notable differences among learners in their tennis skills, people will simply think you weren't very bright for ever presuming otherwise. They'll think you were stupid for doing such a study.

"Thus, what you need is a true issue, one that reasonable people can disagree about. Then, whether you get positive or negative results from your survey or your experiment, the results are meaningful. Such has been the case with your study of lecturing versus a computer program. Before you conducted your experiment, the outcome would have been—in most people's minds—indeterminate; so doing the experiment would be worthwhile, no matter which way it turned out."

## THE MEANING OF "ENOUGH SUBJECTS"

*Student:* "When I told Professor Green about my data, he told me I didn't have enough subjects. He said I'd have to get more. But there aren't that many autistic kids available, and it takes a lot of time—about four months—to apply my training program with each kid."

*Advisor:* "How many children are you using?"

*Student:* "Three—ages 8, 10, and 11."

*Advisor:* "Did Professor Green say how many he thought you needed?"

*Student:* "He said it would be best to have at least 30, so I could use large-sample statistics. And if I don't have that many, I won't find out anything worth talking about."

*Advisor:* "So, what you need is a line of reasoning that persuades potential critics that the result you produce with only three autistic subjects will be of value?"

*Student:* "That's my hope."

*Advisor:* "Well, here's one possible approach. When you are deciding how many subjects you need for an experiment or survey, you answer two questions: *What am I trying to test or reveal? How broadly do I wish to apply the interpretation of my study?* Now, let's direct those questions at your autism project. What's your study supposed to test or reveal?"

*Student:* "A Professor Baron-Cohen at Cambridge University has a theory of autism that assumes that children's social behavior is crucially influenced by their ability to estimate what other people are thinking. According to Baron-Cohen, autistic children suffer from a genetic disorder that damages their ability to estimate other people's thought processes. He's reported some limited success in training children to make better estimates. But apparently nobody has tried to do that with pictures and videos. I've worked out a training system for using photos and videos of people that I think could help autistic kids improve their skill in judging other people's thoughts. I want to test out that training system on these three autistic kids to see if it works at all. And if it does work, is it more effective with one child than with another, and why? I think if I train them over a four-month period it should be long enough to see if my scheme is any good."

*Advisor:* "So, if you get positive results and the children do improve in their social perceptions, what research question does that answer?"

*Student:* "Well, it's this—'Can autistic children's understanding of other people's thought processes be improved by training the children with pictures and videos of people in social situations?'"

*Advisor:* "But what if you get negative results? What if the children's ability to estimate others' thoughts doesn't improve? Is such a result any good? Do you still have a viable thesis—something worth talking about?"

*Student:* "I think so. From Baron-Cohen's theory and the training he's done, I think it's reasonable to try my system. Trying it with three kids should give me some idea whether it's practical."

*Advisor:* "Even though 30 would be better, testing your system on three seems defensible. Now to the second question: How broadly do you wish to apply the results of your study? Do you plan to draw conclusions that can be applied to autistic children other than the three you train?"

*Student:* "Of course. That's why I'm doing it."

*Advisor:* "Then there's a two-part question to ask. It's the question I think Professor Green is concerned about: 'To which people, other than my three subjects, can my conclusions validly be applied; and how should I phrase my interpretation to make clear the conditions under which my results can legitimately be applied to other individuals who display symptoms of autism?'

"Now let's first speculate about how your interpretation might read if your system is at least modestly successful with your three subjects. Here's one way you might interpret such an outcome:

> 'The results of this study suggest that (a) at least some autistic children's ability to estimate other people's thought processes will improve under the study's training program and (b) some children's abilities will improve more than others. The three subjects who participated in this research were all boys, all in the age range of 8 to 11, all from urban U.S. middle-class

> families, and all were outpatients of a child-guidance center. How well the treatment would succeed with girls, with other age levels, and with subjects from other types of homes is unknown. However, the outcomes of the study appear encouraging enough to warrant trying the treatment program with other kinds of autistic individuals to determine the conditions under which such treatment can profitably be employed.'

"It seems to me that such an interpretation would be sufficiently specific and cautious to make the use of only three subjects defensible, since what you are attempting to test is the proposition that your training scheme will work at all."

*Student:* "But what if none of the kids improve? What can I say then?"

*Advisor:* "First, you can argue that it was reasonable to expect your program might work. You base that argument on Baron-Cohen's theory and the success he reported in training autists to recognize other people's thought processes. Next, you explain that your system did not improve your three subjects' social-observation skills. You then speculate about possible causes for such a result; propose what sorts of studies might be conducted to investigate those possibilities; and offer an opinion about whether, in light of your scheme's apparent failure, such studies would be worth the cost and effort.

"So this brings us back to the beginning. The matter of how many subjects you need in an experiment or survey can depend on how you answer those two questions: 'What am I trying to test or reveal? How broadly do I wish to apply the results or interpretation of my study?' If you wanted your study to reveal how effective your scheme would be with all varieties of autists throughout the United States, you would need a large enough sample of subjects to fairly represent the range of influential characteristics within that entire population. In effect, you would need a large sample, drawn in a manner that convinced your readers that the participants indeed typified the nationwide autistic population's influential characteristics. Maybe Professor Green thought you planned to offer such a wide-ranging interpretation on the basis of your three-subject study. Why not organize your rationale so it fits what you are actually trying to do, then talk with him again?"

## NOTHING SHORT OF PERFECT

*Student:* "I still can't decide which method to use for collecting information about people's use of credit cards. Every professor I talk with has a different idea."

*Advisor:* "Such as?"

*Student:* "One says I should do telephone interviews. Another says questionnaires is the way to go. And another recommends face-to-face interviews. Then one says I should do interviews and also get records from the interviewees' credit-card company so I could compare what people say with how they really use their cards."

*Advisor:* "Well, each of those approaches obviously has its own advantages and disadvantages. Any one of them could yield useful results, depending on the exact questions you're trying to answer."

*Student:* "But I have to be sure which method's the right one. I don't want to get in the middle of it and find out I'm doing it wrong."

*Advisor:* "There isn't one perfect method. Each of those options offers a particular perspective toward credit-card use."

*Student:* "But I want my thesis to be recognized as really important, so I want to do it right."

*Advisor:* "Maybe you're demanding too much of yourself—aiming at unquestionable perfection. Your study doesn't have to win a Nobel prize. Naturally you want your work to make a contribution, but you should recognize that doing a thesis is essentially a learning exercise and not your entire life's work. Doing the thesis gives you guided research experience. If you do a good job with any one of those data-collection methods, you'll be making a contribution. Pick one method and go with it."

*Student:* "But I want to be sure it's going to work out right so I won't be criticized."

*Advisor:* "There are no guarantees ahead of time. You have to take a chance. And you can't expect to please everybody. No scholar pleases everyone. I think you've already gotten enough advice from enough professors. Now choose one method that you think has a good chance of answering your credit-card questions, and then start collecting data. Otherwise you'll be around this place all your life."

## STAGE III-B

# ORGANIZING INFORMATION

In every research project, the data you collect need to be arranged in a form that facilitates the interpretation of what those data mean from the perspective of your project. Ways of organizing data are described in the two chapters that comprise Stage III-B.

Organizing data usually involves two opposite, complementary operations—classifying and summarizing.

*Classifying* consists of separating the contents of a mass of information into categories so the contents can be easily compared and contrasted. This operation is the focus of Chapter 10: Classification Patterns.

*Summarizing*—the reverse of classifying—consists of combining a conglomeration of information so the essence and implications of the material can be readily understood. Chapter 11 (Summarizing Information Verbally, Numerically, and Graphically) illustrates popular ways of abstracting and condensing data.

TEN

# CLASSIFICATION PATTERNS

*"What I need to know are the characteristics that a classification scheme should have in order to be accurate and efficient to use."*

One of the most fundamental attributes of human thought is people's propensity to arrange their experiences in terms of categories or classes. By assigning happenings to categories, people render life more comprehensible by revealing how certain events are similar to, and different from, other events. Classifying people, objects, and incidents enables us to compare and contrast our experiences and thereby construct an orderly mental map of reality that helps us cope with life's demands.

The tendency—indeed, the necessity—to classify experiences derives at least partly from the limited capacity of the human mind to simultaneously contemplate a multitude of variables.

> How many comparisons can be assimilated by those who seek an understanding of the patterns of comparisons? Writers on psychology such as Nobel laureate Herbert Simon believe that humans can simultaneously consider only a few items of information, perhaps fewer than four (depending partly on [how much is compressed into a comprehensible "chunk" of information]). For this reason, humans employ categorical ideas to think efficiently about what would be overly complex. (Walberg, Zhang, & Daniel, 1994, p. 80)

The practice of mentally grouping observations has apparently been a natural human function from earliest times. However, the business of rationally devising formal systems for classifying events is of more recent vintage. The science of classification, often called *taxonomy* or *systematics,* probably originated with the ancient Greeks, brought to fruition during the fourth century B.C.E. in the works of Plato and his student Aristotle. The product of systematics can be referred to as a *taxonomy* or, alternatively, as a *typology, classification scheme,* or *codification system.* In the field of biology, the theory of evolution proposed by Charles Darwin (1809–1892) is a taxonomy for codifying the patterns in which the earth's multitude of life forms descended from common beginnings over eons of time. In chemistry, Dimitri Mendeleyev (1834–1907) created the periodic table, a taxonomic system that equips chemists not only to classify known chemical elements but also to predict properties of as-yet-undiscovered elements. In the field of education, Benjamin Bloom (1913–1999) and his associates created a widely used "Taxonomy of Educational Objectives" (Bloom, 1956).

Although we have waited until this point in the book to formally discuss the role that classifying plays in research, it should be apparent that decisions about how you intend to organize your data are profitably made at various steps of your project, from the early stage of defining your research problem through the ultimate stage of interpreting the results. But the reason we have placed this chapter under Stage III-B is because the matter of categorizing information is particularly important during the data-collection process. Your decision about how you are going to classify your data helps you identify the kind of information to collect.

Because ways of adapting and creating classification schemes have already been discussed at some length in Chapter 5, the present chapter need not address such matters. Instead, the following presentation is limited to (a) examples of typical classification schemes and (b) key features of classification systems and implications those features may offer for students' thesis and dissertation plans.

## SOME EXAMPLES OF CLASSIFICATION SCHEMES

As an introduction to the classification task, the following examples illustrate several of the varied patterns that typologies can assume. Each example identifies (a) the title of a study, (b) the study's focal question, (c) the categories into which the collected information is to be located, and (d) the pattern in which the categories are to be organized when the results of the study are finally presented. The examples illustrate classification schemes for six of the approaches to data gathering described in Chapter 7.

## Interpretive History (Economics)

*Title:* "A History of the New York Stock Exchange"

*Focal question:* Through what phases has the New York Stock Exchange developed since its beginning and why those particular phases?

*Categories of information:* (a) aims of the stock exchange, (b) trends in stock prices, (c) policy and practice changes, (d) reasons for such changes (including influential societal conditions), and (e) the names and roles of important people.

*Pattern of organization:* The presentation is organized by development periods that are defined by marked changes in policy and practice. Within each period the exchange's aims, stock price trends, and important people and their roles are identified.

## Face-to-Face Interview Survey (Social Work, Sociology)

*Title:* "People's Reactions to Health Insurance Problems"

*Focal question:* What problems have individuals encountered in obtaining and using medical insurance, what measures have they taken to cope with those problems, how successful were those measures, and why did their efforts turn out the way they did?

*Categories of information:* The categories are of two kinds: (1) respondent-identification classes and (2) type-of-problem classes. The four respondent-identification categories divide interviewees according to their (a) age, (b) gender, (c) health insurance provider (such as Medicare, Medicaid, Prudential Insurance, and the like), and (d) length of time the insurance was held. The type-of-problem classes (problem categories, coping measures, and success of coping measures) are not established ahead of time but will be determined from an inspection of the interview responses after the interviews have been collected. In other words, the researcher does not wish to set classes ahead of time and thereby miss the inclusion of types of problems and coping techniques that were not foreseen earlier.

*Pattern of organization:* The interview results will be arranged in the order of problem incidence, with the most frequent types of problems first and the least frequent last. Within the discussion of each type, the kind of problem and its subtypes will be described first, followed by steps attempted to resolve the problems and the level of success of those attempts. At each stage of the presentation, anecdotal material illustrating various difficulties with insurance claims will be drawn from the interviews and built into the narrative. The final section of the presentation will summarize the results and offer advice to health insurance customers about the effectiveness of different methods of dealing with insurance companies.

### Experience Narrative (Anthropology)

*Title:* "Cheyenne Dreams"

*Focal questions:* What are the forms and contents of representative dreams of members of the Cheyenne nation? In Cheyenne culture, what meanings are attributed to such dreams or what functions are those dreams expected to perform?

*Categories of information:* In this study, the researcher plans to select 10 dreams out of a variety of dreams collected verbatim from Cheyenne informants, then to ask the dreamers or a shaman to tell what the dreams mean or what functions such dreams serve among the Cheyenne.

The categories used for displaying the derived information are of two kinds: (1) respondent-identification types and (2) dream-description types. The first kind divides interviewees according to their (a) age, (b) gender, and (c) type of living context (reservation, city with numerous Cheyenne, city but separated from other Cheyenne, etc.). The dream-description types are divided into (a) the dream narratives themselves and (b) interpretations of the dreams' meanings and functions.

*Pattern of presentation:* The exposition of the dreams will be organized in terms of clusters of dreams that are similar in meaning or function, but the clusters cannot be determined until after the dreams have been collected. An analysis of the collected dreams will permit the investigator to establish dream groupings. Within a group, each dreamer is to be identified by age, gender, and living context. Each dream's description will consist of the dream related verbatim, followed by an interpretation of its meaning and/or assumed function. At the close of the entire set of clusters, the author will summarize the study with generalizations about likenesses and differences among the dreams in regard to their content, attributed meanings, and apparent functions.

### Biography (Education)

*Title:* "Catherine Morton, Pioneer School Mistress"

*Focal question:* What were Catherine Morton's goals at different times of her life, what were her educational achievements, and what people and events influenced her achievements?

*Categories of information:* (a) noteworthy educational accomplishments, (b) influential events, and (c) significant people.

*Pattern of organization:* Each section of the presentation is constructed around a noteworthy accomplishment that is then explained in terms of the people and events that appeared to affect it.

### Questionnaire Survey (Sociology or Religious Studies)

*Title:* "Religious Affiliation and Attitudes Toward Abortion"

*Focal questions:* What relationship obtains between (a) individuals' religious-denomination membership and their level of religious commitment and (b) the beliefs about the suitability of abortion and about the conditions under which abortion would be warranted? What reasons do respondents offer in support of their beliefs?

*Categories of information:* Respondents' (a) gender, (b) age group, (c) religious-denomination affiliation, (d) level of religious commitment (fidelity to the tenets of their denomination), (e) level of religious activity, (f) answers to 12 multiple-choice questions about abortion, and (g) reasons respondents offer in support of their answers. (Beneath each multiple-choice question, space is provided for respondents to write a brief rationale or defense of their answer.)

*Pattern of organization:* The presentation consists of an extensive series of tables showing the relationships between categories (a) through (e) and answers to the 12 multiple-choice questions in terms of both the number and percentage of respondents giving each answer. Figure 10.1 illustrates the blank form of one such display. It is useful to prepare such blank tables (dummy tables) before collecting information so as to ensure that data are gathered in a manner that facilitates their classification and analysis.

The presentation of the data consists of addressing each of the 12 questions in turn, displaying the responses to a question in the form of three tables for each of the questions: (a) gender/age/denomination, (b) level-of-commitment/gender/denomination, and (c) level-of-activity/gender/denomination. Each table is discussed in terms of likenesses and differences among the respondent groups. The presentation closes with (a) an overall summary of the response patterns, (b) the author's speculation about why the responses assumed the configurations revealed in the study, and (c) proposals about what further investigations could be conducted to resolve questions that this study has left unanswered.

### Experiment (Political Science)

*Title:* "Effects of Candidates' Appearance and Speaking Styles in Political Campaigns"

**Question 2: Is there ever any circumstance in which abortion is appropriate? (in %)**

| Age | Catholic | | | | | | Protestant | | | | | | Jewish | | | | | |
|---|---|---|---|---|---|---|---|---|---|---|---|---|---|---|---|---|---|---|
| | Female #= | | | Male #= | | | Female #= | | | Male #= | | | Female #= | | | Male #= | | |
| | Y | N | ? | Y | N | ? | Y | N | ? | Y | N | ? | Y | N | ? | Y | N | ? |
| 15–24 | | | | | | | | | | | | | | | | | | |
| 25–34 | | | | | | | | | | | | | | | | | | |
| 35–44 | | | | | | | | | | | | | | | | | | |
| 45–54 | | | | | | | | | | | | | | | | | | |
| 55–64 | | | | | | | | | | | | | | | | | | |
| 65+ | | | | | | | | | | | | | | | | | | |

# = Number of respondents    Y = Yes    N = No    ? = Undecided

**Figure 10.1** Showing Relationships by Percentages

*Focal question:* In what manner are voters' choices in elections influenced by the physical appearance and the style of speaking of the candidates who are running for office?

*The nature of the experiment:* The experiment involves subjects (college students) viewing videotaped debates between two pairs of candidates who are ostensibly running for office in a city election. After viewing the tapes, the subjects are to (a) mark ballots showing for which candidate they would vote and (b) add any comments about the basis of their choice. The college students who view the tapes are randomly divided into two groups (X and O), with each group containing an equal number of males and females. Group X views a different pair of tapes than does Group O.

The first tape seen by Group X portrays two men competing for the job of city administrator. One man is dressed in a business suit, is clean shaven, and has neatly groomed hair. The other wears a disheveled tie-dyed shirt that is partially open down the front; he has long hair, a stubble beard, and a cigarette tucked over one ear. During the debate, each man speaks clearly and grammatically. Although their speeches are different in pattern, both speeches have been designed by the researcher to be identical in the issues discussed and in the positions the two candidates adopt toward the issues. Thus, the significant difference between the candidates is in their appearance and not in the content of their speeches.

The first tape seen by Group O depicts the same two men running for the city administrator job. But this time the actor who had been neatly groomed in the Group-X tape wears the tie-dyed shirt, long hair, and stubble beard; and the actor who was disheveled in the Group-X tape is now in a business suit, clean shaven, with short, slicked-down hair. Each actor gives the same speech that he gave in the Group-X tape.

After the Group-X and Group-O viewing sessions, the researcher will examine the ballots filled out by the viewers to discover how much influence the candidates' appearance apparently exerted over viewers' choices.

Members of Groups X and O, after marking their ballots following the videotaped debate between the city administrator candidates, will view a second taped debate between two women who are competing for the position of mayor. Both are dressed in a similar fashion, but they differ in their manner of presenting their positions. One of them looks directly at the audience, speaks without hesitation, varies the cadence of her address, smiles, and gestures in keeping with the spirit of what she says. The other woman speaks hesitantly, frequently reads from her prepared paper, adds no gestures, and maintains the same voice volume and pitch throughout. As in the case of the men running for the city administrator position, the speeches of the two women in the mayoralty race differ in their pattern and sequence of topics but are essentially the same in content. Consequently, the difference between the two women is in their manner of presenting their position rather than in the positions they espouse.

The same method used in portraying the city administrator debate is adopted with the mayor debate. The woman who was the animated speaker in the Group-X tape becomes the hesitant speaker in the Group-O tape and vice versa. Therefore, the researcher, when analyzing the ballots for the mayoralty race, should be able to judge how the presentation style, rather than the two women's facial features or grooming, affected the viewers' votes.

*Categories of information:* The categories are of two kinds: (1) respondent identification types and (2) experimental conditions. The identification types include the viewers' (a) gender, (b) age, and (c) number of political science classes previously taken. The experimental-conditions categories are (a) viewing-group membership (X or O), (b) debate type (city administrator or mayor), and (c) comments viewers add to their ballots to explain their choices.

*Pattern of presentation:* After describing the study's aim and experimental design, the author intends to submit the results of the experiment in two parts. The first part will focus on political candidates' grooming, the second part on their speaking style. Within each part, conclusions will be drawn about the apparent influence of the principal variable (grooming in Part I, speaking style in Part II) on voters' choices in relation to the voters' genders, ages, and prior number of political science classes taken.

A different way to analyze classification schemes is in terms of a project's (a) title, (b) types of dimensions or variables within which categories are distinguished, (c) number of categories, and (d) category titles. Here are examples illustrating pairs of variables to be included in three imagined studies.

*Project title:* "Male/Female Wage Differentials"

*Types of dimensions:* gender and average wage

*Number of categories:*

gender = 2

average wage = 10

*Category titles:*

For gender = (1) female, (2) male

For wage = 10 wage groupings in dollar amounts ranging from lowest to highest.

*Project title:* "The United States at War in the 20th Century"

*Types of dimensions:* time in decades and wars by name

*Number of categories:*

time periods = 10

wars = 7

*Category titles:*

For time periods = (1) 1900–1910, (2) 1911–1920, (3) 1920–1930, . . . (10) 1991–2000

For wars = (a) WWI, (b) WWII, (c) Korea, (d) Vietnam, (e) Somalia, (f) Gulf, (g) Kosovo

*Project title:* "The Incidence of Psychoses in Four European Nations"

*Types of dimensions:* nations and psychoses

*Number of categories:*

nations = 4

psychoses = 8

*Category titles:*

For nations = Britain, France, Germany, Spain

For psychoses = (1) schizophrenia, (2) manic depression, . . . (8) paranoia

It should be apparent that classification structures are often far more complex than these three simple examples suggest, since multiple focal characteristics or factors are frequently included in a typology. Such can be the case with the above example of twentieth-century wars, which could include further categories under each decade concerning (a) the names of the combatant nations, (b) the number of members of each combatant's military force, (c) numbers and types of casualties, (d) the dominant weaponry used, (e) which nations were winners and which were losers, and (f) the treatment of the defeated by the victors.

## KEY FEATURES OF CLASSIFICATION SCHEMES: IMPLICATIONS AND APPLICATIONS

Characteristics of classification systems that hold significant implications for planning theses and dissertations include (a) systems' structures, (b) the time and method of creating categories, and (c) precision and clarity.

### Systems' Structures

The term *structure* refers to a classification system's types of categories and the relationship that exists among the categories. From among many possible kinds of structure, those we describe in the following paragraphs concern the quantity of dimensions and the patterning of dimensions.

#### *Quantity of dimensions*

As suggested in our earlier examples, a *dimension*—or *variable* or *taxon* (whose plural is *taxa*)—is the aspect of life that serves as the focus of classification. Thus, dimensions can be age, gender, intelligence, attitude toward dieting, friendship patterns, use of illicit drugs, place of residence, level of formal education, favorite movie, type of physical exercise, frequency of sexual intercourse, and thousands more. The number of dimensions adopted in a thesis or dissertation can vary from one dimension to a great many. For instance, the variable time, as represented by successive historical eras, can be the single classification dimension used in an account of a Crow Indian tribe's migration pattern over a period of three centuries. In our earlier example of attitudes toward abortion, there were 17 variables—5 representing personal-identification dimensions and 12 representing answers to questions about attitudes.

*Patterning of dimensions*

The relationships among variables in a classification system can assume diverse patterns, including *linear versus hierarchical, discrete versus continuous,* and *exclusive versus nonexclusive classes.*

In a linear typology, each variable can be seen as consisting of a single line that extends from an extreme position on the left to an opposite extreme on the right. The categories or choices along the line can vary from two (a dichotomous pattern), to three (a trichotomous pattern), or to any larger number of intervals. The greater the number of intervals along the line, the more the pattern deserves the label *continuous variable.*

An instance of a dichotomous variable is gender, defined as consisting of two categories—male and female. However, sometimes a variable that initially appears dichotomous actually involves far more categories. A case in point is Carl Jung's (Jung, 1921/1971) conception of personality types in terms of *introversion* and *extroversion.* Introverted persons are concerned primarily with their own thoughts and feelings. Extroverts direct their interests outward, to things outside themselves. But rarely does anyone match either the extreme introvert or extrovert description. Most people are some mixture of both traits and therefore belong at some point along the continuum that connects the two so that an introvert/extrovert pattern involves many intervals along a scale. Consequently, a researcher who uses Jung's notion of introversion and extroversion is obliged to classify people's personalities in terms of not just two intervals, but of numerous intervals representing different degrees of the two opposing traits.

In contrast to linear classification schemes are hierarchical systems. Two of the best-known hierarchies are in the field of biology, Carolus Linnaeus' *Animalia* and *Plantae* taxonomies for classifying types of animal and plant life. Each of these systems is organized in seven tiers that form the image of an inverted tree that branches downward. The most inclusive tier at the top—the trunk—is the *kingdom,* encompassing all the phenomena within the field of interest—all fauna in the *Animalia* taxonomy and all flora in the *Plantae.* Six additional tiers that progressively branch out below the kingdom are, in descending order, *phylum, class, order, family, genus,* and *species.* The farther one descends in each hierarchy, the greater the number of defining characteristics that determine the category in which an organism belongs.

Let's now envision a hierarchical scheme that we might create for a study of the extra costs students incur when they enroll in various courses in a university. What we are interested in discovering is how much students can expect to be charged in their courses in addition to their tuition fees—extra charges for books, supplies, equipment, laboratories, field trips, and more. We not only want to know the average extra course expenses across the entire campus, but also how much those costs vary from one department to another, between specializations within a department, and between courses within a specialization. To accomplish this, we create a six-tier hierarchical classification system—an inverted tree—as displayed in Figure 10.2.

The quantities of colleges, departments, specializations, and courses in a typical university are too large to be accommodated in a single diagram, so we have simplified Figure 10.2 by portraying only a sampling of those variables. Tier 1 represents the entire university. On Tier 2 we limit the pictured colleges to a pair—humanities and sciences. Tier 3 limits the number of depicted departments to six in each college. On Tier 4, we illustrate specializations for only two departments—the foreign language department in the humanities college and the biology department in the sciences college. On Tier 5 we distinguish three levels of courses for three foreign-language specialties (French, German, Hindi) and three biology specialties (botany, genetics, biochemistry). The three course levels are defined as follows: (1) lower-division (freshmen and sophomores) introductory survey courses, (2) upper-division (juniors and seniors) advanced courses, and (3) advanced graduate courses. The individual courses within each of these three groups are then found on Tier 6. In the humanities colleges, we have drawn a line under the German-language specialty to identify Level-2 (upper-division advanced) courses on Tier 6. In the sciences colleges, we identify Level-3 (advanced graduate) courses in the genetics specialization. Although our diagram encompasses only this restricted sampling of colleges, departments, specializations, and courses, in our study we intend initially to consider all courses in the university's curriculum.

Consider, now, two ways that our course-analysis classification scheme can help us answer our research questions. First, it seems obvious that trying to discover the extra costs for every course in the university curriculum would be an overwhelming task, far more costly in funds, time, and effort than the desired information is worth. So we need to identify a sample of courses to study, a sample that fairly represents the entire population of courses. Our course-analysis hierarchy can help us with this task. To begin, it is apparent that extra course costs will vary between colleges (humanities versus sciences), among departments, and among specializations within departments. Therefore, we probably should include all departments from both colleges in our sample. And under the specializations (Tier 4), we will likely want to distinguish between lecture and laboratory (practicum) courses so as to be sure that we include some of each type. Some departments—history, literature, philosophy, sociology, and the like—may have no classes that require special equipment or supplies so that we need not make the lecture-and-laboratory distinction in those departments. Hence, descending from Tier 1 through Tier 3, we have included the entire population of colleges and departments. Now, at Tier 4, we begin sampling. Within each department, we draw a selected number of specializations by means of either random or systematic sampling techniques (as described in Chapter 7 under surveys). How many specializations we choose will depend on the number of Tier 6 courses we ultimately plan to analyze. Then, for those selected specializations we move to Tier 5. By random or systematic sampling, we choose a specified number of course levels. Finally, among those course levels in our selected specializations, we choose a sample of courses that we will study.

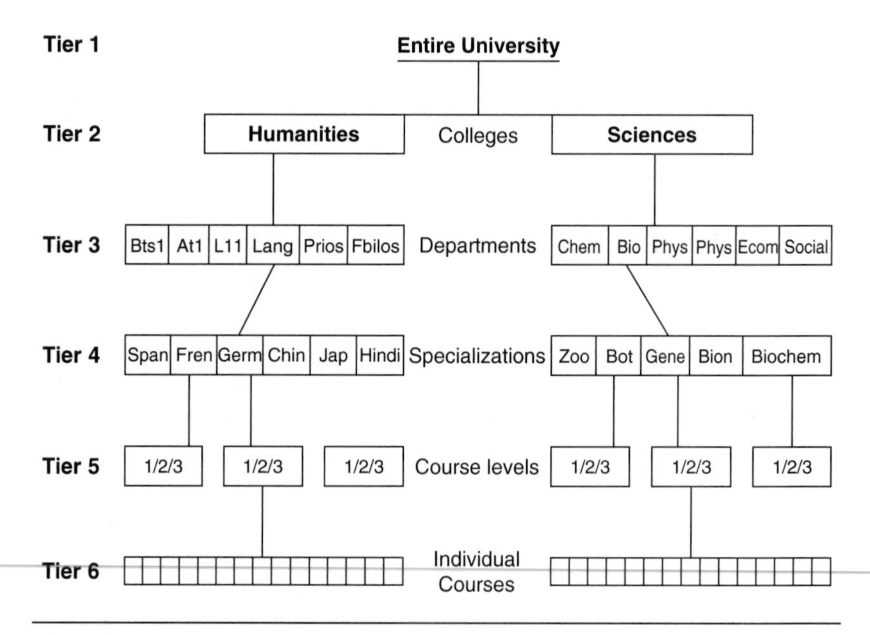


**Figure 10.2** A University Course-Analysis Hierarchy

By the foregoing process, we end up with a sample of courses whose extra costs we can discover by polling a sample of students who have been enrolled in the courses. We can draw a sample of, let us say, four or five students from each course by randomly selecting them from last semester's class rosters in the university registrar's computer data bank. The polling can be done by sending postcard questionnaires (containing prepaid return postage) to the selected students to learn what extra costs they paid—and for what kinds of items—in the course designated on their particular postcard.

Let's imagine that our sampling method worked out well and that a large proportion of the students we polled did, indeed, return the postcards. Our classification hierarchy now equips us to tell a detailed story about extra costs of courses. When the results of our postcard survey are combined in various patterns, we can report the average extra course costs for the typical:

- class in the university as a whole
- lecture versus laboratory course in the university as a whole
- course in the humanities versus course in the sciences
- lecture versus laboratory course in the humanities versus lecture versus laboratory course in the sciences
- course in each department
- lecture versus laboratory course in each department that has both types of courses
- course level (lower division, advanced upper division, graduate) in the university as a whole
- course level (lower division, advanced upper division, graduate) in humanities versus course level in the sciences
- course level (lower division, advanced upper division, graduate) in each department
- course level (lower division, advanced upper division, graduate) in selected specializations

We are also prepared to report the variability of extra costs in each of the above categories; and with examples of specific classes, we can illustrate the course features that lead to such variability. Without the aid of our hierarchical classification system, we would not have been prepared to report so much information in such a systematic fashion.

We turn now to another issue regarding codification schemes, that of exclusive versus nonexclusive classes, as reflected in the question: Within the field of interest, when an item—a bit of information—is to be classified, is there a single category in which the item must be placed, or might it be placed in more than one category? If there is only one site in which an item is properly situated, the system's classes can be considered exclusive or distinct. But if an item might reasonably be put in more than one location, the system's classes are not exclusive or, at best, are only partially so.

Both Linnaeus' *Plantae* taxonomy and a comparative chart of the world's languages are exclusive-class structures. A flower with the characteristics of the buttercup can be properly situated only under the genus *Ranuculus.* A Welshman's native language falls exclusively in the Brythonic branch of the Celtic division of the Indo-European family of languages.

In contrast to such discrete structures, other schemes prove less than perfect in terms of class exclusiveness. Consider, for example, the widely used taxonomy of educational objectives created by Bloom (1956) and Krathwohl, Bloom, and Masia (1964). The method of classifying the goals of education was created to help "teachers, administrators, professional specialists, and research workers who deal with curricula and evaluation problems . . . especially to help them discuss these problems with greater precision" (Bloom, 1956, p. 1). The system was divided into three domains—cognitive (intellectual skills), affective (emotional outcomes), and psychomotor (manipulative or motor skills). A separate subtaxonomy was developed for each domain. The problem of properly classifying educational goals within the cognitive domain can be illustrated with the following objective from a high school literature class:

> Students will be able to compare and contrast three short stories—Poe's *The Purloined Letter,* Steinbeck's *The Red Pony,* and Maugham's *A Friend in Need.*

It can be argued that this goal might reasonably be located under any one or more of the following taxa:

> 1.24 Knowledge of the criteria by which facts, principles, opinions, and conduct are tested or judged.
>
> 4.30 Analysis of organizational principles . . . which hold [a] communication together. . . . It includes the bases, necessary arrangement, and the mechanics which make the communication a unit.
>
> 6.20 Judgments in terms of external criteria. Evaluation of material with reference to selected or remembered criteria. (Bloom, 1956, pp. 203, 206–207)

Hence, when an observed phenomenon is described in terms of Bloom's classification structure, the phenomenon might qualify for placement in more than one category. In effect, the scheme's taxa are not exclusive. Instead, they can represent diverse ways of viewing a phenomenon. This means that people who use the system are required to decide whether an item should be assigned to only one class or to more than one.

## The Time and Method of Creating Categories

As shown by our earlier examples of classification systems, the dimensions and the categories within them can be established at various stages of your research, as influenced by (a) how accurately you can predict ahead of time what sorts of dimensions and their categories will best aid you in answering your research questions and (b) whether new questions arise during the process of conducting your project.

To illustrate the matter of predictive accuracy, let's consider three guide questions that we might include in a study of the incidence and modes of transmittal of infectious diseases in Africa, Europe, and South America over the decade 1995–2005. Our special concern is with the spread of HIV (human immunodeficiency virus) infection compared to the spread of other types of infectious diseases. Among the questions that guide our study, here are three whose answers will require classification schemes. We are interested in deciding how and when we will specify the dimensions and the categories within those dimensions for the three schemes.

1. What was the annual incidence of HIV in Africa, Europe, and South America over the decade 1990–2000?
2. What was the annual incidence of different varieties of infectious disease in Africa, Europe, and South America from 1995 to 2005?
3. What was the frequency of the circumstances in which infected persons incurred HIV in Africa, Europe, and South America during the first half compared to the last half of the decade 1995–2005?

To answer the first two questions, we plan to gather data by examining statistical reports from world health organizations. To answer the third, we plan to interview a representative sample of HIV victims from each of the continents who contracted the infection at different times over the 1995–2005 period.

When, then, do we set up our three classification schemes? The one for recording answers to the first question can be formulated before we collect any data, because we can specify all three dimensions and categories ahead of time. In effect, the focal concern (dimension) of the first question is *incidence of HIV infection.* The second dimension is *time* (10 annual intervals) and the third is *continents* (3 continents). We can also foresee the exact form in which to display our summarized results—a 3-by-10 table in which we enter the focal variable (incidence numbers) in the cells that represent the intersection of the time and continent variables, as suggested by the dummy table in Figure 10.3.

Our second question has the incidence of *different varieties of infectious diseases* as the central concern. Before collecting our information, we can specify the time dimension's categories (10 annual intervals) but not how many different infectious diseases, because we do not know ahead of time what variety of infectious diseases have been identified in world health reports for the three continents. Therefore, we do not know how many diseases or their titles to include in our classification system until we have compiled the data. Consequently, we cannot specify ahead of time the exact size of the table in which we will summarize our results.

The third question poses the same problem as the second. The center of attention (focal variable) is *incidence of circumstances in which HIV was contracted.* Whereas we know at the outset the number (2) and titles (1995–1999 and 2000–2004) of categories along the time variable, we cannot predict with any confidence the variety of *circumstances in which HIV was incurred.* We must analyze the results of our interviews before making that determination.

(number of cases per 100,000 persons in the population)

| | *Africa* | *Europe* | *South America* |
|---|---|---|---|
| 1995 | | | |
| 1996 | | | |
| 1997 | | | |
| 1998 | | | |
| 1999 | | | |
| 2000 | | | |
| 2001 | | | |
| 2002 | | | |
| 2003 | | | |
| 2004 | | | |

**Figure 10.3** Incidence of HIV Infection by Continent, 1990–2000

The question to guide our task of analysis can be "What groups of circumstances can we abstract from the interviews and how should each group be defined and labeled?"

It is useful to recognize advantages and disadvantages of defining categories before data have been collected compared to defining categories after data collection. Consider the *variable circumstances under which HIV was contracted.* If we specify categories of circumstances ahead of time, then when collecting data we can be prepared with a convenient list of the categories, and our respondents need only check the one or more categories that apply in their case. Later, when we compile the results, our task is a simple matter of counting how many respondents checked the different options. However, the disadvantage of this approach is that it can easily miss or distort important features of circumstances that are not accommodated by the preconceived choices that we offer to respondents. Consequently, the final report of the research will fail to acknowledge the effect of those neglected features.

On the other hand, if no categories are defined ahead of time but are extracted only later from the collected data, the task of collecting information via interviews or questionnaires will likely involve the complex process of gathering complete, verbatim accounts of what respondents say or write in narrative form. Then it can be a laborious, demanding challenge to analyze the narratives so as to derive categories that are true to the spirit of the respondents' experiences. However, adopting such an approach does enable us to accommodate features of respondents' experiences that might have been missed if their answers had been limited to those options we might have included in a set of multiple choices.

Two ways that researchers can seek to combine the advantages of both the "check-the-option" and "describe-your-experience" approaches are by (a) preceding the final data collection with a pilot study and/or (b) inviting respondents to attach explanatory comments to each set of the multiple-choice categories they have marked.

In the pilot-study approach, the researcher asks a sample of respondents (via interviews or questionnaires) open-ended questions, such as "As far as you can tell, what was the occasion of your contracting HIV?" Or "Could you describe the situation in which you think you caught HIV—where it occurred, who was involved, how it came about?" The answers to these questions are then analyzed to derive categories, with each category defined in a way that clearly distinguishes it from the others. Then the defined categories are listed on a questionnaire that can be administered either in printed form or as an interview schedule to the participants in the study. Those participants are asked to check the category—or categories—that apply to them.

The second approach to capturing information that could be missed if respondents were offered only multiple-choice options is that of inviting respondents to offer comments about additional factors that apply in their case. The directions on such a multiple-choice questionnaire could then read

> Place an **X** in the box at the left of each of the following statements that tells about the circumstance in which you think you caught HIV. Then, in the space under each statement, write any comments you think will help explain how you contracted HIV.

## Precision and Clarity

A classification problem that can seriously diminish the trustworthiness of a study's results is one caused by the inadequate definition of a variable's categories. There are two principal conditions under which this problem occurs: (a) when respondents fill out questionnaires or answer interview questions and (b) when researchers attempt to classify the contents of people's narratives that are in the form of testimony, letters, written answers to essay questions, interview responses, and the like.

In the first instance, participants are given multiple-choice answers to a question. Their task is to select the choice that is true of their own situation. So, if the outcomes of the research project are to be trusted, then the classification categories—the multiple choices—must be defined precisely enough to enable any reasonably informed person to select the proper choice. Some types of categories are easy to define and recognize. Such is the case with divisions based on gender, age, time interval (year, decade, century), place (school, city, nation), and measures that result in definite quantities (heights, test scores, days absent from school). Any errors made in placing data in their proper categories are the result of respondents' carelessness in selecting a category, not the result of imprecisely defined classes. However, the meanings of the choices are often not obvious, so all respondents may not interpret the choices in the same way. The greater their confusion, and the more they must depend on subjective judgments, the less accurate the results of the study. One way to reduce such ambiguity is to conduct a tryout study of your questionnaire or your interview schedule before you administer it to the participants on whom the results of your study will be founded. The tryout is best conducted with people who are much like your intended respondents. When you administer your questionnaire or interview to the tryout subjects, you can provide some such instructions as these:

> I'm asking you to help me discover if the questions on this sheet—and the choices among the answers—are easy to understand. So, as you read each question and the answers below the question, decide whether you can easily

> decide which answer is best. If you have no trouble deciding on an answer, then write the word *clear* next to that item. But if you have trouble deciding among the answers, write a question mark beside the item. Then, after you finish we can talk about the items with the question marks. That will help me know how I might change those items so they are easier to understand.

Now let's turn to our second circumstance, the situation in which the information the researcher receives from respondents is in narrative form. Such will be the case when an interviewer asks, "What is your opinion of Ms. Kelley as a senatorial candidate?" Or "What was your reaction to the Carswell murder trial?" Or "What problems do you expect if a voucher system is used for determining which schools children will attend?" Or "What social class do you think you belong to, and why do you think you are in that class?" After researchers have collected answers to such open-ended queries, they are obliged to resolve two issues: (a) From the viewpoint of the research study's purpose, into what categories should respondents' answers be placed? (b) How should those categories be defined so that respondents' answers can be located in the proper categories?

To illustrate one way to cope with the first of these issues, consider a study conducted by Johnston (1988) to discover the moral reasoning of adolescents who were asked to offer their opinions about the wrongdoing displayed in two Aesop fables. Johnston's aim was to learn whether 60 adolescents' judgments were determined more by their sense of compassionate caring than by their sense of even-handed justice, so her classification system initially contained two categories—*caring* and *justice.* But after collecting the 60 students' opinions, she discovered that not all answers fit neatly into either the caring class or the justice class. Some answers included an equal measure of caring and justice, so she created a third class to accommodate those mixed responses. Furthermore, a few answers failed to fit any of the three categories, so she relegated them to a fourth class titled *uncodable,* "which meant that the answer did not clearly represent any identified logic" (Johnston, 1988, p. 54).

Now let's look at the second issue, the matter of how accurately members of the research team assign each respondent's answer to a correct category. We should recognize that, in Johnston's study, when students were asked about the moral problem that was embedded in each fable, they could reply in any way they chose. It then became the researcher's task to extract from students' replies (some of which were quite complex) the portions that seemed to reflect either a justice attitude or a caring viewpoint—or both, or neither. But such a task could involve a substantial measure of subjectivity on the part of the person making that decision—subjectivity that might result in one person coding data into different categories than did another. The greater the amount of subjective opinion involved in the coding process, the less trustworthy are the reported outcomes of the research. Three of the ways investigators seek to increase the accuracy of assigning data to categories are those of (a) defining each class in a manner that clearly distinguishes it from any other class, (b) accompanying each definition with examples of the sorts of data (such as the sorts of student replies in the Johnston study) that belong in that category, and (c) conducting training sessions for the people who will do the coding.

Therefore, if the research for your thesis or dissertation involves classifying narrative responses, you may profit from adopting one or both of the following methods for assessing how precisely you have defined your categories. And if this assessment suggests that your classification system is less than satisfactory, you may wish to (a) redefine your classes, (b) add illustrative examples to your definitions, and (c) retrain your coders.

The first assessment method concerns the *successive-judgments consistency* of coders' decisions. Specifically, to what extent does a coder place a particular kind of observation or response consistently in the same category? Imagine that a teacher is judging how logically students argue their position in essays they have written about human rights. The teacher has established five categories of logic in which to locate students' arguments—*superior, above average, moderate, below average,* and *very poor.* Her appraisal technique is deemed perfect in terms of successive-judgments consistency if, when she reevaluates the essays this week, she gives each one exactly the same rating that she gave it last week. In effect, her method is 100% consistent over time. However, such an outcome would be quite unusual. Studies of such matters have shown that raters' successive judgments of narrative data (essays, letters, descriptive oral responses, and the like) are often inconsistent. So, if the results of your coding the same interview or questionnaire responses on more than one occasion show that your successive judgments are consistent less than 85% or 90% of the time, you may wish to adopt one or more of the three remedial techniques mentioned above.

The second method concerns *interrater* reliability: To what extent do two or more judges agree on where to locate a particular observation or response? If multiple judges are in substantial agreement about the placement of data, then the definitions of categories and the training of judges are considered trustworthy. A typical way to assess interrater reliability is to have two or more raters independently classify the same data (narrative answers to questions) into the study's categories. The interrater reliability is then reported as the percentage of times the coders' judgments matched. In the Aesop fables project, Johnston reported intercoder reliability for two raters as 100% agreement on coding students' solutions to *The Dog in the Manger* story and of 90% agreement on coding solutions to *The Porcupine and the Moles* fable (Johnston, 1988, p. 54).

## PLANNING CHECKLIST

In planning the way you intend to classify the information that you gather for your project, you may find it helpful to complete the following steps.

For each question that you hope to answer by the use of your collected information

1. State the question.
2. Name and define each variable (dimension, characteristic) that you will include in your data analysis. Tell when you intend to name and define each of those variables. (Before you gather data? After you gather data?)
3. Name and define the classes (categories) you will employ within each variable. Tell when you intend to name and define each of those categories. (Before you gather data? After you gather data?)
4. State whether the variables are linear or form a hierarchy. If a hierarchy, then draw a diagram showing the hierarchy's structure.
5. Create dummy tables illustrating the form in which you intend to display and analyze your collected information after it has been classified.

ELEVEN

# SUMMARIZING INFORMATION VERBALLY, NUMERICALLY, AND GRAPHICALLY

*"Should I just summarize in words what I did in my study, or should I include statistics or tables or graphs? If so, what sorts of statistics or graphs, where, and why?"*

As noted in the introduction to Stage III-B, the purpose of summarizing data is to simplify an otherwise incomprehensibly complex mass of information so the substance of the information can be readily grasped. This chapter describes three popular forms of summaries—verbal descriptions, statistical reports, and graphic displays. Under each of these forms, we illustrate typical alternatives along with some of their advantages and limitations.

## NARRATIVE SUMMARIES

Narrative summaries are relatively brief statements that offer in condensed form the essence of longer and more detailed descriptions of such phenomena as ideas, events, places, people, organizations, institutions, social movements, periods in history, and more. As will be noted in Chapter 12, summarizing merges into interpreting. Thus, summaries are often indistinguishable from interpretations.

The placement of summaries can vary from one research project to another and even within the same study. For instance, a summary is usually offered at the beginning of a thesis or dissertation in the form of an abstract of the project's overall aims, methods of investigation, and outcomes. Such an introduction is then followed by the main body of the document, which details the evidence in support of the opening summary. In other cases, the data collected for answering a research question are laid out first, followed by a summary of the conclusions that seem warranted by those data. Mini-summaries are often located throughout a document, representing conclusions drawn about individual sections of the presentation. Then a macro-summary is usually placed at the close of the thesis or dissertation as a final chapter that pulls together the principal generalizations extracted from the entire work. The following examples illustrate the functions that summaries perform in relation to where they are placed in a thesis or dissertation—in the first chapter, at the close of a section within a chapter, at the end of a chapter, and at the end of the entire document.

## First-Chapter Summaries

Early in the opening chapter, a synopsis may be introduced to help establish the reader's mental set by guiding the reader's expectation of what the thesis or dissertation is all about and what will be found in subsequent chapters. The following is such a synopsis that serves as an introduction to a study that subsequently offers a detailed analysis of the researcher's main concern—migration.

> *Human Geography, Sociology:* A simple explanation for migration is that one place pulls on a person—with good wages, freedom, land, or peace—while the place in which the person lives pushes because of low incomes, repression, overcrowding, or war. . . . [But migration] is not a matter of each individual deciding rationally and simply where the best hope for freedom or success lies. It is much more complicated and involves each person's history, beliefs, and family; his country's prior relationships with other nations; and the whole interlocking international web of existing migration routes and patterns. (Parfit, 1998, p. 16)

Sometimes an author furnishes a synopsis of each chapter that the study contains. For instance, here is the writer's summary of Chapter 8 ("Intellectual Growth, Autonomy, and Religious Education") in a study titled *For Goodness*

*Sake,* based on the researcher's visits to a variety of Catholic schools in the United States.

> *Moral Education, Religious Studies.* Moral development involves tacking between three moments—standard moral theories and their implications, our own moral intuitions, and the possibility of new moral formulations. The most serious concern about moral education in a religious context is that it can overwhelm moral intuition and moral novelty with premature commitments to established moral theories. The concern is less that students will come to adopt an inadequate moral doctrine than it is that they will come to think that moral agency consists only in conforming to the teachings of authority and that their capacity for independent intellectual thought and moral growth will be aborted. This chapter uses interviews with graduates of Catholic schools to analyze the different ways in which moral novelty is approached from within a religious tradition. (Feinberg, 2006, p. xxvii)

Introductory summaries may consist of both verbal and numerical content. The numbers are intended to lend precision to quantities that would be vague if expressed solely in such terms as *many, few, more, less, often,* or *seldom.*

> *Education, Criminology, Sociology.* Recent years' reports of the frequency of school violence offer both bad news and good news.
>
> The bad news is that violent acts and pupils' fear of danger have continued to be common in the United States. A report by the U.S. Education and Justice Departments noted that in 2003 there were about 738,700 violent crimes involving students at schools, and 846,400 crimes away from schools. Such violence included 28 crimes of rape, sexual assault, robbery, and physical assault for every 1,000 students. The good news is that the incidence of crime in schools during 2003 was only half that of 1993, and crime in general reached a 30-year low. The rate of school violence dropped dramatically between 1993 and 2000, thereafter remaining at a constant level [Sherman, 2005]. High school students who reported being in a physical fight on school grounds decreased from 16% in 1993 to 13% in 2001. The percentage of students who reported being a victim of a crime of violence or theft at school decreased from 10% to 6% [St. Gerard, 2003].
>
> In 85,000 public schools during the 2000–2001 academic year there were 717,400 incidents of reported violence in elementary schools, 441,300 in middle schools, and 261,400 in high schools [CSI, 2004]. The most common types of violence were fist fights, bullying, and shoving matches. Studies of bullying suggest that three out of every 10 students were involved in bullying—13% as bullies, 11% as victims, and 6% as both bullies and victims. "For children in grades 6 through 10, this translates into 3.7 million children who bully other children each year and 3.2 million who are victims"

> [Selekman & Vessey, 2004]. During the 2000 school year, 15% of students in grades nine through twelve reported being in a physical fight on school property [School violence statistics, 2000]. Physical attacks without a weapon and vandalism were far more frequent than such violent crimes as rape, sexual assault, robbery, or aggravated assault that were reported by about 20% of schools [St. Gerard, 2003]. The rate of violent crime has typically risen in grades six through eight, peaked at grade nine, and declined through grade 12 [Cardman, 2003]. Fights with a weapon have been most frequent in middle schools, with 21% of middle schools reporting 7,575 incidents during 2000 [School violence statistics, 2000].
>
> According to analysts, three important factors contributing to the decline in school violence were (a) the installation of metal detectors for screening students in the most troubled schools, (b) the hiring of more security personnel to patrol schools, and (c) the introduction of programs designed to curb bullying that might lead to serious crimes [Sherman, 2005].
>
> In summary, although violence in schools continues to be a significant threat to students' and teachers' welfare and to the efficient conduct of the learning program, there have been positive signs of improvement over the past decade and a half. (Thomas, 2006, p. 3)

This verbal/numerical summary not only offers readers an initial overview of trends in school violence, but also foreshadows the titles of the chapters that comprise the remainder of the document—Deadly Weapons, Fighting, Bullying, Sexual Abuse, Theft, and others.

## Section-Closing Summaries

A chapter that is divided into sections can often profit from a paragraph or two at the end of each section to recapitulate the key points of the section. Such synopses are particularly valuable at the close of long, complex sections.

In a study comparing American Indian religions with Christianity, the section about Indian religions in the chapter titled "Sources of Belief" closes with the following summary:

> *American History, Religious Studies.* The foregoing discussion has illustrated ways that prayers, dreams, visions, inspiration, and instruction have served as channels through which Indians have acquired religious beliefs from the world of spirits. Across the centuries, supernaturalism has pervaded every sphere of tribal life—occupational, marital, economic, spiritual, social, and recreational. Shamans have been—and continue to be—essential to the conduct of religion and to the transmission of religious lore from one generation to the next. (Thomas, 2007)

Section-closing summaries are often used as transition guides, alerting the reader to how the content of the present section merges into the content of the next section. The book *Nationalism in Education* includes a chapter titled "Nationalism in North American Education" that is divided into seven parts. The final paragraph of part three ("Trends in Nationalism Over Two Centuries") leads into part four ("Nationalism in Education") in the following fashion:

> *Education, Sociology, Political Science.* In summary, by the 1990s both Canada and the United States struggled to determine what characteristics all citizens should display in common (their nationalism) in comparison to those characteristics of regionalism and sectarianism that they would embrace. Because the schools in both countries have been seen as crucial determinants of the form of nationalism adopted, the effort to arrive at a viable concept of "nation" is reflected in the idea of nationalism taught in the schools. The following pages address the schools' role in defining and promoting nationalism. (Schleicher, 1993, p. 86)

## A Summary to Close a Chapter

Principal elements of a chapter that the author wants readers to remember can profitably be offered in a summary at the chapter's end.

A typical version of such synopses consists of a paragraph or two that reiterate the main theme of the chapter. Such a summary can be illustrated with the closing paragraphs of the "Nationalism in North American Education" chapter of *Nationalism in Education.*

> *Education, Sociology, Political Science.* Throughout this chapter the picture of nationalism in education has been cast in the form of *isms* that compete for the allegiance of the populace—*nationalism, regionalism, sectarianism,* and *internationalism.* The confluence of a variety of social factors determines the particular relationship obtaining among the four *isms* at any time. A nation's education system serves as a central arena in which the competition among the *isms* is played out.
>
> A key conclusion drawn from the foregoing analysis is that Canada and the United States are currently forging a *multicultural variety of nationalism* that seeks to maintain national unity by accommodating the interests of diverse regions, ethnic groups, and religious sects within each nation's borders, while at the same time achieving an acceptable balance of power with other nations. (Schleicher, 1993, pp. 103–104)

Some chapter-closing summaries assume the form of a list that concisely retraces the sequence of the chapter's content. That approach was used in a research project titled *Financing of Education in Indonesia.*

*Education, Economics.* As this chapter has illustrated, the Indonesian pattern of funding schools reflects an accumulation of practices deriving from key historical events that included:

- Religious groups' early introduction of private (nongovernmental) schools and a commitment to help financing those schools on the part of major religious faiths, principally Muslims, Hindus, Buddhists, and Christians.
- In the mid-1800s, the introduction of publicly supported schools by the Netherlands East Indies government, and the use of public moneys to help fund private schools.
- A commitment of the newly established Republic of Indonesia, by means of the basic education law of 1950, to furnish universal primary schooling, to provide funds to support primary schools, and to offer the entire citizenry opportunities to pursue advanced education that would be financed at least partially by government funds.
- Dividing the responsibility for funding schools among a Ministry of Education, a Ministry of Religion, and a Ministry of Home Affairs.
- Periodic changes in political stability and the vitality of the general economy that influenced the capacity of the government and of families to support schooling for the nation's youth. (Bray, 1998, pp. 23–24)

Another variation of the chapter-closing summary includes additional features that were not in the body of the chapter. For instance, the following example from the earlier-mentioned study of American Indian religions and Christianity is written as a comparison of the two belief systems—a comparison that did not appear earlier in the chapter where the descriptions of the two worldviews were entirely separate. The chapter was titled "Spirits."

*American History, Religious Studies.* As a way of summarizing this chapter's content, the two religious persuasions can now be compared in terms of their likenesses and differences.

**Similarities**

One way that Indian religions and Christian culture are alike is in their both recognizing multiple deities. In Christian culture and in most—if not all—Indian cultures, the spirits are arranged in a hierarchy, with those on the upper steps of the structure wielding greater power and commanding larger realms of life than those on the lower steps. Thus, the Christian God is more potent and affects more aspects of life than do either the angels or Christian saints. In like manner, the Algonquins' Gitche Manitou, the Siouxs' Wankan Tanka, and the Cheyennes' Heammawihio are more influential than any other deities in those tribes' spirit registries.

In both Indian and Christian traditions, believers can adopt guardian spirits to ward off evil and furnish aid in time of need. For Christians, that protector can be Jesus, the Holy Ghost, an angel, or a saint. For Indians, the guardian has most often been an animal—a bear for its strength, a spider for its cleverness, or an eagle for its imposing power and air of command. Hassrick [1964, p. 167] has suggested that the Sioux "deliberately placed themselves upon a lower plane [than the animals] with respect to rapport with the universe and its Controllers. With complete devotion, the Sioux appealed to the animals as emissaries in tune with the gods for guidance and help in all matters."

**Differences**

Perhaps the two most dramatic differences between Amerindian and Christian spirit worlds are in (a) the far greater number of deities in the Indian pantheon than in the Christian and (b) the Indians assuming that animals and inanimate objects of nature can be spirits while Christians limit the concept *spirit* to select humans (saints) and personified deities (God, angels).

The combined total of spirits in American Indian religions extends beyond the billions, if we grant that all things in nature have spirit qualities. In contrast, the number of spirits in Christian tradition is perhaps in the thousands, composed of the Trinity (God, Jesus, Holy Spirit), an indeterminate quantity of angels, and perhaps 10,000 saints.

Not only have Indian religions taught that animals can assume spirit form but, in at least some tribes' belief systems, animals rank above humans because they allegedly arrived in the universe before people and wield power over events. "The Sioux may have been envious of animals, whom they unconsciously felt have a more efficient ecological adjustment" [Hassrick, 1964, p. 267]. This notion of animal superiority is a claim rejected by Christian clerics.

A final way that Indian and Christian traditions differ is in the sources they trust for identifying spirits and spirits' traits. Christian culture depends on the Bible for knowledge of the trinity and angels, whereas church organizations create saints. In contrast, Indian cultures accept as spirits all those beings depicted as deities in the thousands of stories recounted by tribal tellers of tales. (Thomas, 2007, pp. 41–43)

## Last-Chapter Summaries

The final chapter of a thesis or dissertation usually includes a summary of the entire study. For convenience of discussion, we divide last-chapter summaries into three types—*bare-bones, embellished,* and *plus-addenda*—which can overlap, so that one type may include some aspect of another type.

*Bare-bones summaries*

The components of a bare-bones summary reflect the main divisions of the entire study, such as:

1. The question or questions the research was designed to answer.
2. The kinds of information (data) needed to answer the question.
3. The sources of that information (publications? people?).
4. The process used to collect the information (content analysis? interviews? questionnaires? experiment?).
5. The compilation and organization of the collected information.
6. The interpretation of the information, especially in terms of how well it answered the research question.

*Embellished summaries*

Whereas a bare-bones summary offers only a minimal description of each component, an embellished summary includes explanations intended to enrich readers' understanding of what occurred during the study, why that occurred, and with what result. By way of illustration, consider the following reasons that summaries of studies' components would be augmented with explanation beyond a meager portrayal of the research.

1. *Research question—examples of reasons:* During the data-collection phase, the original question had to be broken down into subquestions that would reflect the complexity of interviewees' opinions. Or, the original question had to be rephrased to include a quantitative element that would permit the application of statistical analysis.
2. *Kinds of information—examples of reasons:* The initial plan to collect college students' opinions of the candidates for the state senate was changed when one of the dissertation-committee members warned that conclusions about the public's opinions of the candidates on the basis of such a sample of respondents would be biased. Or, the police captain said that estimates of the frequency of juvenile crime could not be founded solely on official police reports, because many crimes were never reported or never officially recorded.

3. *Information sources—examples of reasons:* The discovery of a valuable Internet website during a literature survey led the researcher to add information from websites to the original plan of using only questionnaire responses. Or, the university's human-subjects committee would not permit the use of kindergarten children in an experiment about racial stereotypes.

4. *Data-collection process—examples of reasons:* The hurricane destruction at a school during the collection of classroom observations required the substitution of a different school. Or, the manner of administering a mail-in questionnaire was changed because of a low rate of return of questionnaires in the initial mailing. Or, the plan to interview respondents in a variety of counseling centers had to be abandoned because the travel costs were prohibitive.

5. *Data compilation—examples of reasons:* The intended method of coding interview responses was altered because too many responses failed to fit any of the original classification categories. Or, a low level of agreement between the people who did the coding of questionnaire answers required that the coding guide-sheet be revised and the coders retrained.

6. *Interpretation—examples of reasons:* The results of this study suggest that the theory proposed by Professor X is inadequate for explaining people's behavior in crisis situations. Or, the views expressed by participants in the research reported in this thesis do, in the main, support the findings of Smith (1999), Jones, (2002), Doe and Roe (2004), and Brown (2005).

*A summary plus addenda*

The final chapter of a thesis or dissertation may offer—in addition to a bare-bones or embellished summary—material that extends beyond the study's contents. Such addenda may include:

- Suggestions for kinds of research that focus on issues related to this present study's questions not answered completely by the present study.
- Proposed research designs for answering the present investigation's key questions from different perspectives (different samples of respondents, different data-collection techniques, different patterns of data organization).

- Ways of applying the results of this study to improve individuals' lives, the society and its culture, or the operation of organizations.
- Lessons learned, kinds of knowledge gained, and skills developed by the researcher while carrying out the thesis or dissertation project.

## Diverse Contents of Summaries

Summaries can differ from each other in a number of ways—in (a) length, (b) the type of phenomena addressed, (c) the quantity of phenomena encompassed, (d) the amount of detail and number of examples included, (e) the presence or absence of value judgments, (f) estimates of what caused the phenomena, and more. The following three summaries from research in the social sciences and humanities illustrate how such variables may appear in different kinds of studies.

In the first example from the realm of philosophy, the type of phenomenon addressed is different writers' opinions of the postmodern movement, with the range of opinions embraced by the summary extending from the very positive to the very negative.

> *Philosophy:* Postmodernism has been the leading fashion in academia for the last two decades. It has been variously described as the greatest intellectual advance since the eighteenth-century Enlightenment, and as the death knell of the Enlightenment's age of reason. It has been credited with opening academia to a greater diversity of values and truths, and accused of paving the way for nihilism and even fascism. (Cherry, 1998, p. 20)

The field of interest in the second example is sex typing. The phenomena included in the summary are a culture's stereotypical gender characteristics that boys and girls acquire during the first half decade of their development. The author includes one illustrative example to help clarify the nature of the topic being discussed.

> *Developmental Psychology:* Male and female children become "masculine" and "feminine," respectively, at a very early age. By the time they are four or five, for example, girls and boys have typically come to prefer activities defined by their culture as appropriate for their sex and also to prefer same-sex peers. The acquisition of sex-appropriate preferences, skills, personality attributes, behaviors, and self-concepts is typically referred to within psychology as the process of sex typing. (Bem, 1987, p. 226)

The focal topic in the third example is the original Aztec culture as affected by Spanish colonialism. The quantity of phenomena encompassed by the summary is very large, including (a) thousands of Aztec/Spanish cultural encounters across several centuries and (b) multiple aspects of culture. The summary also includes value judgments in the form of appraisals of cultural events from a perspective that favors the Aztecs and faults the Spanish.

> *History/Anthropology:* Much of what we know about the Aztecs and their religion comes filtered through Spanish [priests' and conquistadors'] minds that could not help but seize on the practices most shocking to, and least understood by, them. Across an enormous gulf of language, culture, religion, and ways of organizing the world, the Spaniards tried to reconstruct a coherent system of Aztec beliefs and rituals. Inevitably this attempt led to misinterpretation, oversimplification, distortion, and exaggeration. (J. I. Gardner, 1986, p. 289)

Finally, it is useful to recognize a feature that often distinguishes popular publications from such scholarly products as theses and dissertations. Publications intended for a general reading public (entries in encyclopedias, articles in magazines and newspapers, textbooks, essays, nonfiction/nontechnical books) commonly offer summaries without furnishing the raw data on which the summaries were based. In contrast, theses and dissertations are expected to provide readers with the array of information on which the author's summary was founded so readers can judge whether the synopsis is consistent with the data on which it has been based.

## STATISTICAL SUMMARIES

Verbal summaries not only describe qualities of phenomena but sometimes also refer to quantities, though often in a rather imprecise manner—*more, less, many, few, larger, smaller,* and the like. But such inexact signifiers of quantity are not nearly as helpful as specific numerical amounts. Thus, in studies that concern numbers of phenomena, numerical summaries in the form of statistics are much preferred. The following discussion depicts the use of statistics from two perspectives: (a) how to select the statistic most appropriate for answering a particular research question and (b) how to get help with calculating and interpreting the chosen statistic.

### Matching Statistics to Research Questions

When selecting a type of statistic that will be most suitable for answering the question at hand, it is useful to recognize that statistics in research reports typically perform one or both of two functions—the descriptive and the inferential.

The descriptive involves summarizing information in an easily comprehended, quantitative form. The inferential involves providing an estimate of how likely a sample of people or events accurately represents a broader population of people or events. The following discussion first identifies a variety of descriptive statistics, then turns to matters of inference. The aim of the discussion is limited to suggesting which sorts of statistics are most suitable for answering which kinds of research questions. The aim does not include explaining the mathematical foundations underlying statistical procedures or demonstrating methods of computation. Nor does the aim include specifying (a) the assumptions on which each procedure is based or (b) the detailed advantages and disadvantages of the various procedures. Such mathematical foundations, computational techniques, underlying assumptions, and precise advantages/disadvantages of different forms of statistical analysis will be found in the kinds of books listed at the end of this section.

## Descriptive Statistics

As mentioned above, description involves summarizing information in an easily comprehended, quantitative form. The kinds of descriptive statistics included in the following discussion are percentages, percentiles, measures of central tendency, measures of variability, and correlation techniques. The presentation of each type identifies the sort of research questions the statistic is designed to answer.

Throughout this presentation, the word *distribution* refers to a collection of quantities (groups of people or objects, costs of goods, amounts of income, and more) that are arranged in a sequence from the highest to the lowest or from the most to the least. For example, employees' efficiency ratings would be listed from the employee judged the most efficient to the employee judged the least efficient. Students' grade-point averages would be arrayed from the highest to the lowest.

### *Percentages*

***The research question:*** What proportion of a variable (such as candidates for office, nations' population growth rates, a student's test results, a company's budget, or the like) displays a particular characteristic?

> In the election for state attorney general, 43% of the women voted for Johnson, 40% for Trang, and 17% for Coronado. Among the men, 31% voted for Johnson, 27% for Trang, and 42% for Coronado.

The annual urban population growth rate in Argentina is 1.65%, in Afghanistan 4.84%, and in Tanzania 9.59%.

Natalie's test scores were: 86% in language usage, 68% in mathematics, 72% in science, and 93% in social studies.

The company's budget allocated 67% of the funds for personnel salaries, 13% for equipment and supplies, 8% for travel, 7% for administrative expenses, and 5% for miscellaneous costs.

A valued feature of percentages is their ability to translate disparate measures into a common coin that permits easy comparisons among the measures. Another advantage of percentages is that they are a familiar part of the general public's everyday living, so research results expressed in percentages can be readily understood by a very broad audience.

*Percentiles*

***The research questions:*** What proportion of a variable falls below a designated point on a 100-unit scale? Within a collection of items (people, institutions, objects, events, or the like) where does one item rank in comparison with the others?

The meanings of *percentage* and of *percentile* are closely linked but not identical, which is a distinction sometimes missed by people not well acquainted with the two terms. Whereas a *percentage* tells the proportion (on a 100-unit scale) of a variable that displays a given characteristic, a *percentile* is the point on the scale below which a given percentage of people, objects, or events are located. Thus, a percentile tells where a particular person, object, or event stands in relation to the total number of other persons, objects, or events in terms of some specified feature. Let's say that Natalie was in a class of 33 students. Of the 50 items on the language-usage test, Natalie answered 43 (86%) correctly. However, 16 of Natalie's classmates did better than she by answering 44 or more items correctly. This means that in the class of 33 students, 16 of them (48.5%) scored higher than Natalie and 16 (48.5%) scored lower. Hence, Natalie was in the middle, at the 50th percentile—the point below which nearly half of the students' scores fell. In like manner, we could determine Natalie's percentiles in the other three subject areas by computing where she ranked in relation to her classmates on the math, science, and social-studies tests. Furthermore, by learning the annual urban-population growth rates of an additional 17 countries, we could determine the percentile ranks of Argentina, Afghanistan, and Tanzania in comparison to the others. We could then conclude that:

Natalie's percentile ranks in the four tested subjects were: 50th percentile in language usage, 15th percentile in math, 67th percentile in science, and 88th percentile in social studies.

In urban-population growth rate for 20 developing nations, Argentina is at the 10th percentile, Afghanistan at the 65th percentile, and Tanzania at the 95th percentile.

Percentiles thus provide a convenient way to show one unit's (person's, nation's, college's, company's, or such) position on some measure in relation to the other units in the group under consideration. Like percentages, percentiles allow a researcher to compare disparate rankings in terms of a single, readily comprehended scale.

*Measures of central tendency*

***The research question:*** What single number can show the level reached by a group in terms of some measure? In other words, how did one group fare, in general, compared to another group? The measure in question can be any one of many kinds—annual family income, amount of time watching television, level of formal education, numbers of days employees were on sick leave, incidence of teenagers using illicit drugs, frequency of manic-depressive psychosis, scores on an intelligence test, and much more.

The three most commonly used central-tendency statistics are the *arithmetic mean,* the *median,* and the *mode.* Each is designed to answer a particular central-tendency question.

*Mean. The research question:* What was the average among the measures of some characteristic?

Ratings on leadership ability among tall men were 17.3 points higher on average than ratings of short men.

The cost of a personal computer this year declined by $217 from last year's cost.

The average school class size in Monarch City is 25.7 students, in Desert Wells 30.8, and in Langston 33.7.

The arithmetic mean is computed by adding together all of the measures attained by the members of a group, then dividing the sum by the number of members. Groups can then be conveniently compared in regard to how well they performed in general or in the main or on the average.

*Median (50th percentile). The research questions:* What score separated the upper half of the group from the lower half? Which score fell in the exact middle of the group's distribution of scores?

Whereas the mean for a group of students that took a test is computed by totaling their scores and dividing by the number of students, the median is determined by listing the students' test scores from the highest to the lowest, then counting up this list to find the halfway point. The median is that halfway score (if there is an uneven number of students) or is the space between the two scores that lie just above and below the middle (if there is an even number of students). The median obviously is the same as the 50th percentile.

The median household income in Preston is $41,000 and in Marline $59,000.

The median times spent on homework assignments by sophomores over the past month were mathematics 25 hours, science 16 hours, foreign language 22 hours, and history 19 hours.

*Mode. The research question:* Which is the most popular amount in a collection of amounts?

In an array of test results, the mode is the one score that the greatest number of students earned. In a survey of the family incomes in a town, the mode is the particular amount of income received by the greatest number of people. As a measure of central tendency, the mode is usually less helpful than either the mean or the median, because the mode might occur at any place in the distribution other than near the middle.

### *Measures of variability*

***The research question:*** What kind of number can best reflect the degree to which a collection of measurements stretch out? For many research interests, it is not sufficient to learn only the average of an array of measurements. It's also important to learn how much the measurements are bunched together or spread out. For this purpose, we need statistics that summarize the extent of variability or dispersion in a distribution. Several kinds of variability measures are available. Those described in the following pages include the total range, distance between percentiles, interquartile range, standard deviation, and variance.

*Range. The research question:* What is the distance between the highest score and the lowest score?

At first glance, it might appear that the range is a desirable measure of dispersion, since it's easy to compute and understand. However, the range is determined entirely by the two scores at the opposite ends of a distribution. Consequently, it fails to show whether the bulk of the scores between those extremes are bunched together or spread out. When people ask for a report about the variability within a group's performance, they typically want to know about the group in general, not simply about the two extreme individuals at the opposite ends of the array. Thus, in research projects, the range is rarely useful. Unlike the range, the following statistics depict the variability of the bulk of the items in a distribution, not just the two at the extreme ends.

*Distance between percentiles. The research question:* How many units of measurement or of scores lie between a selected percentile in the upper half of a distribution and another selected percentile in the lower half?

As explained earlier, along a 100-point scale a percentile is the point below which a specified fraction of the measurements or scores are located. A girl who is taller than 78% of her agemates is at the 78th percentile in height. A boy who runs faster than 43% of other 9-year-olds is at the 43rd percentile in speed.

The distance between selected percentiles can be used to describe the extent of variability among measurements in a distribution. To choose which percentiles to use, we need to estimate what portion of extreme scores at the opposite ends of the scale we wish to disregard in order to report how much the majority of the scores were spread out or clustered together. If we decide that eliminating 10% at each end would be sufficient to prevent extreme scores from affecting the impression of group variability, then our measure of dispersion will consist of reporting the distance between the 10th percentile and the 90th percentile, thereby encompassing the middle 80% of the scores in our report. Or if we think it best to disregard 15% at each end, we will report the distance between the 15th percentile and the 85th percentile, thus focusing on the middle 70% of the measurements. In choosing which pair of percentiles to adopt, we wish to (a) prevent extreme measurements—outliers or deviants—from distorting the picture of variability for the group in general, but at the same time (b) avoid cutting off so many measurements that we end up telling more about central tendency than about dispersion.

One popular version of distance-between-percentiles is the interquartile range, which reports the distance between the 25th percentile (first quartile) and the 75th percentile (third quartile). The interquartile range, therefore, reflects the extent of dispersion among the middle 50% of a distribution's measurements. Sometimes the interquartile range is divided by 2, thereby producing the *semi-interquartile range.*

It is useful to note that the principal types of central-tendency and variability measures form two families of statistics. First, in the percentiles family the measure of central tendency is the median (50th percentile), while variability is determined by some version of distance between percentiles (including the interquartile and semi-interquartile ranges). Therefore, if the median is used to report the general success of a group of students, the accompanying measure of variability can reasonably be a version of distance between percentiles.

We turn now to the second family of variability measures.

*Variance and standard deviation. The research question:* How much do measurements or scores in a distribution stretch above and below the mean?

As noted above, calculating the median and allied percentiles consists of counting the number of scores extending from the lowest and highest. In contrast, computing the mean involves totaling all the measurements or scores, then dividing the sum by the number of measurements or scores. Two measures of dispersion related to the mean are ones determined by calculating how far a distribution's scores deviate from the mean. These measures are the *variance* and *standard deviation.*

Consider the example of a study of finger dexterity among employees of a clock manufacturer. The variance of a distribution of employee's scores on a finger dexterity test is computed by (a) calculating how far each score deviates from the mean, (b) squaring that deviation, and then (c) adding all the squared deviations together. In brief, the variance is the average of the scores' squared distances from the mean. The act of squaring the deviations from the mean has the obvious effect of lending greater weight to deviations as they extend farther away from the mean—providing greater recognition of extreme high and low scores. Once the variance has been calculated, the standard deviation is easy to determine. You simply find the square root of the variance.

### *Correlation techniques*

***The research question:*** The general question that correlation statistics are designed to answer is: When a change occurs in one variable, how much change—if any—occurs in another variable?

The general question, when recast in terms of particular variables, results in such queries as the following:

*Ethnic status and academic achievement.* Are students from certain ethnic groups more successful at academic studies than students from other ethnic groups?

*Television viewing and violent behavior.* What is the relationship between the number and kinds of television programs children watch and the number and types of violent acts in which children engage?

*Mothers' intelligence and daughters' intelligence.* How closely do mothers' IQs (intelligence quotients) correspond to their daughters' IQs?

*Identical twins' confidence.* In pairs of identical twin girls, how does the level of confidence of a typical girl compare with the level of confidence of her twin sister?

*Administrative style and employee satisfaction.* Are the administrative styles of factory managers related to the degree of satisfaction expressed by workers who serve under those managers' supervision?

A variety of statistical procedures are available for answering such questions. Which procedure will be appropriate in a given case depends on the kind of data found in the variables being compared. Variables appear in two principal forms: (a) as a distribution of scores or measurements ranging from low to high and (b) as a series of rankings. Table 11.1 indicates which correlation method is suited to which pattern of data. Each of the correlation procedures listed in the right-hand column of Table 11.1 is described briefly in the following pages.

*Pearson product-moment correlation. The research question:* What is the degree of relationship between two variables if each variable is a set of measurements along a scale that consists of a series of equal intervals?

In judging whether the Pearson product-moment method (symbolized by the letter *r*) is appropriate for a given study, the researcher needs to decide whether both of the variables being compared represent equal-interval scales. Strictly speaking, an equal-interval scale is one in which the distance from one step to the next is precisely the same through the entire length of the scale. Measures of height fulfill this equal-interval requirement, because the distance from

**Table 11.1** Kinds of Data and Correlation Procedures

| *Variable A* | *Variable B* | *Correlation Technique* |
|---|---|---|
| Measurement series | Measurement series | Pearson product-moment ($r$) |
| Ranks | Ranks | Spearman rank-order (*rho* or $\rho$) |
| Measurement series | Dichotomy | Biserial ($r_b$) |
| Separate categories | Separate categories | Phi coefficient ($\phi$) |

25 cm to 30 cm is exactly the same as from 60 cm to 65 cm or from 105 cm to 110 cm, and so on. Measures of temperature, of weight, of time, of speed, of dollars, and of distance on a running track also involve equal-unit scales. In contrast, some scales used in the social sciences may appear at first glance to be composed of equal intervals, but upon closer inspection it becomes clear that they are not. Scoring intelligence-test results in terms of IQ levels is a familiar example. The difference in intellectual ability between an IQ of 100 and one of 105 is not the same as the difference between 120 and 125, because the questions that make up the test are not all of equal difficulty. Test items that differentiate between IQs 120 and 125 are probably more demanding than those that distinguish between IQs 100 and 105. Likewise, a distribution of scores on a test of English usage or of science facts does not produce an equal-interval scale in the strict meaning of the term, because the items that differentiate between scores 80 and 90 are likely more difficult than those that differentiate between scores of 30 and 40. In effect, a 10-point difference in one segment of the scale is not equal to a 10-point difference in another segment.

This distinction between truly equal-interval scales and scales that contain intervals that are only approximately equal has caused some critics to condemn the use of the Pearson method in a great many of the studies that have employed the procedure. (More than 90% of all correlation coefficients reported in the research literature within the behavioral sciences are Pearson *r*'s.) However, Heermann and Braskamp's (1970, pp. 30–110) analysis of a host of investigations suggests that using Pearson's technique with variables involving intervals that are no more than approximately or partially equal is still warranted. Glass and Hopkins (1984, p. 9) have observed that the critics' "disenchantment with the classical methods was premature." Thus, it is generally acceptable to apply Pearson's *r* in studies whose variables consist of test scores or involve ratings of performance or of attitude.

*Spearman rank correlation. The research question:* What is the degree of relationship between two variables if each variable consists of ranks along a scale rather than measured intervals?

Frequently research data are not in the form needed to compute a Pearson *r*, because one or both of the variables consist of ranks instead of measured amounts. Sometimes data are originally collected as rankings, as when teachers are ranked in terms of popularity with students, basketball players ranked by overall ability, and nations ranked by the prestige of their higher-education systems. Other times the data are collected as quantities, which are then converted into ranks for convenience of computation. Thus, provinces can be ranked by per-pupil expenditures, colleges by their graduation rates, and students by their grade point averages. Probably the most popular rank-order correlation statistic is Spearman's *rho* ($\rho$).

*Biserial correlation. The research question:* What is the degree of relationship between two variables if one is measured in a graduated fashion so as to produce a sequence of quantities and the other variable is in the form of a dichotomy?

Two computational techniques for determining the association between such variables are the *biserial* and *point-biserial* methods. Each yields correlation coefficients that are estimates of what the Pearson $r$ would be if both variables were normally distributed arrays rather than one of them being in the form of a dichotomy.

Deciding whether the biserial technique is appropriate in a given research situation depends on the researcher's assumption about the nature of the dichotomous variable. The biserial method is not appropriate in cases of *true* dichotomies, such as sex (male/female) or employees' attendance at work on a particular day (present/absent). However, it is applicable when the dichotomy appears to be an artifact of crude measurement. For instance, in a survey of parents' opinions about teaching birth control methods in high school, data may be collected in the form of a dichotomy (*agree/disagree*). But it is likely that parents' opinions are actually far more varied than the resulting data suggest—some parents will have strong objections to birth control instruction, some will disagree moderately, others will object mildly, some will agree but with serious reservations, and so on. If a more precise scaling approach had been used in gathering opinions, the results would have assumed the form of a distribution of graduated steps. Thus, the dichotomized variable in this instance was not truly discrete. Therefore, it is this latter type of spurious, crude-measurement dichotomy for which the biserial correlation technique is designed.

On the other hand, if the dichotomous feature is truly discrete (male/female, citizen/alien, fourth-grade pupil/non-fourth-grade pupil), an estimate of $r$ can still be obtained by applying the point-biserial method.

*Phi coefficient. The research question:* What is the degree of relationship between two variables if both of them consist of sets of discrete categories?

The phi ($\phi$) coefficient is the product-moment correlation between two variables when each variable is scored as discrete points rather than as a series of measured steps. For example, assume that we wish to determine among political party activists the direction and degree of relationship on a given work day between two variables: (a) the activists' marital status and (b) promptness. We identify two types of marital status (married and single) and two levels of promptness in arriving at work (on-time and late). We then construct a 2-by-2 table with the marital-status variable on the horizontal axis and promptness variable on the vertical axis. We can now enter data about the relationship between an individual's marital condition and promptness into the four cells of our 2-by-2 table. This then permits us to compute a phi coefficient reflecting the degree of relationship between our two variables.

The data used in computing phi coefficients need not be restricted to two discrete positions on each of the variables. For instance, comparing college students' class levels (freshman, sophomore, junior, senior) and those students' use of alcohol during a given week (did drink vs. did not drink) would produce a 4-by-2 table. In like manner, other variables represented in discrete types or steps could produce larger size tables—4-by-4, 3-by-6, and such.

*Other correlation options.* The correlation methods described in the above paragraphs are only four of the more commonly used techniques. Numerous other approaches found in statistics textbooks and journal articles are designed to suit additional conditions of the data that a researcher has at hand. For instance, in some situations the relationship between two series of measures may not assume the shape of a straight diagonal line. As scores on one variable increase, the scores on the other do not increase regularly in a similar manner. Such a relationship results if people's ages over their life span are compared with their eye-hand coordination scores. Whereas age increases in regular steps, eye-hand skills do not; instead, such skills increase in early life, remain at a high level for much of adulthood, then decline in old age, thereby rendering their progression *curvilinear.* In such cases, an eta ($\eta$) coefficient can be computed to reflect the association between the variables. As a second example, under certain conditions a *tetrachoric coefficient* ($r_t$) rather than a phi coefficient can usefully be calculated to determine the magnitude of the relationship between two variables, each of which is a dichotomy.

The term *factor analysis* identifies several alternative procedures for estimating which features are common to a series of correlations that have been computed from a variety of measures of a group of individuals. For example, a large number of students can be administered tests intended to assess their mental abilities. Correlations can then be computed to determine which test items are highly related to each other and which ones appear to be mainly independent of each other. The assumption is that when certain items are closely associated (so that students who do well on one item in the cluster also do well on the others, and vice versa), a particular mental ability or mental factor underlies that group of items. Typically, a label is assigned to that cluster of closely related items, with the label intended to reflect the cognitive skill—or *factor*—that binds the cluster together. For example, the labels applied to factors found in such test batteries as the Primary Mental Abilities (Thurstone, 1938) and Differential Aptitude Tests (Bennett, Seashore, & Wesman, 1952) are number comprehension, verbal reasoning, verbal comprehension, abstract reasoning, clerical speed and accuracy, mechanical reasoning, space relations, language usage, and word fluency.

> In applications in education, factor analytic studies have been undertaken in such diverse areas as prose style, administrative behavior, occupational classification, attitudes and belief systems, and the economics of education. The technique is still in extensive use in the exploration of abilities, in the refining of tests and scales, and in the development of composite variables for use in research studies. Its most promising applications in recent years, however, have been concerned with the testing of explicit hypotheses about the structure of sets of variables, as in the study of growth models. It has also facilitated the comparison of the factorial structure of different subpopulations, allowing investigators to determine whether the factorial structure of a given set of variables varies, for example, with sex, age, ethnicity, socioeconomic status, or political affiliation. (Spearritt, 1985, pp. 1822–1823)

## Drawing Inferences From Samples

As noted earlier, descriptive statistics summarize in a concise form the results of measurements of a group of individuals or events. Sometimes researchers are interested only in what such statistics tell about that group. However, other times they want to apply the group's results to a larger population. In other words, as described in Chapter 7, the measured group is considered to be a sample of a larger population that has not been measured. Hence, from testing the reading ability of 200 nine-year-olds, an investigator may intend to draw inferences about the reading skills of all of a city's or state's nine-year-olds. From a statistical summary of 350 religious workers' expressed attitudes about the use of marijuana, a researcher may hope to estimate the attitudes toward illicit drugs of all such religious workers. However, extending the conclusions about a tested group to a larger population always entails a risk of error, since the sample group may not truly represent the larger population. In effect, the sample may be biased. Therefore, it's important for researchers to have ways of judging how likely the statistics gathered about a sample will accurately portray the features of an intended population. Or, stated as a question, what is the probability of making an error when using descriptive statistics as the basis for drawing inferences about a population? The procedures for answering such a question are called *inferential statistics.*

It's useful at this point to consider the sources of errors that may distort the conclusions drawn from assessing people or events. In the case of descriptive statistics, inaccurate conclusions derive from measurement errors. For instance, the purpose of having students take a history test is to discover precisely their knowledge of historical facts, concepts, trends, theories, and the like. However, various kinds of errors can render the assessment inaccurate. The directions for taking the test may be unclear, some test items may be badly phrased, noises in the classroom may disrupt students' attempt to concentrate, the time to complete the test may be too short, the tester's method of correcting the students' answers may be faulty, and more. Such measurement errors can be reduced by careful attention to the preparation of the test, to the manner of administering it, and to the method of correcting it. However, if the results of testing a sample of students are used as the foundation for drawing inferences about the broader population of students from which the sample was drawn, another source of inaccuracy can distort the inferred picture of the population's knowledge of history. That source is *sampling error,* meaning the degree to which inferences about a population likely deviate from the true characteristics of that population. The following discussion identifies two popular statistical procedures for estimating the magnitude of sampling error.

As noted in Chapter 7, researchers can never know for sure how accurately a sample drawn from a population reflects the characteristics of that population. For example, assume that you conduct telephone interviews with 100 consumers to learn which TV programs they prefer, and you compute the percentages of your respondents who prefer various programs. What you now want to know is how likely those percentages are an accurate reflection of the preferences of all 500,000 residents of the city in which you are conducting your survey. The only way you can know for sure the accuracy of your results is to interview all 500,000. But since interviewing the entire population would be impractical, the best you can do is to estimate the probability that the sample percentages are close to the population's true percentages. Inferential statistics are designed to furnish that estimate. We will briefly inspect two of the ways to arrive at such estimates—the *t*-test and the analysis of variance.

### *The* t-*test*

Researchers often compare two groups in terms of their means. If the means are found to differ, the question arises: Does each group represent a different population in relation to the characteristic that was measured, so the difference in these sample means reflects an actual difference in the means of the underlying populations? Or are the two groups just slightly biased samples from the same population, whose true mean we really don't know? To illustrate, imagine that 50 women and 50 men are enrolled in a college class titled "Methods of Logic." On the final test at the end of the semester, the mean for the women is 83.6 and for the men 78.9. We may now ask whether these scores reflect a difference only between female and male members of that particular class, or is the population of the kind of college women who enrolled in the class generally more adept at learning the methods of logic taught in the class than is the population of the kind of college men who enrolled? The *t*-test provides an estimated answer to this query.

By applying the appropriate computation procedure (found in nearly any statistics textbook), we learn that there apparently is less than 1 chance in 1000 that the two groups represent the same population and that the obtained means are different simply because of bias in drawing the samples. In other words, our results support the conclusion that the population of women (of the kind enrolled in the logic class) is on the average somewhat more skilled at learning the methods of logic taught in the class than is the population of men (of the kind that enrolled). There is a 999 chance in 1,000 that this conclusion is warranted.

However, if the means for women in our hypothetical logic class had been 81.0 and the men 83.6 (with the standard deviations $\sigma = 6.7$ and $\sigma = 6.3$), we would learn that there are likely 5 chances out of 100 that there is no real difference in the means of the populations from which these women and men were drawn. In effect, there are 5 chances in 100 that the difference between 81.0 and 83.6 is simply the result of sampling error—the men's sample just happened to include more adept logic learners—and that both the men and women represent the same population in terms of ability to master the logic techniques taught in the class. But there are 95 chances in 100 that the obtained differences actually do reflect a difference that would be found in the mean scores of the two populations of the kinds of women and men who took the test.

Thus, the *t*-test is designed to help researchers estimate the probability that measures of a sample of people or events accurately portray the broader populations of people or events from which the sample was apparently drawn. In addition to testing the representativeness of obtained means, there are *t*-tests for pairs of medians, percentages, standard deviations, and correlations.

In the above brief sketch of the *t*-test procedure, we have not taken the space to point out several important assumptions about the way samples are drawn from populations, assumptions that significantly affect the appropriateness of *t*-tests in particular studies. For explanations of those assumptions, readers are directed to the suggested readings at the end of this section.

*Analysis of variance*

As explained earlier, the variance ($\sigma^2$) is a description of how much measurements spread away from the center of a distribution. Specifically, the variance is the average of the squared measurement-deviations from the mean.

We have seen that the *t*-test is used to estimate whether the means from two samples represent the same population or two different populations. The analysis of variance (ANOVA) is a procedure for simultaneously testing how likely three or more means represent samples drawn from the same population or, in contrast, are means representing different populations. One example of comparing three or more means is found in attitudes toward birth control methods as expressed by parents, teachers, police officers, and teenagers. Another example is found in a study of mathematics test scores of high school students representing six ethnic groups—Anglos, Latinos, African Americans, Asians, Native Americans, and Pacific Islanders.

Not only does ANOVA permit the simultaneous comparison of multiple means, but the results are more accurate than if *t*-tests were applied to each pairing of the multiple means being studied. Glass and Hopkins (1984, p. 324) point out that "ANOVA is the most common of all inferential statistical techniques in education and the behavioral sciences."

ANOVA results are interpreted in much the same way as those of the *t*-test, that is, in terms of the probability that a difference between sample means are the result of sampling error rather than the result of a difference in the true means of the populations from which the compared samples were drawn. Thus, a difference among sample means that could occur by chance (by sampling error) at a probability level of only 1 time in 100 gives the researcher more confidence in believing that the means of the represented populations are truly different than does a difference among sample means that could occur by chance 5 times in 100 or 10 times in 100.

ANOVA can also be extended to test the likelihood of interactions among factors. For instance, one researcher used ANOVA to discover whether teachers' ethnic status affected their perceptions of how adaptable Anglo and Latino students were. The results showed that there was indeed interaction between teacher and student ethnic types. Latino teachers more often judged Latino students as more adaptive, whereas Anglo teachers more frequently considered Anglo students more adaptive (Glass & Hopkins, 1984, p. 404).

*Additional options*

In the foregoing pages we have introduced a few types of statistics commonly used in research and have suggested which of the types are most useful for answering various kinds of research questions. There are, however, far more statistical procedures than those reviewed in this chapter, procedures well suited to answering additional kinds of research questions. Such additional types of statistical treatments are identified by such titles as chi square, partial correlation, one-way analysis of variance, two-way analysis of variance, the analysis of covariance, linear and nonlinear regression, Kendall's tau coefficient, Kendall's coefficient of concordance, the median test, the Mann-Whitney *U* test, the Wald-Wolfowitz runs test, and others.

Descriptions of a wide range of statistical procedures, as well as their computational steps, are found in such sources as the following.

Glass, G. V., & Hopkins, K. D. (1996). *Statistical methods in education and psychology* (3rd ed.). Boston: Allyn & Bacon.

Gravetter, F. J. (2006). *Statistics for the behavioral sciences* (6th ed.). St. Paul, MN: West.

Hays, W. L. (1994). *Statistics* (5th ed.). Fort Worth, TX: Harcourt Brace.

Jaccard, J., & Becker, M. A. (1990). *Statistics for the behavioral sciences* (2nd ed.). Belmont, CA: Wadsworth.

Popham, W. J., & Sirotnkik, K. A. (1992). *Understanding statistics in education.* Itasca, IL: Peacock.

Siegel, S., & Castellan, N. J., Jr. (1988). *Nonparametric statistics for the behavioral sciences* (2nd ed.). New York: McGraw-Hill.

Sirkin, R. M. (2005). *Statistics for the social sciences* (3rd ed.). Thousand Oaks, CA: Sage.

Sprinthall, R. C. (2002). *Basic statistical analysis* (7th ed.). Boston, MA: Allyn & Bacon.

## Getting Help With Computation and Interpretation

A problem frequently faced by students whose thesis or dissertation research involves the analysis and summarization of quantitative data is that the students lack the statistical expertise needed for selecting the most appropriate modes of analysis, for organizing their data in a form well suited to the chosen mode, for carrying out the steps of computation, and for displaying and interpreting the results.

Your first step toward solving such statistical problems is that of stating the question—or series of questions—you hope to answer with the numerical data you plan to collect. Our saying "plan to collect" is intended to suggest that you are best prepared if you select your statistics at the time you devise your research design, that is, before you actually gather your data. By thus planning ahead, you better ensure that your data will be compiled in a form well suited to the statistical treatment you will ultimately apply. However, it is not uncommon for students to collect their quantitative data before they choose their type of statistics. It is also the case that additional research questions may arise during the data-gathering stage so that the statistical treatment needed for answering those further questions could not have been anticipated at the research-design stage. Under either of these post–data-collection circumstances, the statistical decisions will be made during or after the information has been collected.

So, with your questions in hand, you face the second step of the process—that of selecting modes of statistical analysis that will yield convincing answers to such questions. At this point you may find that you need help. Your feasible options include:

- Inspecting scholarly journals to locate published studies that were guided by questions similar to your own questions. You can then analyze the statistical treatments used in those studies to decide whether you might profitably adopt the same approaches.
- Seeking the aid of fellow graduate students skilled in statistical applications.
- Asking the advice of faculty members who are experts in research design and statistical analysis.
- Searching through statistics books, such as those listed above, to find methods suited to your questions.

These same sources of help can be useful in taking the subsequent steps of casting the data in an appropriate form, conducting the calculations, and displaying and interpreting the outcomes. At the stage of carrying out the calculations, you can profitably avail yourself of the statistical programs available for both personal and mainframe computers. Calculations that, in the past, were laboriously done by hand with the aid of a calculator can now be performed flawlessly and within a few seconds, simultaneously yielding a variety of types of statistics. The following are examples of statistical packages for use with personal computers.

AB-STAT, Version 2.0. Distributed by Allyn & Bacon, Boston, MA, 02116. This package is free with the Sprinthall text on page 241.

(The following items are also found on the Internet in World Wide Web pages with more information for readers.)

DataDesk from Data Description, P.O. Box 4555, Ithaca, NY 14852, www.datadesk.com

Sigmund from Psychsoft, Inc., 2275 Lake Whatcom Blvd., Suite 177, Bellingham, WA 98226, www.Psychsoft.com

Statistica, 800 South Frederick Ave., Suite 204, Gaithersburg, MD 20877-4150, www.statistica.com

StatView from SAS Institute, SAS Campus Dr., Cary, NC 27513, www.sas.com

SYSTAT from SPSS, 233 South Wacker Dr., 11th Floor, Chicago, IL 60606-6307, www.SPSS.com

## TABULAR AND GRAPHIC SUMMARIES

An economical method of presenting a summary of complex information is to cast it in tabular or graphic form. Narrative descriptions of data necessarily arrange ideas in linear order, one idea after another in single file. In contrast, tables and graphs are able to display a quantity of information concurrently, enabling readers not only to view a variety of items simultaneously but also to grasp the items' interrelationships.

### Tabular Summaries

Tables consist of lists of items arranged in rows and columns. The simplest type is a list of items, such as (a) nations listed by population size, (b) students listed by grade point average, (c) occupations ranked by average income, (d) neuroses listed by number of cases, or (e) cell-phone models ranked by popularity. Another common kind of table shows the interaction of two variables by arranging one variable along the vertical axis and the other along the horizontal axis. Then, within the body of the table, data are entered to show how the variables interact. Several dimensions can be accommodated in a matrix if, along both axes, subcategories of variables are included.

By such a device, Table 11.2 accommodates four variables on the horizontal and vertical axes (grade level and sex on the x axis, district and school on the y axis) plus a fifth variable within the cells (average mathematics test scores). A narrative accompanying Table 11.2 can direct readers' attention to features of the data. For example, girls tended to score slightly higher than boys at the third-grade level in Districts 3 and 8. However, at the sixth-grade level in all three districts, boys scored slightly higher than girls. In addition, the lowest (Bayside) and the highest (Carlton and Elm Grove) scores occurred in the same district (District 8) at both the third-grade and sixth-grade levels.

**Table 11.2** Average Math Test Scores in Two School Districts

| | *Grade 3* | | | *Grade 6* | | |
|---|---|---|---|---|---|---|
| | *Boys* | *Girls* | *All* | *Boys* | *Girls* | *All* |
| District 3 | | | | | | |
| J.Q. Adams School | 62 | 72 | 67 | 81 | 79 | 80 |
| M.L. King School | 58 | 64 | 61 | 84 | 82 | 83 |
| J.F. Kennedy School | 67 | 69 | 68 | 82 | 84 | 83 |
| **District 3 Average** | **62.3** | **68.3** | **65.3** | **82.3** | **81.7** | **82** |
| District 7 | | | | | | |
| Oakdale School | 51 | 47 | 49 | 64 | 60 | 62 |
| East Lane School | 48 | 41 | 45 | 58 | 64 | 61 |
| Central School | 57 | 61 | 59 | 73 | 70 | 72 |
| El Monte School | 61 | 58 | 60 | 76 | 74 | 75 |
| **District 7 Average** | **54.3** | **51.8** | **53.3** | **67.8** | **67.0** | **67.5** |
| District 8 | | | | | | |
| Carlton School | 73 | 73 | 73 | 84 | 82 | 83 |
| Elm Grove School | 70 | 76 | 73 | 86 | 87 | 87 |
| Bayside School | 56 | 60 | 58 | 70 | 66 | 68 |
| **District 8 Average** | **66.3** | **69.7** | **68.0** | **80.0** | **78.3** | **79.3** |
| **Districts Combined** | **61.0** | **63.3** | **62.2** | **76.7** | **75.7** | **76.3** |

SOURCE: Thomas, 1998, p. 225.

NOTE: Potential scores ranged from 0 to 100. More advanced mathematical operations were required on the sixth-grade test than on the third-grade test.

## Graphic Summaries

Graphs are diagrams that communicate multiple variables and their interrelationships in a way that would be difficult to convey in a narrative. Graphic displays include pie charts, trend graphs, time lines, histograms, path analyses, theory structure charts, maps, flow charts, and organization charts.

### *Pie charts*

As Figure 11.1 shows, pie-shaped charts are useful for graphically conveying the meaning of percentages.

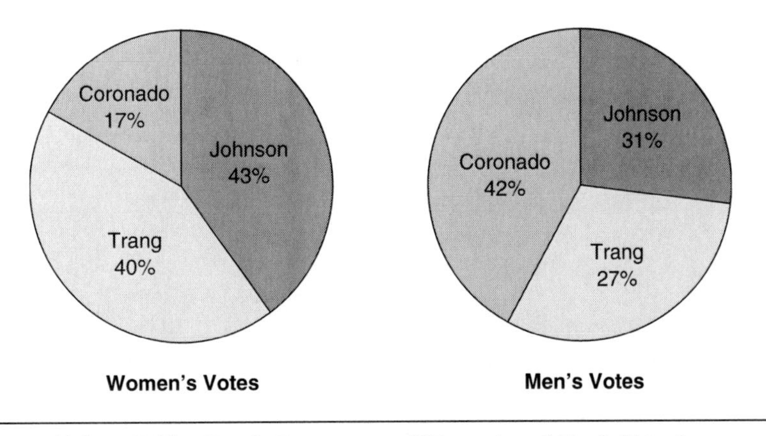


**Figure 11.1** Polling Result: Percentages of Women's and Men's Votes in an Election for County Commissioner

SOURCE: *Conducting Educational Research* by Thomas, R. M. Copyright © 1998. Reproduced with permission of Greenwood Publishing Group, Inc. Westport, CT.

*Trend graphs*

Depicting the pace of change over time is illustrated in Figure 11.2, which shows the estimated growth in the world's population by year 2050. When trends for a variety of variables are displayed, it is appropriate to apply a different style to each line (solid, dotted, dashed, dash-dot lines) so as to distinguish clearly among the variables. The following type of explanation can suggest educational implications of the trend.

> Virtually all of the next half-century's population increase will occur in developing nations, since the advanced industrial societies have by now nearly reached a steady state of growth due to family-planning practices and other social conditions that cause the developed countries to produce hardly more than enough children to replace their elders in the population. This means that the most serious educational problems associated with population growth will be suffered by developing societies. (Thomas, 1990, p. 304)

*Histograms*

As Figure 11.3 demonstrates, bar charts—sometimes called histograms—are convenient devices for graphically comparing groups and for comparing individuals within groups. Even a brief glance at the distributions of reading-test scores in the two rural schools shows that students in School B generally performed better than students in School A. The charts also aid us in comparing

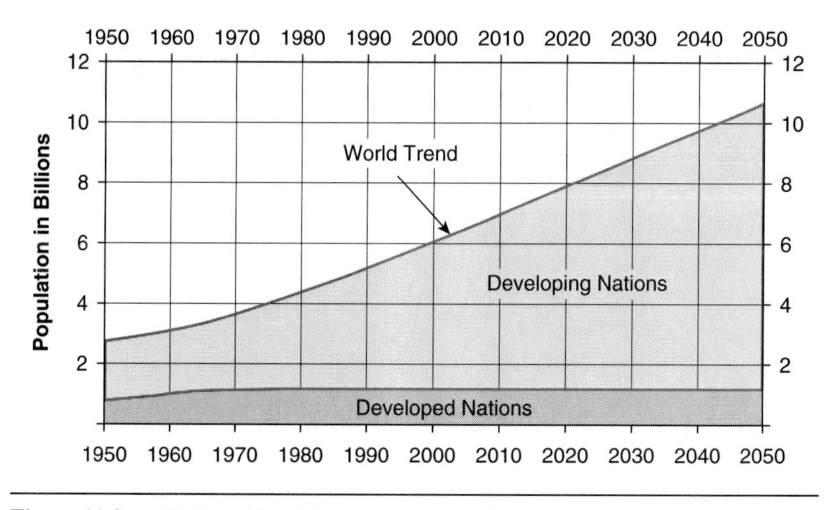


**Figure 11.2** Projected World Population Increase

students. When we learn that Anne earned a score of 68 in School A, we recognize that she was one of the better readers among her classmates. But if she were in School B, she would be slightly below average. And judging from the test results, the best reader was in School B with a score of 75.

*Time lines*

A time line portrays chronological relationships among events. Compared with verbal descriptions, time lines are more effective in delineating the length of periods between events and in presenting all events simultaneously. Figure 11.4 illustrates a time line focusing on inventions that fostered rapid and accurate communication.

The task of composing a time line consists of choosing a theme (such as *significant communication inventions*), identifying the length of time to portray, and selecting the items to include. The following are samples of themes and time spans—American wars (1775–2007), a city's succession of school superintendents (1850–2006), a school's athletic championships (1930–2000), local political parties' periods of control of county offices (1955–2005), and stock-market boom and bust periods (1900–2000).

*Path analyses*

Path analysis equips researchers to estimate the route through which causal factors influence outcomes. The procedure involves calculating the correlations

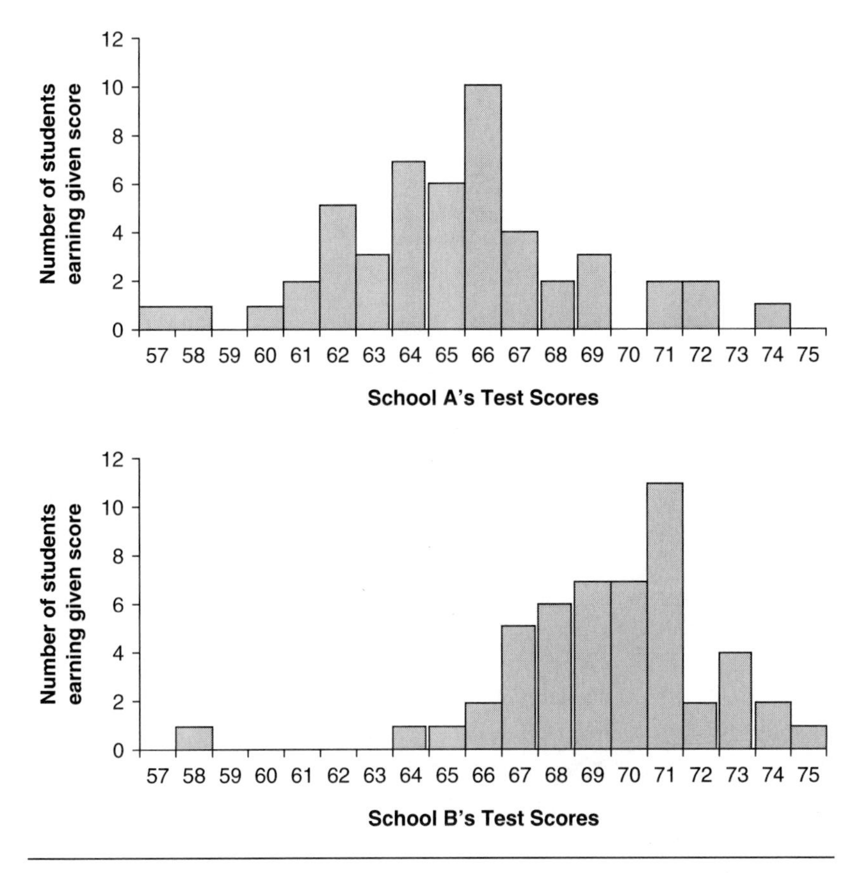


**Figure 11.3** Distributions of Reading-Test Scores in Two Rural Schools

SOURCE: Adapted from Thomas, 1998, p. 196.

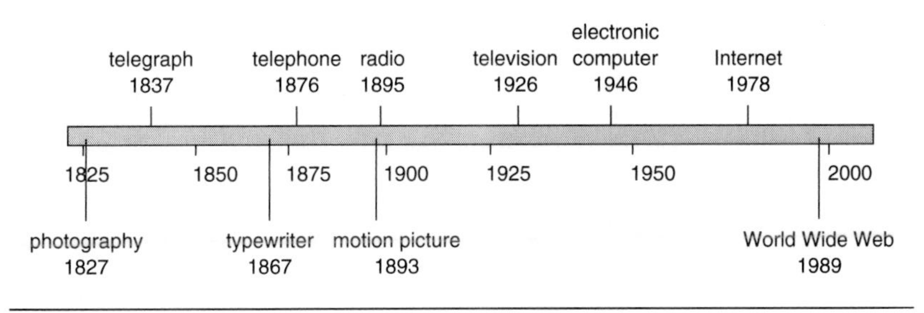


**Figure 11.4** Landmark Communication Inventions

SOURCE: From *Conducting Educational Research* by Thomas, R. M. Copyright © 1998. Reproduced with permission of Greenwood Publishing Group, Inc. Westport, CT.

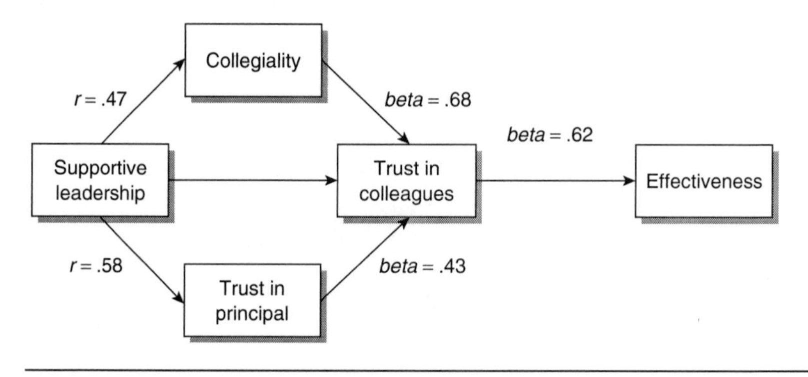


**Figure 11.5** Path Analysis of School Principals' Influence

SOURCE: From Hoy, W. K., Tarter, C. J., & Witkoskie, L. (1992). Faculty trust in colleagues: Linking the school principal with school effectiveness. *Journal of Research and Development in Education, 26*(1), 38–45. By permission of the publisher.

among variables that are measured in a research project. For instance, Hoy, Tarter, and Witkoskie (1992) assessed five variables relating to the attitudes of school personnel and the effectiveness of a school: (a) how supportive the school principal appeared as a leader of the faculty, (b) teachers' interactions with their peers (collegiality), (c) teachers' trust in the principal, (d) teachers' trust in their colleagues, and (e) the effectiveness of the school (Figure 11.5).

The authors explained that:

> The results demonstrated the complexity of the relationships. Supportive principal leadership produced colleagiality and trust in principals, but not trust in colleagues. Teacher trust in colleagues, not leadership behavior of the principal, explained effectiveness in schools. (Hoy, Tarter, & Witkoskie, 1992, p. 38)

### *Theory-structure charts*

A theory is often easier for readers to grasp if the verbal description is accompanied by a diagram identifying the model's components and the interactions among the components. Figure 11.6, illustrating such a diagram, was created from a study of the conception of human personality embedded in Hindu religious doctrine (Thomas, 1997, Chap. 11). The author was unable to find a consolidated Hindu description of personality structure and thus was obliged to collect elements of such a structure from diverse writings and to combine the elements in the following description, which was then cast in the graphic form shown in Figure 11.6.

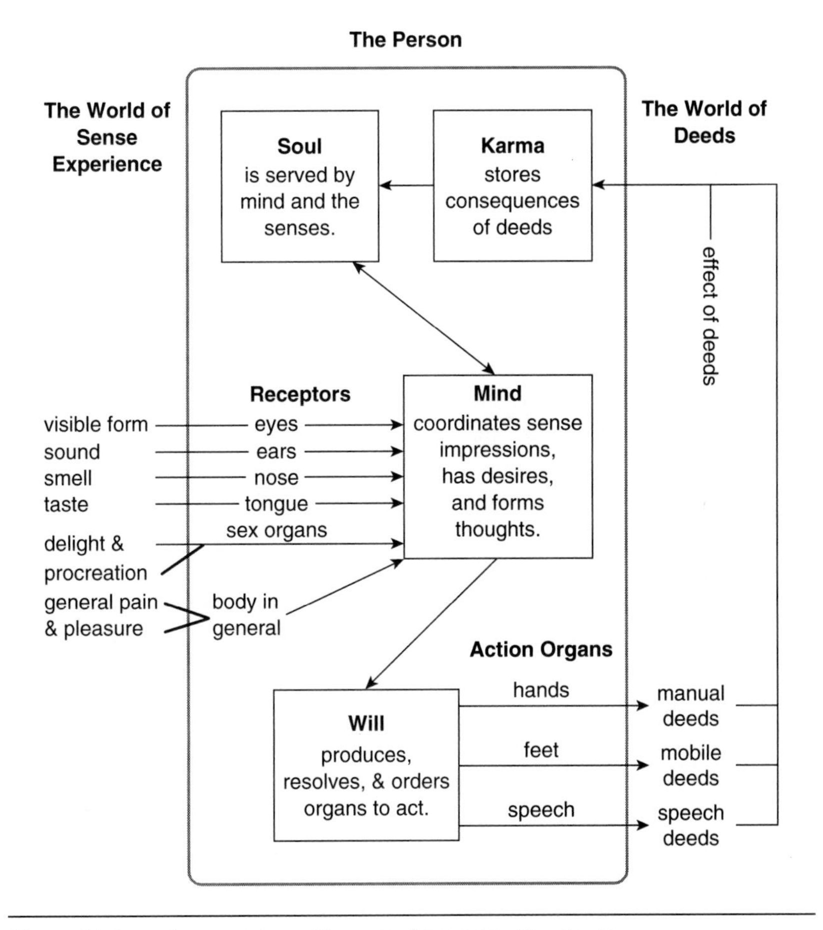


**Figure 11.6** Summarizing a Theoretical Model in Graphic Form

SOURCE: From *Conducting Educational Research* by Thomas, R. M. Copyright © 1998. Reproduced with permission of Greenwood Publishing Group, Inc. Westport, CT.

Hindu theory divides the human being into two general parts—the physical (the visible body) and the nonphysical (consisting of mind, soul, will, and karma). When a person dies, the physical aspect gradually disintegrates and the mind and will disappear, but the soul that contains the karma continues to exist, ready to inhabit a new body for another sojourn on earth. The soul and karma, in effect, transmigrate into a new body upon the demise of the present body.

The term *karma* identifies both a product and a process. The process is founded on the following convictions:

(a) People's actions can be either morally good (faithful to the revered religious doctrine), or morally bad (in violation of the doctrine), or neutral (unrelated to the doctrine).

> (b) Good behavior produces a positive effect or residue in the soul, bad behavior produces a negative effect, and neutral behavior produces no effect.
>
> (c) Karma, as a product, consists of the algebraic sum of the positive and negative effects in a person's soul up to the present time. Karma is thus a kind of moral bank balance, with the bad deeds subtracted from the good deeds to yield a total which can be either dominantly negative or dominantly positive.
>
> Hindu authorities agree that key features of the body-soul configuration include the senses, which vary in different accounts from eight to ten in number. Each sense is a seeker or grasper (ghraha) of a particular sort of experience (atigraha). In contrast to Western conceptions, the senses in Hindu theory include both receptors, such as the eyes, and executors of deeds, such as the hands. The senses and their external experiences form pairings, like the following from the Kausitaki Upanishads: Ear is paired with sound, tongue with taste, eye with visible form, smell with odor, speech with name, hands with action, feet with movement, the body in general with pleasure and pain, the sex organs with delight and procreation. (Keith, 1925, p. 556)

A typical way Hindu theory interrelates these pairings is to envision the mind as the integrating center for the senses and to assign the mind the tasks of governing "desire, judgment, belief, doubt, unbelief, firmness, weakness, modesty, knowledge, fear. . . . Mind, therefore, is responsible for forming into ideas the impressions of the senses (sight, hearing, taste, smell, touch), which mind then—in the form of *will* motivated by *desire*—transforms into resolves that are carried out by the organs of action" (Keith, 1925, pp. 554–555).

One way the components of personality change with the passing of time is in the maturation of the mind—the accumulation of knowledge cultivated by the study of holy texts, by daily experiences, and by meditation. In addition, a person's karma is expected to change as thoughts and deeds add to, or subtract from, the existing sum of karma.

### *Maps*

Maps offer readers an instant impression of the comparative locations of regions, nations, districts, institutions, or events, as illustrated in Figure 11.7, which shows the sections of the United States with the greatest concentrations of Spanish language speakers.

The Internet is helpful in providing maps that can be adapted for inclusion in theses and dissertations. If you enter the word *maps* into such a search engine as *Google* or *Ask,* you generate millions of websites that concern maps. Ones you find there range from those depicting the entire world to ones portraying individual nations, individual states, cities, and even neighborhoods. You can slide such a map onto your computer "desktop" to use as a model for drawing

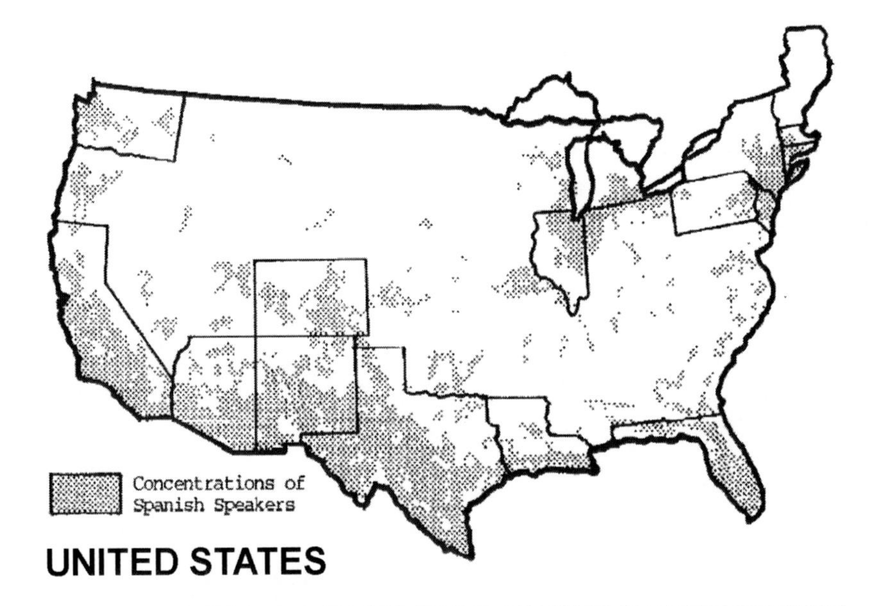


**Figure 11.7** Concentrations of Spanish Language Speakers

SOURCE: From *Conducting Educational Research* by Thomas, R. M. Copyright © 1998. Reproduced with permission of Greenwood Publishing Group, Inc. Westport, CT.

(either on the computer or by hand) the sort of map you need. Or you can use your computer's "copy" function to enter the Internet map into the chapter you are currently writing, then adapting that map to your needs by adding symbols or words from your word-processing program's drawing tools.

*Flow charts*

The step-by-step operation of a process can be summarized in the form of a flow chart. The example in Figure 11.8 shows the phases through which a project proposal in a research bureau will pass from the initial introduction of the project to its final review stage.

*Organization charts*

Diagrams depicting the components of an organization are useful in delineating how the various parts of a social structure are related to each other. Figure 11.9 offers an example of a diagram depicting power and communication relationships within the authority structure of a school system. This diagram also reveals how a single diagram can depict both the intended and the

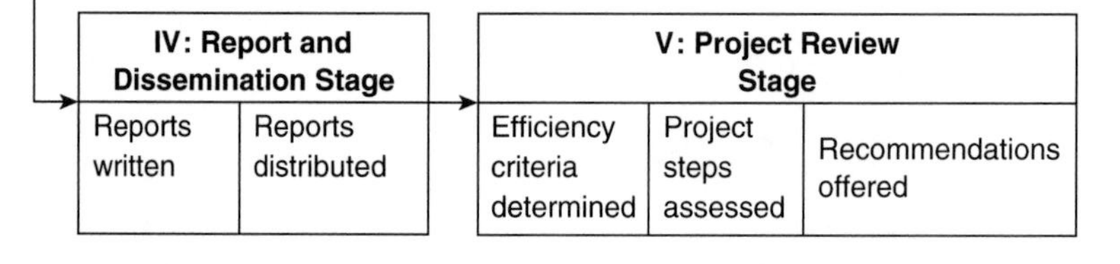
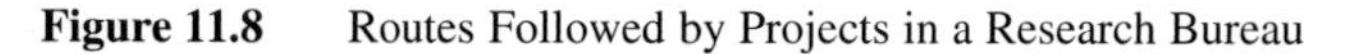


**Figure 11.8** Routes Followed by Projects in a Research Bureau

SOURCE: From *Conducting Educational Research* by Thomas, R. M. Copyright © 1998. Reproduced with permission of Greenwood Publishing Group, Inc. Westport, CT.

actual authority and communication channels of an organization. The intended operation of a hypothetical small city's school-administration hierarchy is shown in lines connecting the rectangles.

Authority (decisions and power) is expected to flow from the board of education at the top, down through the administration's officers and bureaus, to the school principals, then to the teachers. Decisions are to be communicated along those same routes. However, an inspection of events in the schools shows that power and communication often flow along channels other than those pictured in the system's formal structure. Four such exceptions to the formal plan are identified by the shaded arrows superimposed over the formal diagram. Arrow (1) connects a school board member with a primary school teacher who happens to be the member's sister. Because brother and sister maintain a close, friendly relationship and frequently discuss school business, the sister is able to wield greater influence over educational policies and practices than can the typical teacher. Arrow (2) signifies an informal relationship between

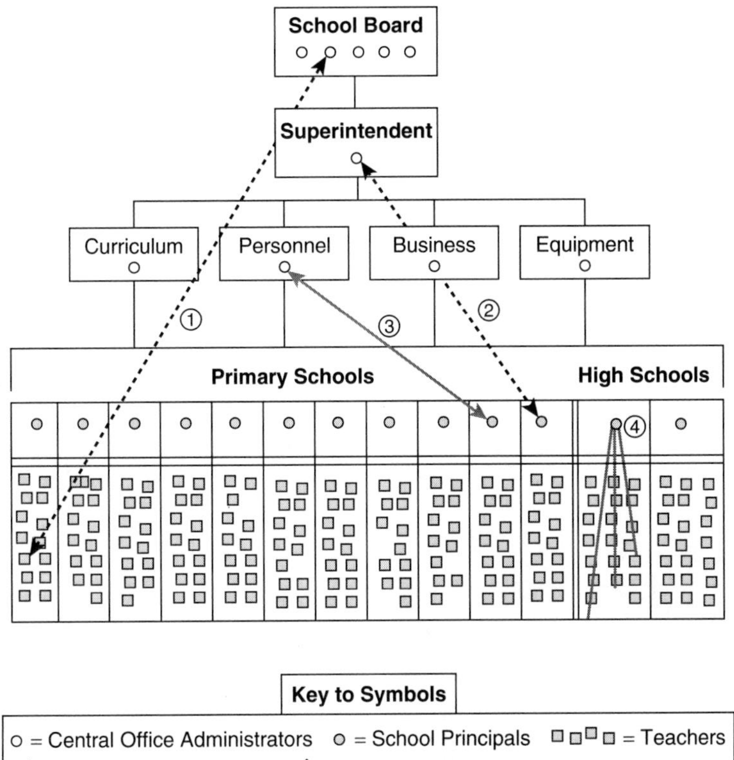


**Figure 11.9** Formal and Informal Routes of Influence in a School System

SOURCE: From *Conducting Educational Research* by Thomas, R. M. Copyright © 1998. Reproduced with permission of Greenwood Publishing Group, Inc. Westport, CT.

the superintendent of schools and a primary school principal who is the superintendent's golf partner. Their weekly game of golf provides the principal information about school affairs before other principals learn of such matters through official channels.

Arrows (3) and (4) identify antagonistic relationships that detract from the smooth operation of the administrative system. Link (3) represents a feud between a school principal and the director of personnel services—a feud affecting the appointment of teachers to the school. Link (4) signifies a conflict between a high school principal and a group of teachers who frequently refuse to carry out the principal's directives.

## PLANNING CHECKLIST

Although it is likely not possible for you to predict all of the places in which you will want to create summaries throughout your thesis or dissertation, you may find it useful to try foreseeing at least some of those locations and to envision the form the summaries could assume. Perhaps the following checklist can aid you with that task.

1. **Narrative summaries.** On a sheet of paper, list the questions that should be answered in your project's final version with a narrative/verbal summary.

2. **Statistical summaries.** Write an **X** on the line in front of each type of statistic that you intend to use in your study. On a sheet of paper, write the names of each type of statistic that you have marked with an **X**. Then, beside each name, write the question that your use of that statistic is intended to answer.

   ___ 2.1 Percentages

   ___ 2.2 Percentiles

   ___ 2.3 Measures of central tendency

      ___ 2.3.1 Mean

      ___ 2.3.2 Median

      ___ 2.3.3 Mode

   ___ 2.4 Measures of variability/dispersion

      ___ 2.4.1 Range

      ___ 2.4.2 Distance between percentiles

      ___ 2.4.3 Variance or standard deviation

      ___ 2.4.4 Other (specify) ______________________________

   ___ 2.5 Correlation methods

      ___ 2.5.1 Pearson product-moment ($r$)

      ___ 2.5.2 Spearman rank-order (*rho* or $\rho$)

      ___ 2.5.3 Biserial ($r_b$)

      ___ 2.5.4 Phi coefficient ($\phi$)

      ___ 2.5.5 Other (specify) ____________________________

   ___ 2.6 Other kinds of statistical treatments (specify) ________________

   ______________________________________________________________

3. **Tabular and graphic summaries.** Write an **X** on the line in front of each type of table or graph that you intend to use in your study. On a sheet of paper, write the names of each type of table or graph that you marked with

an **X**. Beside each name, write the question you intend to answer with that table or graph.

___ 3.1 Table

___ 3.2 Pie chart

___ 3.3 Trend graph

___ 3.4 Time line

___ 3.5 Histogram, bar chart

___ 3.6 Path analysis

___ 3.7 Map

___ 3.8 Organization chart

___ 3.9 Flow chart

___ 3.10 Theory structure chart

___ 3.11 Other (specify) ________________________________

# STAGE IV

# INTERPRETING THE RESULTS

The single chapter (Chapter 12: Modes of Interpretation) in Stage IV concerns ways of proposing what the outcomes of your investigation mean. This is the stage at which you explain the usefulness of what you discovered.

TWELVE

# MODES OF INTERPRETATION

*"I've heard that I could use hermeneutics for explaining the meaning of my project. But what precisely are hermeneutics?"*

Throughout this book, *interpretation* refers to students *assigning meaning* to an aspect of their research project by answering a question about that aspect. In effect, *the meaning* of the aspect resides in the answer to the question about it. To illustrate this point, we will use the following pair of studies, each of them designed to answer a principal question.

> *Title:* "An Investigation of Reading-Textbooks' Effectiveness"
>
> *Principal question:* In a comparison between two textbooks, is one book more effective than the other for improving fifth-graders' reading skills?
>
> *Title:* "Predicting College Success"
>
> *Principal question:* What characteristics of high school graduates are most useful for predicting how successful they will be in college?

The argument we use to support our definition of *interpretation* consists of four propositions.

***Proposition 1:*** *Information (data) has no meaning in itself.* Some people seem to believe that information is, in itself, meaningful, but such is not the case. For example, two sets of fifth-grade reading textbooks mean nothing until a question is answered about the texts. Hence, different meanings are derived from different questions whose answers use the same data, such as:

- Is one text more efficient than the other for improving fifth-graders' reading skills?
- Which text has more pictures?
- Which text is more expensive?
- How do the texts compare in their portrayal of different ethnic groups?
- How do the texts compare in the moral values they promote?

Likewise, in the second of our illustrative studies, students' high school grade-point averages mean nothing until they are used in answering a question.

- What characteristics of high school graduates are most useful for predicting how successful they will be in college?
- What are alternative methods of determining high school students' grade-point averages?
- How can computer hackers alter students' grade-point averages?
- How often are grade-point averages mentioned in letters of recommendation that students submit in their applications to colleges?

***Proposition 2:*** *Questions usually serve as the guide to what data to collect.* Researchers typically begin by posing a question or hypothesis, then think of the kind of information that will most effectively answer the question or test the hypothesis.

But it is also true that researchers sometimes operate the other way around. They first collect—or happen upon—information, and then ask, "What kind of question could these data help me answer?" The data might be in the form of (a) a diary written by a pioneer schoolmarm, (b) third-grade children's essays about "my favorite TV star," (c) a social-service agency's records of juvenile delinquents' family conditions, (d) the number of days students were absent in five high schools, or (e) the price of gasoline at different times during the past century.

But in either case—first the question or first the data—the question and its answer determine the meaning of the data.

***Proposition 3:*** *Guide questions can be either explicit or implied.* The expression *explicit* refers to questions or hypotheses you specifically identified as ones your project would address. There can be two sorts of explicit questions. The first consists of the original issues you intended to investigate. The second involves unanticipated questions or issues that emerged during the process of conducting the research, questions you then intentionally adopt as further matters to be included in the study. The term *implied questions* identifies material you include in your interpretation as answers to questions that were never directly asked. The following example illustrates the distinctions among these three sorts of questions—original questions, explicit emerging questions, and implied questions.

Imagine a study titled "Ways of Conducting a Census: A Comparative Analysis" in which the author in the opening pages of her dissertation explains that she initially designed her research to answer this three-part query:

> What are common methods of conducting a population census, what criteria have most frequently been used for evaluating those methods, and which methods are judged best and which poorest when they are assessed by means of such criteria?

However, in the process of collecting data to find answers, she is obliged to recognize that a variety of social and cultural conditions influence the census methods adopted in a particular society. Consequently, explaining why a given method was chosen calls for describing how influential conditions within each society affected that choice. Thus, she adds a further question that she would attempt to answer:

> What social and cultural conditions within a society significantly influence the selection of how the census will be conducted?

In the final writing of the dissertation, this question is appended to the original one, and the student explains how such a question was generated during the process of data collection.

Later, in the final pages of the dissertation, after she has described the way she collected and organized her data, she first writes an interpretation of the answers to her explicit questions, then attaches this paragraph.

> The extent to which—and the manner in which—census outcomes are publicized affects how census data are applied in decision-making by government agencies, educational institutions, and business enterprises. This point is demonstrated by the following comparison among the five nations that have been included in the present investigation.

Her comparison then assumes the form of statistical evidence and a discussion of how the five nations' census practices have been analyzed. This attached material is an example of an implied question. That is, the inclusion of information about the manner of reporting census results and the practical applications of census information does not derive from a question posed earlier in the dissertation. Instead, it reflects a latent question—one not central to, but nevertheless relevant to, the main thrust of the study and thus is considered appropriate for inclusion among the project's interpretations.

***Proposition 4:*** *Questions that guide interpretations can appear at many places in a thesis or dissertation.* Interpretation appears—or is needed—at every juncture in your research report where a reader of your work wonders "exactly what does this mean"? This is particularly true of key terms you use in your report (as illustrated in Chapter 6). Therefore, there will be many explicit and implicit questions throughout your work. The following section describes in some detail the diversity of meanings that various research questions can denote.

## MEANINGS DENOTED BY TYPES OF GUIDE QUESTIONS

If interpretation does indeed consist of describing the meanings reflected in the answers to research questions, then it becomes apparent that there are many kinds of meaning associated with various types of questions. The following discussion is divided into two parts. The first part identifies several general kinds of interpretation. The second part is devoted to kinds of interpretation that we believe qualify as hermeneutics.

Throughout the presentation, we begin by describing each kind of interpretation in relation to the type of meaning it yields. Then we offer questions that would call for such an interpretation. It will be apparent that the few types of interpretation reviewed in this chapter have been selected from the broader range of meanings that are possible in research. In effect, there are more available types than the few reviewed in this chapter.

### Some General Varieties of Interpretation

The eight common forms of interpretation described in the following paragraphs involve (a) comparing and contrasting, (b) proposing causes (explanatory, predictive), (c) revealing trends, (d) confirming beliefs and practices, (e) challenging conventional wisdom, (f) proposing alternative meanings, (g) attempting to alter beliefs and behavior, and (h) evaluating events, people, policies, or practices.

#### *Comparing and contrasting*

In compare-and-contrast analyses, meaning derives from recognizing how two or more phenomena are alike and are different. *Comparing* involves identifying similarities among phenomena, whereas *contrasting* consists of recognizing differences among them. Many things can be the objects of compare-and-contrast interpretation—individuals, groups, institutions, activities, belief systems, attitudes, emotions, and more.

*Individuals:* In terms of contributions to the nation's welfare, how have historians rated presidents Theodore Roosevelt and Franklin Roosevelt?

*Groups:* In what ways are devoted Catholics, Muslims, and Buddhists alike and different?

*Institutions:* How do public schools in the Netherlands and in Scotland compare in regard to their curricula, financial support, mode of governance, and students' achievement?

*Activities:* What are the strengths and weaknesses of playing chess versus working crossword puzzles as activities to sustain mental alertness and memory accuracy among the elderly?

*Belief systems:* What are the comparative advantages and disadvantages of the British capitalistic economy and the North Korean state-socialist economy from the viewpoints of production efficiency and distributing the society's wealth equitably throughout the populace?

*Attitudes:* How do opinions about birth control vary by social-class level—upper class, middle class, lower class?

*Emotions:* How similar are adolescent girls and adolescent boys in their feelings about the death of a parent?

*Proposing causes*

The process of causal analysis involves two steps: (1) identifying a correlation between two or more phenomena and (2) providing a line of logic that suggests that one of those phenomena is the result—at least partially—of the other. The first step—demonstrating a correlation—is descriptive; it consists of showing that when one factor changed, the other also changed, at least to some degree. The second step—establishing a causal link—is speculative, representing the analyst's estimate of how one of the factors has caused, or could cause, a related one.

Two versions of causal interpretation are the explanatory and the predictive.

***Explanatory interpretation:*** Explanatory analysis is concerned with the past by focusing on events that have already occurred. In one form of explanation, the researcher's purpose is to detect the influence of earlier events (the antecedent or independent variable) on subsequent events (the outcome or dependent variable). The connection the analyst is seeking to establish can be expressed as a question.

> In what ways did changes in the sexual-harassment legislation alter male-female relationships in the workplace?
>
> In a sample of 1,000 New York City adolescents, what difference did being raised in a one-parent home rather than in a two-parent home make in students' mental health and academic success?
>
> What influence did the amount of financial and technical aid provided by the Allied nations to defeated nations in World War II exert on the speed and strength of defeated nations' economic recovery?
>
> Why did Richard Nixon lose to John Kennedy in the 1960 presidential election?
>
> What has caused the rise in the divorce rate in recent decades?
>
> What lasting influence did Sigmund Freud's writings exert on European and American psychology and psychiatry?
>
> Why was Effraim Schultz able to rise from a family background of poverty and crime to become a wealthy entrepreneur and highly regarded social-welfare philanthropist?

In contrast to the people who analyze events and documents in order to explain causal influences, there are critics who play the role of debunkers, disputing the validity of such analyses. Debunkers operate either by doubting that an investigator of documents truly understood the documents' import or by disputing the line of logic with which the investigator has connected the contents of documents to events. An example is Walford's quarreling with the argument put forward in a book focusing on connections between education and poverty.

> The authors claim that the first of [their] chapters uses data from up to 40 countries to investigate the effect of education on reducing poverty. . . . What the chapter actually does is provide some interesting correlations between various factors for the countries selected. . . . But it is positively misleading for the authors to infer causation from correlation . . . [in that] they do not overcome the simple problem of untangling whether, for example, more equitable income distributions are caused by improvements in education or vice versa. The reality is probably a lot more complex than either possibility. (Walford, 1993, p. 84)

Typical questions that lead to debunkers' contributions include:

What was wrong with the line of logic that led the author to such conclusions?
What data were either ignored or misrepresented in the author's analysis?
What ill-founded, unstated assumptions underlay the analyst's reasoning about causes of crime?
How has a postmodern deconstruction of the concepts of race and gender invalidated the influence of traditional marriage laws on the quality of individuals' lives and of society?

***Predictive interpretation:*** Predictive analysis addresses the future. Its aim is to estimate the influence that presently existing or expected new events will exert on conditions that will appear in the days or years ahead. A predictive interpretation is thus an inference about a likely causal connection between present times and a specified future time.

Would the proposed flat tax provide more revenue for the federal government than is obtained from the present form of income tax?
What changes can be expected in the contents of science textbooks if religious groups' criticisms of humanistic secularism replace prevailing publishing guidelines?
Will the recently published statistics on immigration trends affect regulations governing the conditions that aliens must fulfill in order to earn U.S. citizenship?

*Revealing trends*

Trends are patterns of change over time. Interpreting a sequence of events in terms of trends involves identifying the nature of those patterns, thereby making patterns of change the meaning of trend analysis. As demonstrated in the following examples, a trend interpretation is frequently directed by a guide question that is accompanied by a further query regarding the cause of the trend.

In what ways have women's styles of dressing changed over the twentieth century? What have been the principal reasons behind those changes?
What pattern did the cycles of economic prosperity and depression assume between 1920 and 1990? What factors determined that pattern?
In traditional Zuñi culture, what stages have been identified in the development of obedience during children's and youths' growing years? Why did those stages appear in such a sequence?

*Confirming beliefs and practices*

Interpretation performs a confirmative function whenever information is seen as corroborating a belief the analyst wishes to advance. One sort of confirmative inquiry is the manifold-support type, guided by the question: How much documentary evidence can I compile in support of my position? Another is the conflicting-version variety, derived from answering the question: Which of several contradictory accounts of an event do I believe is the most convincing?

In the manifold-support type, multiple documents are interpreted as substantiating the hypothesis, viewpoint, policy, or practice the analyst is advocating. In other words, the analyst seeks to convince others of the soundness of his or her stance by offering not just one, but a multitude of materials in support of that position. In way of illustration, Cremin (1970, p. 657) cites 12 "recent works" that represent the "serious and systematic study of characteristic family life" on which he based his own rendition of family influences on education in colonial America. Other studies that also involve manifold support include ones designed to answer the following questions.

What evidence from present-day Cuban society supports the contention that the adoption of Marxist political-economic principles promotes the greatest good for the majority of citizens?

What fallacies in the logic presented by supporters of the death penalty weaken those supporters' assertions about the death penalty's usefulness for reducing violent crime?

In what ways do the results of empirical research studies demonstrate the superiority of conflict theory over social-exchange theory for explaining the treatment of prisoners of war in the Vietnam and Iraq wars?

*Challenging conventional wisdom*

Sometimes investigators conduct research intended to test popular beliefs that have derived from cultural traditions or from an accumulation of previous studies. When the results of the research are at odds with conventional wisdom, it means that conventional wisdom has ostensibly been wrong, at least for the circumstances under which the present study was conducted. The researcher's task of interpretation is one of accounting for the apparent discrepancy between what tradition would have predicted and what the study produced. This can involve the author comparing the contradictory accounts, then adducing an argument showing that the rationale supporting his or her position is the more logical of the pair and the one better buttressed by empirical evidence.

How do recent studies of cross-cultural relations in the United States cast doubt on the traditional belief that American society represents a unified nationwide cultural "melting pot"?

What's wrong with schools' promotion policies which require that a child be "at grade level in academic achievement" before the child is permitted to advance to the next grade?

*Proposing alternative meanings*

Frequently a critical researcher will accept at face value a document's descriptive content but will question the author's interpretation of the material and then will suggest a different meaning for the data. The guide question for conducting such a reappraisal can be: What is the political, moral, social-class, ethnic, or gender vantage point from which the original author viewed the events depicted in this document, and how might the account have been different if the author had assumed another vantage point?

This type has been most prominent in recent decades in formerly colonized nations whose people have sought to revise, from their own viewpoint rather than the perspective of the colonialists, the region's history during colonial times. But such revisionism is not limited to cases of newly independent peoples. It can occur as readily whenever the political control of a state falls into new hands, and the leaders of the new regime choose to recast historical accounts by reinterpreting the previously presented evidence. The resulting revised interpretation typically attributes ignoble motives to the people involved in the original account or else suggests that the policies and practices of those earlier times produced different consequences than the ones described in the original document.

The researcher's methods for determining the accuracy of a work's interpretation can involve:

1. Estimating the way political, economic, and social motives of various groups in the society would likely have influenced their explanation of the events depicted in the original document, then

2. Comparing the analysis found in a communication with the explanation that might derive from each group's motives in order to determine whether the communication's interpretation was biased or else was a balanced representation of different groups' viewpoints.

What often stimulates a scholar to initiate an alternative interpretation is the philosophical or theoretical persuasion to which the scholar subscribes, a persuasion different from that of the original author of the documents under question. For example, Marxist theory may be used for reinterpreting an account of nineteenth-century schooling in the Pacific Islands that had been written by a Christian missionary who founded schools there. Or conflict theory may be used to reassess changes in Eastern Germany's social-class structure as described by a Russian historian after the Soviet Union took political control of Eastern Germany following World War II. When researchers thus intentionally bring a different theoretical perspective to interpreting a communication, they add further items to their list of guide questions: What were the philosophical assumptions and investigative methods of the original author, and how do those compare with the ones I bring to the reinterpretation of the work? What additional kinds of information do I require for my reappraisal, and why are these new kinds needed?

Why can a postmodern perspective furnish a better explanation of ethnic groups' worldviews than can logical positivism?

How does adopting a radical/libertarian feminist theory alter the expectations women hold for what constitutes "equitable opportunities and treatment"?

*Attempting to alter beliefs and behavior*

Sometimes the intent behind a communication is to promote particular policies, practices, individuals, organizations, or ideologies. Such communications represent efforts to persuade an audience to adopt convictions the author favors. In effect, the meaning of such a hortatory effort is found in the author's motives and the type of change the author intends in the chosen audience. The interpreter's task is therefore to discern what it is the author is trying to sell, to whom, how, and why.

In the Islamic Quran, what sorts of arguments are offered to convince readers that they should subscribe to the doctrines and abide by the dictates espoused in the book?

What was the motive behind Senator Sturdlee's criticism of the leaders of his own party?

*Evaluating events, people, policies, or practices*

Evaluative analysis is concerned with judging whether a communication is desirable in terms of specified characteristics, such as cost, social equity, clarity, user convenience, functional efficiency, aesthetic appeal, or the like.

Oftentimes the comparison is not based on a single document that is intended to represent a given practice but, rather, is founded on a series of related documents.

*Events:* Did the Woodstock rock concerts exert a positive or negative influence in American society?

*People:* Which U.S. president was more effective in getting important legislation enacted, John Kennedy or Lyndon Johnson?

*Policies:* How have regulations that govern the protection of Native Americans' sacred grounds affected projects of real estate developers? Who profits from the proposed changes in Medicare legislation and who suffers damage?

*Practices:* What are the advantages and disadvantages of medical treatments offered by Navajo shamans?

### Hermeneutics

The word *hermeneutics* has been around for centuries, particularly in reference to interpreting the meaning of biblical writings. However, the present-day heightened popularity of hermeneutics in the humanities and social sciences is of rather recent origin, dating principally from the early 1960s. The popularity ranges far beyond the realm of biblical exegesis to include the interpretation of any sort of communication—legal documents, speeches, letters, newspaper articles, books, movies, radio and television broadcasts, and more. Along with this heightened interest has come a fair amount of puzzlement arising from a lack of consensus among writers about precisely what the aims and methods of hermeneutics are. This lack of agreement even extends to the pronunciation of the term itself. (Is it best as *her-me-NOO-tics, her-me-NYOO-tics,* or *her-me-NOY-tics?*) One result of the confusion is that potential users of hermeneutics fail to understand when or how to apply its methods.

Hermeneutics, in its most general sense, has been broadly defined as the art or science of interpretation. Under such an all-encompassing definition, any assignment of meaning to data could be considered an application of hermeneutics, including all of the types in this chapter. And, indeed, there are people who use the term in that way, as a synonym for *interpretation.* However, other users place greater restrictions on the concept. The problem, then, becomes that of discovering how to distinguish hermeneutic analysis from other forms of interpretation.

A search of the literature to learn how *hermeneutics* has been defined yields a harvest of mixed worth. Wilhelm Dilthey (1833–1911), the German philosopher most often credited with stimulating the modern-day movement, defined hermeneutics as "understanding social phenomena in terms of the motives of the participants and the meanings [that such motives] give to institutions and events" (Macsporran, 1982, p. 47).

Less clear than Dilthey's statement is Bubner's assertion: "For hermeneutics, understanding means a fundamental apprehension of truth which takes place in intersubjective processes of communication and in the mediation through history" (Bubner in Mannien & Tuomela, 1976, p. 69).

Equally elusive seems the meaning Giddens intended when writing that hermeneutics involves "grasping frames of meaning contextually as elements of the practice of particular forms of life—and not only consistencies with frames, but also inconsistencies and disputed or contested meanings" (Macsporran, 1982, p. 48).

In view of this murky condition of much of the discourse about hermeneutics, our problem of explaining the technique's exact aims and methods became one of determining more precisely what part hermeneutics might play in doing theses and dissertations. We approached the problem by reviewing key writings bearing on document interpretation in various disciplines, then extracting from those writings six functions that might adequately qualify as hermeneutic activities applicable to research in the humanities and the social and behavioral sciences (Bozarth-Campbell, 1979; Gadamar, 1975; Garfinkel, 1981; Habermas, 1972; Held, 1980; Macsporran, 1982; Mazzeo, 1978; Odman, 1985; Palmer, 1969; Ricoeur, 1976; Thomas, 1987; von Wright, 1971). The six functions are those of (a) extracting the essence of a body of data, (b) locating a communication in its original context, (c) verifying the authenticity of an account, (d) judging the accuracy of information, (e) clarifying the meaning of a communication, and (f) translating symbols. Hence, for us the task of *hermeneutic analysis* consists of seeking to determine the original meaning intended by the author of a communication.

### *Extracting the essence of a body of data*

An important act of interpretation performed by any researcher is that of condensing a large quantity of information into a concise account that accurately reflects the most fundamental meanings of that body of information. The following are two forms of that act.

***Synoptic interpretation:*** In synoptic interpretation, the analyst endeavors to provide a concise version of a longer communication. This is the summarization function described in Chapter 11. The analysis is guided by the question: How can I best prepare a brief version that is true to the spirit and content of the original large body of information?

A synopsis may be brief, identifying no more than key themes that run through the work or works that are being summarized, or it may be more extensive, providing considerable detail, and in some cases attempting to maintain a sense of the original authors' writing styles. In the comparative form of synoptic interpretation, summaries of two or more communications are placed side by side, with the analyst usually pointing out what could be regarded as significant similarities and differences.

What were the common features shared by the Parnack and Stackhouse election campaigns in the race for the post of county commissioner?

What was the main lesson implied in the Algonquin myth of Glooskap's death and his subsequent revival?

In brief, what method did Hanafia and Sumantri use for studying social stratification in Sundanese villages, and what were the chief results of their study?

What was self-contradictory in French philosopher Michel Foucault's contending that valid generalizations could be drawn only from very specific events and that those generalizations would be applicable only within the context of those events?

***Personal qualities interpretation:*** Often an analyst, when abstracting from documents, seeks to summarize prominent features of an individual's or a group's personality. The documents that frequently serve this purpose are biographies, letters, speeches, and regulations that the individual or group has produced. Or the personal qualities may be drawn from interviews with people who have known the individual or group. The question guiding such inquiry is this: What characteristics typify this individual's or group's beliefs and actions?

What were Benjamin Franklin's most admirable qualities, and which of his qualities were subject to censure?

How well did Eleanor Roosevelt's abilities and temperament suit her for the role of wife to the president of the United States?

What skills and personality characteristics are needed in a woman if she is to function as a successful chief administrative officer of a large entertainment conglomerate, such as the Disney Corporation or Turner Broadcasting?

Are there really such things as "national character traits"? If so, what traits distinguish the French, the Germans, the Chinese, and the Japanese?

*Locating a communication in its original context*

Contextual interpretation refers to how an account of an event has been affected by the historical or sociocultural context within which the account was composed. This form of interpretation is frequently applied in historical and anthropological investigations in which a researcher is seeking to determine the meaning intended by someone who wrote or spoke from a perspective distant in time, space, or culture from that of the researcher. The investigator endeavors to fathom the intent of the original author by comprehending the social-class system, political pressures, religious beliefs, etiquette, knowledge structures, and other circumstances from which that author operated. That sort of understanding is pursued by such means as learning the language of the author, reading extensively about the author's life and times, and interviewing people who knew the author or who have authoritative knowledge of the society in which the author lived.

What was the intent of the creators of the U.S. Constitution when they included in the Bill of Rights the provision for citizens to bear arms? How did social conditions in those days influence the addition of such a provision to the Bill of Rights? From the viewpoint of the public welfare, how appropriate is that provision under present-day social conditions in the United States?

What characteristics of the worldview of typical Christian Science practitioners affect their either rejecting or accepting various sorts of medical treatment?

*Verifying the authenticity of an account*

Verification analysis is aimed at determining the authenticity of a communication. The purpose is to help the analyst decide whether an account is actually what it is purported to be. Verification interpretation, in its comparative version, involves ascertaining which of two or more communications is the most authentic. This mode of analysis can result in such appraisals as Cremin's conclusion: "The literature on Horatio Alger, Jr., is replete with legend and even some fraudulent biography based on a nonexistent diary. But Edwin P. Hoyt's *Horatio's Boys: The Life and Works of Horatio Alger, Jr.* appears to be authoritative" (Cremin, 1980, p. 565).

One common sort of verification analysis is reflected in the question: When there are two somewhat contradictory accounts of an event, which account is the more accurate? In attempting to answer this question, the experienced investigator will typically depend on both internal and external sources of evidence.

*Internal* refers to characteristics of the documents themselves, such things as factual consistency, completeness of presentation, chronological accuracy, and writing style. *External* refers to evidence from outside the document that either corroborates the account or casts doubt on it. External evidence usually consists of information about the same event as provided by other documents or witnesses.

To what extent were reports of the Lincoln-Douglas debates, as published in newspapers of the day, accurate, verbatim accounts of the men's speeches? And if the published speeches were edited versions, how might the mode of editing have affected readers' understanding of Lincoln's and Douglas's political beliefs and styles of oratory?

In certain respects, the Book of Job in the Old Testament of the Christian Bible reads somewhat differently in the King James Authorized Version than in the New American Version. Which of these versions is truer to the original Hebrew on which the two English-language translations were based?

In the O. J. Simpson murder case, what means could have been used to resolve the conflicts between the accounts of the affair offered by different witnesses who spoke at the trial?

*Judging the accuracy of information*

Whereas the aim of verification interpretation is to determine whether a communication is what it claims to be, data-accuracy analysis is intended to discover whether the information in a document or in someone's testimony faithfully depicts what happened.

In assessing the validity of historical accounts, the researcher's guide questions become these: To what extent are the episodes or information in the document complete, or at least representative of conditions at the time? What other information should have been included in the document to ensure that the data were accurate? Techniques for answering such queries include

1. Reviewing the apparent sources of the original author's data to estimate whether the author had extracted from them a balanced description of conditions at the time.

2. Searching for new sources of information so as to check the contents of the new sources against the contents of the original author's work to learn whether adding the new information warrants changing the conclusions drawn in the original work.

3. Estimating reasons for any data inaccuracies that have been discovered in the communication.

In judging the accuracy of the accounts offered by witnesses or informants, an investigator can consider the likely motives of the witnesses, the skills of observation and description that the witnesses commanded (acuity of sight and hearing, verbal proficiency), and the context in which the witnessed events occurred (political convention hall, emotionally charged confrontation between husband and wife, high school football game).

In the confrontation between FBI agents and the Branch Dravidian religious cult near Waco, Texas, whose depiction of the episode represents what really occurred?

How likely is it that the girl who testified in the robbery case could have identified the suspect at dusk when the girl was still half a block from the gas station?

What was the author's motive for taking credit for the success of the research project when he himself had not conducted the study?

*Clarifying the meaning of a communication*

The aim of this type is to render the meaning of a communication more easily understood than it was in its original form. In attempting to create a more lucid version of a work, the analyst is essentially saying, "What the author *really* meant was this." The rationale behind producing a clarifying interpretation is that the original version would be inordinately abstruse for potential readers. In other words, phrasings and concepts in the original work would be unduly archaic, foreign, technical, or ambiguous for the audience that the analyst hopes to reach.

When postmodern authors' writings are explained with the use of examples from everyday life events, what do we discover those authors mean by such expressions as foundationalism, epistemological essentialism, postmodern negations, politics of voice, grand narratives of legitimation, counter-narratives, language games, structuralism, and metalanguage?

How can D'queljoe's description of Basque social structure be rewritten so it is readily understood by people who know little of anthropologists' technical jargon?

*Translating symbols*

Much of language is symbolic, in the sense of words being used to convey meanings that differ from the literal meanings originally attached to those words. For example, an aggressively ambitious young woman may be referred to as "a social climber." A politician who wildly launches irrational accusations at his opponents may be deemed "a loose cannon." A self-styled reformer who launches campaigns about issues that others consider ridiculous may be referred to as "the Don Quixote of Sixth Avenue."

Not only do authors use individual words and phrases symbolically, but they also sometimes speak in parables, describing an event or telling a tale whose meaning is not to be accepted literally but, rather, viewed symbolically as a representation of similar conditions at a different time or place. One of the best-known parables bearing on politics and social organization is George Orwell's *Animal Farm* (1946), which ostensibly describes the social relations among domesticated animals but is actually a commentary on human societies. Jonathan Swift's eighteenth-century *Gulliver's Travels* (1726/1980) is a well-known parable from the past that holds implications for understanding people's attitudes about the acceptability of individuals from unfamiliar cultures. Jean-Jacques Rousseau's *Emile* (1773), although cast as a novel, is a broad-ranging treatise on child rearing and education.

We can thus suggest that researchers who seek to interpret a communication's symbols can be led by such questions as these: Is the entire document symbolic—a fable, parable, or analog—so its literal meaning is not the one intended by the writer? Or does the document offer two meanings, one literal and the other symbolic? Is most of the meaning of the document intended to be direct and literal, but within the work are there symbolic meanings found in proverbs, aphorisms, or allusions? How can a researcher recognize symbolic contents?

The investigator can seek answers for these queries through the use of such tools as dictionaries that trace word etymology, collections of proverbs, and literary works from the time the document was written. In societies that have depended more on oral rather than written history and literature, clues to symbolic meanings may be sought through interviewing elderly members of the society. Essays, letters, or diaries that the original author produced may address themselves to matters of writing style, including how symbols are employed. If the document under consideration is a translation of a work originally produced in another language, then bilingual dictionaries can prove useful.

In Samoan culture, what figurative meanings are assigned to these proverbs?
"Pepe made a strange catch."
"Tufugaluli's ears go wandering about."
"Heaven was spat on."

In what way does the function of an electronic computer serve as an analog of the human information-processing system? Or, stated differently, why can the performance of a computer qualify as "artificial intelligence"?

What personality characteristics have been attributed to the following creatures by North American Indian tribes?
the owl by the Creeks
the rattlesnake by the Shawnees
the eagle by the Cherokees
the dove by the Hurons

What are the following expressions interpreted to mean in American business and political circles?
(business) Wall Street, bull market, bear market, whistle blower, negative cash flow, blue chip
(politics) lame duck, red herring

## CONCLUSION

The purpose of this chapter has been to demonstrate types of interpretation that authors of theses and dissertations may adopt for revealing the meanings they assign to the information they assemble. A key feature of the demonstration has been the use of guide questions to identify kinds of meaning being proposed in a given study. It should be apparent that the types of interpretation illustrated in the chapter represent only a portion of many available kinds.

## PLANNING CHECKLIST

Decisions about the specific interpretations you will draw in your project will likely be made at various stages of the project. At the stage of first launching your research, your initial guide questions will imply some of the core meanings you hope to derive from the study. Other questions that will lead to interpretations can arise during the process of choosing and applying information-collection techniques. Still other guide questions may appear only after the results have been compiled. Furthermore, various kinds of interpretation can be called for at the different stages of your work—proposing causes, comparing/contrasting, evaluating, challenging conventional wisdom, explaining symbols, or others. Therefore, how completely you are able to fill out the following checklist will likely depend on how far along you presently are in your work. Nevertheless, even though you may not be prepared at this time to do a thorough job of identifying the sorts of meanings you expect to draw from your study, you may still find it useful to fill out the checklist as a way of stimulating thoughtful consideration of what kinds of interpretation you might employ in your thesis or dissertation.

To complete the checklist, first place an X on the line in front of each type of interpretation you expect to propose in your study. Then, on a separate sheet of paper, write the guide question that you would use to identify the kind of meaning that each of your chosen types of interpretation is expected to yield.

____ 1. Comparing and contrasting

____ 2. Proposing causes

    ____ 2.1 Explaining past events

    ____ 2.2 Predicting future events

    ____ 2.3 Suggesting possible implications

____ 3. Revealing trends

____ 4. Confirming beliefs and practices

____ 5. Challenging conventional wisdom

____ 6. Proposing alternative meanings

____ 7. Attempting to alter beliefs and behavior

____ 8. Evaluating events, people, policies, or practices

____ 9. Extracting the essence of a body of data

    ____ 9.1 Synoptic interpretation

    ____ 9.2 Personal-qualities interpretation

____ 10. Locating a communication in its original context

____ 11. Verifying the authenticity of an account

____ 12. Judging the accuracy of information

____ 13. Clarifying the meaning of a communication

____ 14. Explaining symbols

____ 15. Other (explain) ______________________________

STAGE V

# PRESENTING THE FINISHED PRODUCT

The three chapters that comprise this final stage focus on methods of (a) writing the final version of your project (Chapter 13: Writing the Final Version), (b) convincingly defending your research before your advisor and before other faculty members who are assigned to evaluate your work (Chapter 14: Mounting a Persuasive Defense), and (c) extending the account of your research to audiences beyond your own campus (Chapter 15: Reaching a Wider Audience).

THIRTEEN

# WRITING THE FINAL VERSION

*"A friend told me his advisory committee turned down the first version of his dissertation because they said it was badly written. What precisely is the difference between a well written and a badly written dissertation?"*

This chapter offers suggestions about how to produce the ultimate document that will earn your graduate degree. The chapter addresses two sets of issues:

- Meeting the university's thesis or dissertation requirements as well as accommodating your supervising committee's preferences.
- Writing a skillfully crafted, readable document.

## FULFILLING REQUIREMENTS AND PREFERENCES

Two sources of expectations that your final work is expected to meet are (a) your university's or department's standards and (b) the preferences of your major advisor and members of your supervising committee.

### University and Department Requirements

Graduate students sometimes are unaware of the requirements set by their university or department regarding (a) deadlines for submitting theses and dissertations and (b) the form in which theses and dissertations must be written. Therefore, early in the process of conducting your research—and certainly before writing the final version—you'll profit from inspecting those requirements. How you find such information can vary from one institution to another. A place to start hunting is the university's graduate school catalog or bulletin, where guidance about such matters may be found in the index under the words *thesis* and *dissertation.* The catalog may mention a *Guide for Preparation of Theses and Dissertations,* which you can obtain from the graduate school office, the central library, or the campus bookstore.

Deadline dates usually identify the final day for submitting your application for graduation, the final date for an oral examination (if required), the last day for filing one or more signed copies of your study, and the final date for the clearance of candidates for degrees, including the last day for depositing copies of your document with the graduate school or central library. You may find it wise to keep a careful record of the occasions when you spoke with graduate school personnel, to whom you spoke, and the outcome of your conversation. You may need this record in case you are later obliged to resolve misunderstandings about your case.

Among the requirements that warrant your attention are the guidebook's specifications about such matters as the proper sizes of margins, acceptable bibliographic styles, footnotes, how to cite references within the body of the work, the quality of paper to use, type size, how to have the final version bound, the number of copies of the document to submit, and more.

Here is a sampling of requirements from a typical guide pamphlet for theses and dissertations.

The body of the work should be printed double-spaced on one side of a sheet. The reverse side of the sheet should be left blank.

Use the same typeface and type size consistently throughout the body of the work. Section headings should be in boldface type.

Paragraphs should be indented five spaces. A new paragraph should not begin at the bottom of a page unless there is adequate space for at least two lines.

Limited use of quotations and extracts is permitted. Usually, material from professional journals and books that does not exceed several hundred words may be quoted without requiring the permission of the copyright owner. However, copies of pictures, charts, tables, tests, and questionnaires should not be reproduced without permission.

Quotations that do not exceed three lines in length can be inserted within quotation marks in the paragraph to which they apply. However, quotations that exceed three lines should be inserted in a block (indented five spaces from the left and right margins) beneath the paragraph that introduces them. Such quotations are separated from the text by a triple space before and after.

References listed at the end of the thesis or dissertation must include all work cited in the main body of the document.

Appendices must be clearly titled, with references to those appendices offered at appropriate locations in the body of the work.

An abstract, no longer than 350 words or 35 lines, should precede the title page. The abstract is a brief summary of the body of the work. The abstract is an important part of the thesis or dissertation as other scholars will peruse it in order to see if they wish to read the entire work.

An acknowledgments page is optional. It should be brief, simple, and free of sentimentality or trivia. It is customary to acknowledge the work of the advisor and committee members. Help offered by others may also be recognized. Credit for financial assistance should be given if such assistance made this study possible.

The document should be printed on 100% rag bond paper.

Any duplicating process (such as printing from a computer or photocopier) must produce sharp, high-contrast, black images suitable for microfilming. No smudges, spots, inadvertent lines, or other blemishes are acceptable.

For binding purposes, the center of the page should be three spaces to the right of the exact center of the page. Backs of pages are to be left blank. Each page should have a uniform margin of one-and-one-half inches at the top and left, and one inch at the right and bottom. However, the first page of a chapter should have a two-inch top margin.

In recent years, more colleges and universities have required students to submit the final version of theses and dissertations in electronic, rather than paper, form. As an example of the rationale supporting this practice, note the following segment from the University of North Carolina at Greensboro website that explains the document-submission process.

> An electronic thesis or dissertation is the student's original research produced, submitted, archived and accessed in an electronic format. The components and structure of the document are basically the same as paper theses and dissertations. However, in the final stage, the documents are converted to and stored as pdf files instead of printed and bound as books. A pdf is a Portable Document File, created in a universal file format that allows data saved in one format to be converted into a format that can be read on any computer utilizing free Adobe Acrobat Reader.
>
> The University of North Carolina at Greensboro, together with universities around the world, is accepting electronic theses and dissertations (ETD's). The submission of electronic theses/dissertations offers numerous benefits. The ETD process helps to train students in the electronic publishing and technical skills they will need as professionals. On a larger scale, the immediate and widespread availability of ETD documents provides worldwide access to scholarship. ETD's allow researchers to build on the work of those before them, even those whose work was completed in recent months or even weeks. (Graduate School UNCG, 2007)

Not only is there a move toward requiring the submission of the final product in electronic form, but professors at an increasing pace are insisting that students send them early drafts of chapters by e-mail—instead of on paper—for evaluation and feedback. This means that the thesis or dissertation must be composed on a computer so it can be transmitted to advisory-committee members' computers.

### Advisors' Standards and Preferences

In addition to fulfilling institutional requirements, you are also obliged to satisfy the standards and preferences of your major advisor and other members of the committee that must approve of your work. As explained in Chapter 2, faculty members can differ markedly from each other in their conceptions of proper research topics, suitable methods of collecting information, and ways of interpreting the results. They can also disagree about how the research project can best be described in its final version. Therefore, it's helpful if, during the final writing process, you can receive feedback from your advisors regarding the way you are presenting your work. This may involve your asking them to review a chapter or two early in the final writing process so they can comment on your writing style. However, some professors refuse to inspect a candidate's work bit by bit. They are willing to judge the document only when a completed draft is available. In that event, you are compelled to wait until a final corrected version is ready.

## CREATING A READABLE DOCUMENT

The following discussion about creating readable theses and dissertations (a) distinguishes between good writing and bad writing, (b) suggests ways of rendering the task efficient and less burdensome, and (c) addresses the matter of writing an abstract of your work.

### Good Writing, Bad Writing

We are defining *good writing* as "writing that is easily and accurately understood by the audience for whom it's intended." In contrast, *bad writing* is "writing that is difficult to understand and/or is misunderstood by the audience for whom it's intended."

When the contents of scholarly journals, books, theses, and dissertations are judged by this standard of ease and accuracy of reader comprehension, it's apparent that there is a considerable quantity of bad writing in academia. So if you accept our definition of good writing, then you may find the following paragraphs useful. Our purpose is to describe characteristics of good and bad writing in terms of (a) the intended reading audience, (b) expression and communication, (c) organizing the manuscript, (d) the meanings of key terms, and (e) preparing readers for what they will encounter.

#### *The intended reading audience*

Your most immediate audience consists of the members of your advisory committee—the people who decide whether your document warrants the award of a graduate degree. Therefore, at the very least your writing style and the way you organize your manuscript must satisfy those members' standards of acceptability. However, most students hope their work will appeal to others as well—other faculty members, graduate students, journal editors, perhaps book publishers, and even an informed general public. Consequently, you will find it helpful if, at the outset of the writing task, you determine which sort of audience—or audiences—you wish to reach. This decision can influence the vocabulary you employ, the sorts of examples you include, and the manner in which you explain your research procedures. For example, expecting that your readers will be prepared to assign suitable meanings to technical words (*phonemes, family nuclearization and gentrification, transfer of learning, endorphins, macroeconomics, homosexual mentorship, chi-square*) will affect your writing differently than if you imagine your readers won't know what you mean by such terms.

You can probably expand your audience to include a greater variety of readers by employing such techniques as those described in the following passages.

*Expression and communication*

Bad writing can result from an author's failing to recognize the distinction between *expressing* and *communicating.* When you write solely to express what you think and feel, you can use any style that gets your notions out, so long as you can conclude that "I put down exactly what I feel." However, your way of expressing what you feel may not make much sense to someone who tries to read your document. Therefore, writing a thesis or dissertation requires not only that you express yourself but also that your intended readers readily and precisely grasp your meanings. This means that your writing should both express and communicate. We are convinced that the likelihood you will communicate effectively can be increased if you approach your writing from a reader's vantage point. By *reader's vantage point* we mean that instead of planning simply to "put down what I know about my project," you say to yourself,

> Let's assume that I know nothing about this project's topic, and I want to understand what it's all about, what was done, and why. In that event, what questions would I want the author to answer; and how would I like to have those answers worded?

By adopting a reader's perspective, you can find yourself defining more terms, explaining procedures in greater detail, including more clarifying examples, and placing ideas in a psychologically more sensible sequence than would be true if you had intended only to "express what I had in mind."

*Organizing your manuscript*

The pattern in which you will organize the final version of your thesis or dissertation may already have been determined for you by your faculty advisor or by traditions in your department or in your academic discipline. That pattern may take a form similar to the following one that we identified in Chapter 3 as one popular structure.

Chapter 1: Introduction
Chapter 2: Review of the Literature
Chapter 3: Methodology
Chapter 4: Results/Findings

Chapter 5: Analysis and Interpretation of the Findings
Chapter 6: Conclusions, Applications, and Recommendations for Further Study

A slightly different alternative that features the application of a theory assumes this pattern:

Chapter 1: The Nature of the Problem and Its Significance
Chapter 2: A Theory for Interpreting the Phenomenon That Is Studied
Chapter 3: The Research Design for Testing the Theory
Chapter 4: Data Collection
Chapter 5: A Report of the Results
Chapter 6: An Analysis of the Results
Chapter 7: Implications of the Study's Outcomes

However, even if your chapter headings have been predetermined for you, the way the material within chapters will be arranged usually depends on your own decision. In any case, you face a task of determining the order in which readers will meet the contents of your work. One way to approach that task is to adopt the reader's vantage point described above. Here is a series of three steps that such an approach can involve. (You may recognize this approach as much like one we introduced in Chapter 3.) The steps are illustrated in reference to an envisioned study titled *Family Correlates of Academic Performance.*

***Step 1.*** Ask yourself, "If I knew nothing about this project's topic and I wanted to understand what it's all about, what questions would I want the author to answer; and how would I like to have those answers worded?"

***Your response:*** Write down all questions that you think an interested but uninformed reader would ask. The questions can be listed in whatever order they come to mind. The following partial list demonstrates how this first step can be taken.

What is this research about?
Which characteristics of students' families are associated with students' high academic performance and which characteristics are associated with low performance?
What kind of information should be gathered to answer the above question?

What techniques and instruments should be used for collecting information?
What topics should be taken up in the final report of the study?
Why is a study of this kind worth doing? Why is it important?
Exactly what is meant by academic performance?
Precisely what is meant by family characteristics?
Can the results of such a study be used to improve family conditions or students' academic performance? If so, how?
Who participates in the study? That is, which students and their families are to be used, and why those families?
Who collects the information?
Who analyzes the collected information? What methods of analysis do they use?
Is information already available about family characteristics and students' academic achievement? If so, how can that information be obtained, and what does that information tell about the relationship between family characteristics and students' academic performance?
What do the results mean?
Is there a causal relation between family characteristics and students' academic performance? In other words, do family traits influence academic performance or vice versa?

***Step 2.*** Ask yourself, "In my imagined role as a reader, in what sequence would I want the author to answer my questions?"

***Your response:*** Rearrange your list of questions into what you regard as a psychologically sound order, that is, in an order that you believe a typical reader would wish to meet answers. Probably some of your questions will be subparts of more general ones. This means that it would be helpful to cast your list in outline form, with major (level 1) items representing chapters and with minor items subsumed under major items to represent issues addressed within chapters. During this process, you may think of additional questions that should be incorporated into the outline. In the following illustration, each additional question is identified by an asterisk (*).

The first two questions in our randomly ordered list identified the overall issue that the hypothetical study is intended to investigate.

What is this research about?
Which characteristics of students' families are associated with students' high academic performance and which characteristics are associated with low performance?

Because those questions identify the general focus of the study, they can be reflected in the title: *Family Correlates of Academic Performance.* The remaining items in the list represent issues to be treated within the body of the dissertation.

In the process of arranging the questions in sequence, you decide which major questions can properly serve as chapter topics and which minor questions can represent subsections within chapters.

---

1. What is this research about? *(Chapter 1: The Nature of the Investigation)*

   1.1 Which characteristics of students' families are associated with high academic performance and which characteristics are associated with low performance?

   1.2 Why is a study of this kind worth doing? Why is it important?

   1.3 Exactly what is meant by academic performance?

   1.4 Precisely what is meant by family characteristics?

   *1.5 In general, how will the central research question be investigated in the present study? In other words, what can I expect to find in the remaining chapters of the dissertation?

2. What information is already available about family characteristics and students' academic achievement? *(Chapter 2: Past Studies of Family Traits and Students' Academic Achievement)*

   2.1 How can that information be obtained?

   2.2 What does that information tell about the relationship between family characteristics and students' academic performance?

   *2.3 What implications does the survey of past studies hold for the conduct of the present study?

*3. What specific subquestions must be answered to provide a convincing resolution of the central research question? (*Chapter 3: The Detailed Research Problem*)

4. What kind of information should be gathered to answer the research questions? (*Chapter 4: The Research Methodology*)

   4.1 What techniques and instruments should be used for collecting information?

   *4.2 Who designs or obtains the techniques and instruments?

   4.3 Who participates in the study? That is, which students and their families are used?

   4.4 Why use those students and families?

   *4.5 How are the students and their families recruited?

   4.6 Who collects the information?

   *4.7 What are the steps of the information collection process?

*5. How are the collected data classified and summarized? (*Chapter 5: The Compiled Results*)

6. What do the results mean? (*Chapter 6: An Interpretation of the Results*)

   6.1 Who analyzes the compiled information?

   6.2 What methods of analysis do they use?

   6.3 Is there a causal relation between family characteristics and students' academic performance? In other words, do family traits influence academic performance?

   6.4 Can the results of such a study be used to improve family conditions or students' academic performance? If so, how?

*7. What questions about correlates of family traits and student performance have been left unanswered by this study and by previous ones? What sorts of research might provide the sought-for answers? (*Chapter 7: A Need for Further Research*)

***Step 3.*** Ask yourself: As I consider the contents of each chapter in turn, can I identify additional, more detailed questions for which I seek answers? If so, in what order can those questions profitably be addressed within the chapter?

***Your response:*** At Step 2 you began identifying kinds of material that would compose the contents of each chapter. At Step 3 you can continue this process in greater detail by approaching each chapter in the same way you approached the task of identifying the principal contents of the entire dissertation. That is, you (a) generate questions at random, and then (b) reorganize the questions in what appears to be a psychologically sound sequence from a reader's vantage point. By way of illustration, consider the following outline of the first half of our imagined Chapter 5 that could result from applying the Step-3 process.

---

Chapter 5: The Compiled Results

5. How are the data classified and summarized?

5.1 What classification procedure is used?

5.1.1 In what form will the collected information be received?

5.1.2 What characteristics are required of the classification system? That is, what criteria should the system meet?

5.1.3 What system of classification will be used?

5.1.3.1 Is there such a system already available; if so, what is its source?

5.1.3.2 If no appropriate system is available, who creates the one that is needed?

5.1.4 What are the steps in the classification process?

5.1.5 What technological aids (such as computer programs) are used in that process?

5.1.6 Who does the classifying?

5.1.7 How is the classifying process monitored to ensure its accuracy?

---

The job of identifying the remaining parts of Chapter 5 would then continue with our generating questions about how the classified data are to be summarized in preparation for interpretations that will be offered in Chapter 6.

It should be apparent that the outline resulting from such a planning approach will be subject to revision and improvement at each stage of the research until the thesis or dissertation arrives at its final version.

*Meanings of key terms*

The act of reading can be defined as "the process of bringing meanings to the words authors use." An author's task then becomes one of conveying new meanings to readers by casting familiar words into unfamiliar patterns. In effect, new meanings are generated by sentences that represent novel arrangements of already known words. By the same token, incomprehensible or mistaken reading results whenever readers fail to assign the author's intended meanings to the author's words. Hence, if authors believe readers may not accurately grasp their meanings, those authors should take pains to delineate precisely what they intend, using such approaches to definitions as those described in Chapter 6.

So, if your writing is to be correctly understood, it's important for readers to bring the same meanings to words as the meanings you have in mind. As illustrated in Chapter 6, accurate communication is more likely to occur if you clearly define for your readers the key terms you use than if you neglect to elucidate those terms. But apparently—for any of several reasons—writers often fail to clarify important words. Some authors of theses and dissertations apparently cannot imagine that there could be any question about what their expressions mean. Some authors may fear that the kind of reader to whom their writing is directed would feel insulted if they paused to define concepts. This is the fear that such readers would resent the author's adopting the condescending habit of "talking down" to them.

However, it is useful to recognize that two sorts of audiences—both the uninformed and the well-informed—appreciate precise definitions of critical words and phrases. Uninformed readers profit from a definition because they have no idea what the meaning of the term might be. In effect, the word or phrase is entirely new to them, so they need examples of how the author intends it. In contrast, well-informed readers have the opposite problem. They know multiple meanings that can be assigned to the term. What they need is an explanation of which of several potential meanings is the correct one for the present setting. So both types of readers can be well served by an explanation of terms, an explanation phrased in a fashion that both types can accept without feeling confused or patronized. To illustrate, consider the following explanation of two quite ordinary words—*education* and *religion*—that appeared at the beginning of a study of diverse modes of religious education around the world.

> Because there exists no universal agreement about the meaning of either religion or education, there is likewise no agreement about what constitutes the field of religious education. Therefore, at the outset of this study of religious education around the world, it is useful to recognize which meanings will be assigned to those two terms.
>
> Writers who conceptualize religion in a broadly inclusive way define it variously as "the collective expression of human values," as "the zealous and devout pursuit of any objective," or as "a system of values or preferences—an

inferential value system." Such definitions are so broad that they encompass not only the belief systems of Christianity, Islam, and Hinduism but also those of communism, democracy, logical positivism, and even anarchism.

Other writers place far greater limitations on the term *religion,* proposing that a conceptual scheme qualifying as religion must be an integrated system of specified components, including the nature of a supreme being or of gods (theology), the origin and condition of the universe (cosmology), rules governing human relations (ethics, moral values), the proper behavior of people toward superhuman powers (rites, rituals, worship), the nature of knowledge and its proper sources (epistemology), and the goal of life (teleology). Under this second sort of definition, Christianity, Islam, and Hinduism are religions but communism, democracy, logical positivism, and anarchism are not.

The second of these conceptions of religion seems to be the one intended by most people who write or speak about religious education, so it is the one adopted in the present study for identifying matters which rightly belong in the field of religious education.

Just as religion has been conceived in various ways by different writers, so has education. In its broadest sense, education can be equated with learning. And learning can be defined as "changes in mental process and overt behavior as a result of experience." However, in the following study, education is defined in a narrower sense to mean "the activity carried on by a society's institutions of systematic, planned instruction." Such a definition eliminates from consideration kinds of learning informally acquired during people's daily social life, as through their conversations in the family or through models of behavior offered by their companions. That definition eliminates as well learning acquired through the incidental use of libraries, book shops, newspapers, and recreational radio and television.

When the foregoing preferred definitions are combined, they identify the realm of religious education as that of "systematic, planned instruction in beliefs about the nature of the cosmos and of supernatural powers, about rites and worship, about personal moral values and the ethics of human relations, and about the meaning and goal of life." (Thomas, 1985, p. 4275)

Consider three devices the author used in the foregoing passage. First, he noted alternative definitions of each target term—*religion* and *education.* This device not only enables readers to recognize varied meanings, but also suggests that the author is well versed in his field of research. Second, the writer identified which of the alternative definitions would be used throughout the ensuing account. Third, he indicated how the chosen definition excludes from the study certain philosophical positions (communism, democracy, etc.) and sources of skill and knowledge (family conversations, libraries, etc.) that readers might otherwise include in their conceptions of religion and education.

*Preparing readers for what they will encounter*

Mystery novels and detective stories quite properly confront readers with sudden surprises. But such unanticipated events are seldom, if ever, desired features of research studies. Consumers of theses and dissertations are better served if continually informed about what to expect ahead.

You can satisfy your readers' need to know what to expect in your document if, at each stage of the narrative, you apply that oft-quoted, tripartite advice about how to structure a speech. First, you tell the audience what sort of matter you are going to explain. Next, you explain that matter in detail. Finally, at the end you summarize for the audience what you had explained.

We've adopted such an approach in this book. Our first chapter offered an overview of the volume's contents and organizational plan. Then each subsequent chapter opened with a description of what that chapter would include. Next, in the body of the chapter we provided the detailed description of the chapter's topics. Finally, at the end of the chapter when appropriate, the planning checklist served to summarize the topics that had been addressed in detail.

One way to determine whether your presentation has properly prepared readers for what they will meet is to ask a sample of readers if they were surprised at, or puzzled about, what they met at some place in your narrative. In effect, your presentation failed to prepare them properly if, at any point, they found themselves wondering, "What's this all about?" or "Why take up such a matter at this juncture?" or "How is this relevant?"

## A Few Details About the Mechanics of Writing

Perhaps you are well in control of all the mechanical aspects of producing your document. If so, you may wish to skip this section, which offers suggestions about a few details that usually warrant students' attention at the final stage of their project. Those details concern (a) the question of using first-person pronouns and contractions in your document, (b) typing the manuscript, and (c) editing and proofreading it.

*Personal pronouns and contractions*

Traditionally, students have not been allowed to use the pronouns *I, me,* or *we* in theses and dissertations. Their need to circumvent such direct self-references has led to a pair of stratagems intended to distance writers from what they have written. One ploy has been that of referring to one's self as "the present author" or "the writer" or "the investigator." Another has involved the grammatical device known as "third-person omniscient," implying that the author's statements are objective truths rather than personal opinions or interpretations. Here are four such distancing phrasings:

The evidence supported the proposition that . . .

The standards for evaluating the outcomes were as follows . . .

Research shows that . . .

One can reasonably conclude that . . .

However, in more recent times some faculty members have permitted—or even urged—students to use first-person pronouns, in the belief that doing so more accurately reflects the subjective judgments that enter into research efforts. Thus, occasionally we find theses and dissertations in which *I, me, we, us, mine,* and *our* appear. Consequently, it can be important for you to learn the opinions of your advisory committee about which personal-pronoun practices are acceptable in the final version of your own project.

As another tradition in writing style, contractions have not been permitted in theses and dissertations. Such colloquialisms as *doesn't, don't, can't, won't, they've, ain't,* and similar others are proscribed. The only acceptable forms are *does not, do not, cannot, will not, they have,* and *are not.* Unless your advisory committee directs otherwise, you are wise to avoid contractions, even though contractions are becoming more common in textbooks. As you've noticed, throughout this book we've used both first-person pronouns and contractions so as to lend the writing a conversational flavor.

*Typing the final version*

Three decades ago, nearly all final versions of theses and dissertations were produced on a typewriter. Today that is rarely the case. Nearly all are the result of a word-processing program in a computer. Because of the advantages of computers' ability to correct errors, check spelling automatically, and print multiple copies of professional-quality documents, more students produce their own final versions than was true in the past. But if you don't plan to produce the final manuscript yourself, you may find it useful to ask faculty members or your fellow graduate students how to find a first-rate word-processing person whom you can hire to do the job for you. By *first-rate* we mean someone who has had successful experience typing theses and dissertations, is not unduly expensive, and can be counted on to finish the task within the time period you specify.

If you are doing your own word processing, always back up each portion of your work on a disk that you keep in a different location than the place in which you have your computer. The halls of graduate schools are replete with horror stories about former students whose projects were the victims of fire, flood, loss, thievery, and the like when authors had not bothered to back up their work.

*Copyediting and proofreading*

Even if you are already a skilled writer, you may value the help of a copy editor who can identify weaknesses in your document—typographical errors, grammatical mistakes, the misplacement of topics, confusing explanations, undefined terms, infelicitous phrasings. Your faculty advisor or fellow graduate students can perhaps direct you to a skilled copy editor or proofreader. But you should recognize that not everyone who has majored in English will be an efficient copy editor.

Some students expect their advisor or members of their supervising committee to do the copyediting. However, most advisors and committee members are unwilling to take on that task, particularly if the manuscript needs multiple repairs. Faculty members' attention is most often dedicated toward correcting difficulties with the document's organization, the validity of its contents, and the author's line of reasoning rather than toward spelling errors and awkward syntax.

*Resources*

Further aid in producing a well-written thesis or dissertations is offered in

Glatthorn, A. (2005). *Writing the winning dissertation* (2nd ed.). Thousand Oaks, CA: Corwin Press.

Lester, J. D. (2004). *Writing research papers* (11th ed.). Glenview, IL: Scott Foresman.

Strunk, W., Jr., & White, E. B. (2006). *The elements of style* (4th ed.). New York: Macmillan.

Thiroux, E. (1999). *The critical edge: Thinking and researching in a virtual society.* Upper Saddle River, NJ: Prentice Hall.

Webster, W. G. (1998). *Developing and writing your thesis, dissertation or project.* San Ramon, CA: Academic Scholarwrite.

## Writing an Abstract

Students are typically required to include an abstract as part of the final version of their study. The abstract is expected to serve as a concise summary of the research project—its objectives, data-gathering methods, results, and perhaps a proposal about the significance and applications of the results. The maximum allowable length of abstracts is usually specified in the university's or department's guidebook for preparing theses and dissertations. The abstract is usually located at the beginning of the manuscript, where it provides readers a brief overview of the entire project.

Abstracts can have additional uses as well. They are available for publicizing a student's work in such resources as *Dissertation Abstracts International,* which acquaints readers around the world with descriptions of dissertation projects from leading higher-education institutions. And if you envision publishing your study in condensed form as an article in an academic journal or as a chapter in someone's compilation of studies related to your topic, the abstract furnishes the editor a preview of your work.

Here, then, is an example of an abstract from a PhD dissertation at the State University of New York, Stony Brook.

> Dissertation Title: The Political Economy of State Environmental Policy Innovations (1997)
>
> Author: Alka Kuldeep Sapat.
>
> Abstract: The major research goal of the dissertation is to explain variations in state environmental policy innovations and to analyze the importance of the American states as experimental policy laboratories for the federal government. Innovations research theory and studies of regulatory enforcement were fused together to develop a theoretical model explaining variations in the adoption of state innovations. Chapters 1–3 provide the introduction, a literature review, and a discussion of the theoretical framework of the dissertation. The next two chapters explore the relative influence of political institutions, industry and environmental interest groups, and economic factors on state adoption of hazardous waste and groundwater protection innovations; in doing so, a distinction is drawn between "consensual" and "conflictual" innovations. Data for the dissertation were drawn from secondary sources and from a survey of state administrators in environmental protection agencies. Event-history analysis was used to test the model of policy innovation. The results indicated that the ideology and capability of institutional actors were more important than the role of interest groups and the severity of the problem in both policy areas and for both "consensual" and "conflictual" innovations. The last part of the dissertation focuses on the vertical diffusion of policy innovations into the federal level and actors in this process. The policy ramifications of the study for devolution and state-federal relations are addressed in the conclusion. (Sapat, 1998, p. 308-A)

If you do, indeed, publish a version of your work as a journal article, you may be expected to preface the body of the work with an abstract. In this event, the abstract prepared for the journal will usually be shorter than the one you wrote for your thesis or dissertation. In other words, you will be writing an abstract of an abstract. Here is an example from the beginning of a journal article titled "Gender Stereotypes and Partner Preferences of Asian Women in Masculine and Feminine Cultures."

> A Japanese market research unit, Wacoal, has published a survey among single working women aged 20–30 years in Bangkok, Beijing, Hong Kong, Jakarta, Seoul, Singapore, Taipei, and Tokyo. Gender stereotypes as found in the Wacoal survey have been correlated with Masculinity Index scores from Hofstede's IBM studies. In the more masculine cultures [such as Japan], as compared to the more feminine ones [such as Thailand], *sense of responsibility, decisiveness, liveliness,* and *ambitiousness* were less often seen as feminine; caring and gentleness were more often seen as feminine. Meaningful correlations were also found for partner preferences (husbands compared to steady boyfriends). In the more masculine cultures, husbands should be more healthy, rich, and understanding; boyfriends should have more personality, affection, intelligence, and sense of humor. In the more feminine cultures, there was hardly any difference between preferred characteristics in husbands versus boyfriends. (Hofstede, 1996, p. 533)

## PLANNING CHECKLIST

As you prepare to compose the final version of your thesis or dissertation, you may find it useful to perform the following activities.

1. Obtain a copy of your college or university's regulations governing theses and dissertations. As you read the document, place a check mark in the margin beside each of the regulations that apply to your project.
   - On a calendar, write a reminder note on each date that represents a deadline for submitting material relating to your thesis or dissertation.

2. Discuss the following issues with your faculty advisor or other members of the committee that supervises your work on your project:
   - When you submit your work for the faculty member's evaluation, should you hand in each chapter as that chapter is completed, or should you wait until you have finished a complete draft before you submit any of your work?
   - For what sorts of errors or weaknesses in your document will that faculty member be willing to offer suggested improvements, and what sorts will be left to others (such as a copy editor or proofreader) to correct?
   - Will you be permitted to use such first-person pronouns as *I, me, my,* and *mine* throughout your document. Or should you refer to yourself solely by such phrases as "the present writer" or "the investigator" or "the author of this work"?

3. If you plan to have someone other than you yourself type the final version of your document, how do you intend to find that someone?

4. Experiment with outlining the structure of your thesis or dissertation from a reader's vantage point. First, generate in a random fashion the questions that you believe readers would want your document to answer. Then arrange the questions in a psychologically appealing sequence, identifying which questions represent separate chapters and which represent subsections within chapters.

FOURTEEN

# MOUNTING A PERSUASIVE DEFENSE

*"I've heard some very scary stories about professors demolishing candidates' dissertations during the final defense. How do I avoid that happening to me?"*

The usual ultimate step in the pursuit of a doctorate involves the candidate meeting with a panel of professors to defend the dissertation. Whether a master's degree thesis must also be defended orally depends on the policies of the institution the student attends.

It is not uncommon for the oral defense to be only the penultimate event—the next-to-last step—if the examining committee decides that improvements are needed in the student's product. In that case, the session with the candidate includes committee members specifying desired changes. Then the candidate's chief advisor or another member of the committee accepts responsibility for ensuring that the revisions are completed satisfactorily before the committee members affirm their approval by placing their signatures on the work.

Difficulties that may arise during the oral defense can often be foreseen, so that candidates who are aware of potential problems can be prepared ahead of time to wend their way safely through the minefield of professors' questions and suggestions. Thus, it is essential that, prior to the defense session, you confer with your advisor in order to prepare for questions, challenges, and criticisms that may arise during the session and to decide how you should respond to such possibilities.

The purpose of this chapter is to identify some of the more common problems and to propose ways of solving them. The style of presentation is the same as that of Chapter 9: Things That Go Wrong. In each of the following cases, a student describes worrisome incidents that may occur during the oral defense, and a faculty advisor suggests ways to cope with those incidents.

The seven cases concern (a) the validity of research findings, (b) a study's significance, (c) the candidate's proper role, (d) the advisor's proper role, (e) professors objecting to the student's research method, (f) committee member debates, and (g) inadequate proofreading.

## THE QUESTION OF VALIDITY

***Student:*** "Dr. Johnson looked over my research plan and said my study lacked validity. He says there's no way to validate people's expressed feelings about being Latin American immigrants. When I asked what kind of validity he wanted, he said I needed to do a study in which I could use predictive validity or concurrent validity or something of the kind. How can I defend my study as valid?"

***Advisor:*** "You can start by adopting a general definition of *validity,* then show how your study qualifies under that definition. Perhaps Dr. Johnson has a different definition, so what you are doing in your project may not meet his criteria. In that case, when you defend your work before the thesis committee, you can hope that the majority of the committee members—and maybe Dr. Johnson as well—will be persuaded by the way you argue your case. I'll suggest one approach you might try.

"You start with some such definition as this: 'Research is valid to the extent that its outcomes convincingly answer the questions on which the study has focused—including both the original questions and ones that may have emerged during the study.' This definition should encompass the kinds of validity that Dr. Johnson seems to have in mind as well as a kind you can offer for your study. You should realize that Dr. Johnson is a psychologist who works with tests. Psychologists typically say that a test is valid if it measures what it is supposed to measure. So, a test has *predictive validity* if it accurately prophesies some future outcome. For example, a college aptitude test is valid if it accurately predicts the grade-point-average students will have compiled by their senior year in college. Thus, the question answered by predictive validity is: How well does an evaluation of a phenomenon at an earlier time foretell the status of that phenomenon at a later time?

"*Concurrent validity* means that an assessment—as with a test or interview—correlates highly with a different sort of appraisal made during the same period of time. Therefore, a type of interview that leads to the same assessment of workers' abilities as that found in their on-the-job productivity can be considered to have high concurrent validity. In the case of both predictive and concurrent validity, statistical evidence—such as a correlation coefficient—is typically used to reflect the level of validity. The closer a coefficient approaches 1.00, the greater confidence one can place in predictive or concurrent validity. So a correlation of .85 is more convincing than one of .36 or .19.

"But many studies don't lend themselves to quantitative appraisals, so you need to depend on other means of convincing people that your results satisfactorily answer your research question. For instance, in writing history, you are obliged to furnish persuasive evidence and a line of logic to support your contention that the events you depict did, indeed, happen as you declare. This can involve your drawing from different descriptions of the same episodes to show consistencies among different witnesses' accounts, or it may include demonstrating how the varied motives of different narrators explain their conflicting interpretations of events.

"In your study of Latin American immigrants' attitudes, your problem is to present a compelling argument that their expressed attitudes are your respondents' true feelings. There are several ways to build your case. First, you can demonstrate that your methods of gathering information—your interview technique—did not cause the interviewees to give false answers, either inadvertently or intentionally. Inadvertent distortion could result from a respondent's not understanding the language adequately, so you need to show that the interviews were conducted in language that respondents could comprehend. And your immigrants could have intentionally falsified their answers if they thought you wanted them to report a particular kind of feeling, so they expressed such an attitude in order to please you. Or they may have feared that admitting to certain feelings would get them into trouble, so they feigned opinions that they thought would be more acceptable. Therefore, you need to convince readers of your dissertation that your data-gathering procedures were ones that would evoke respondents' authentic beliefs.

"Next, in your presentation of your interview results you can buttress your claim of validity in several ways. First, you can identify common themes that run through several respondents' tales, thereby suggesting that Latin American immigrants share certain attitudes in common because of their similar origins and their current status as immigrants. Second, when you find differences among respondents' expressed attitudes, you can hunt for reasonable explanations of those exceptions. Frequently the explanation will be reflected in the respondents' own phrasings, which you can quote in support of your interpretation. Third, you can compare your findings with ones in the professional literature to show how your results are in concert with other researchers' views.

"Some professors avoid debates about traditional experimental concepts of validity by adopting other terms—*verisimilitude, authenticity, trustworthiness, cogency, quality,* or *conviction*—to represent the truthfulness of research interpretations. For instance, consider this passage from Lee Shulman's discussion of such matters:

> Narrative modes [of research] are specific, local personal, and conceptualized. We do not speak of the validity of a narrative, but of its verisimilitude. Does it ring true? Is it a compelling and persuasive story? A good piece of physics [research] demonstrates its validity through meeting standards of prediction and control. A good work of tragedy demonstrates its verisimilitude by evoking in its audience feelings of pity and fear. (Shulman, 1992, p. 23)

"Then see in Glesne's book how she summarizes Cresswell's (1998) eight ways to foster the validity of qualitative studies:

1. Prolonged engagement and persistent observation [such as spending] extended time in the field so that you are able to develop trust, learn the culture, and check out your hunches.
2. Triangulation—use of multiple data-collection methods, multiple sources, multiple investigators, and/or multiple theoretical perspectives.
3. Peer review [that provides] external reflection and input on your work.
4. Negative case analysis [in the form of] conscious search for negative cases and unconfirming evidence so that you can refine your working hypotheses.
5. Clarification of researcher bias—reflection upon your own subjectivity and how you will use and monitor it in your research.
6. Member checking [in the form of] sharing interview transcripts, analytical thoughts, and/or drafts of the final report with research participants to make sure you are representing them and their ideas accurately.
7. Rich, thick description [in the form of] writing that allows the reader to enter the research context.
8. External audit, [having] an outside person examine the research process and product through 'auditing' your field notes, research journal, analytic coding scheme, etc. (Glesne, 1999, p. 32)

"If you want more about such matters, try these sources:

Bogdan, R., & Biklen, S. (2006). *Qualitative Research for Education* (5th ed.). Boston: Allyn & Bacon.
Creswell, J. (2006). *Qualitative Inquiry and Research Design.* Thousand Oaks, CA: Sage.
Lincoln, Y. S., & Guba, E. G. (1985). *Naturalistic Inquiry.* Beverly Hills, CA: Sage.
Maxwell, J. (2004). *Qualitative Research Design: An Interactive Approach.* Thousand Oaks, CA: Sage."

## THE QUESTION OF SIGNIFICANCE

***Student:*** "During lunch we were talking about the surprise Harry got during his oral exam. Professor Brown asked him, 'Now that you've done all this work, what does it mean?' Harry didn't know what to say. What should he have said?"

***Advisor:*** "Yes, that happens a lot. But don't fault the professor. It's a proper question. Your friend Harry seems to have been so busy with the details of his study that he hadn't come to a clear decision about the significance—or lack of significance—of what he's done.

"Here's one way to answer 'What does it mean?' First, you explain various kinds of meaning that can derive from—or be attributed to—a piece of research. Explaining various kinds shows you have a broad understanding of *meaning.* For example, meaning can be *causal,* providing a new or revised explanation of why events occurred as they did. Meaning can be *evaluative,* a test or appraisal of something. Meaning can assume the form of *practical application,* showing a better way—or at least an alternative way—to carry out some task. Meaning can portray *relationship* or *correspondence,* showing how one thing is similar to (compared) and different from (contrasted) another. Meaning can be *predictive,* indicating what future results can be expected from earlier conditions. So there are many kinds of meanings that you could mention.

"After recounting different meanings of 'meaning,' you can tell which of those you believe apply to your project, and then explain your kind in some detail. Therefore, to prepare yourself ahead of time for such a question, you can do a bit of roleplaying. Try explaining the meaning of your work to some of your fellow graduate students who assume the role of committee members trying to poke holes in your reasoning.

"But you shouldn't wait till the oral defense before you describe what your project means. That description should be part of the final chapter of the thesis itself."

## WHO'S IN CHARGE?

***Student:*** "In the oral exam, what can I expect to happen first?"

***Advisor:*** "You can't be sure, but usually the committee chairman will ask you to give a brief summary of the study—its purpose, the method used, and the outcome. The intent is to give you a chance to explain something that you are intimately acquainted with and, in doing so, you conquer your initial nervousness. But as you summarize, some committee members won't seem to be listening to you. They may be inspecting the copy of the dissertation you gave them. Don't let that upset you. There are several reasons that they may be inattentive. Those members who have already studied your work carefully don't need your summary, so they may be checking on specific passages in your document. Others who haven't studied your dissertation before coming to the meeting may be hurriedly trying to catch up with their homework. So if they seem distracted, just plow ahead as if everyone were enthralled with your summary."

***Student:*** "But that's so rude. Why couldn't I just stop and politely ask them to pay attention?"

***Advisor:*** "One of my advisees tried that, and it was nearly a disaster. You need to remember that you're not in charge. The professors are. You're at their mercy. My advisee had told the committee, 'I'm not going to continue until I have your attention.' So I asked her to step out of the room while I talked to the committee. I apologized to the committee members for the young woman's behavior and asked their forbearance. I then went into the hall and cautioned her not to treat the committee members as if they were recalcitrant fourth-graders but just to answer their questions as concisely as possible. When the meeting continued, the young woman obviously felt threatened by the frigid social atmosphere she had generated by admonishing the professors, so she didn't perform as well as she might have. Fortunately, the committee did approve her dissertation.

"But at the same time that you recognize that the professors are in charge, you should also recognize that—if you've done your job properly—you are now an expert in the matters on which your research focused. So you can defend your work with a measure of confidence and conviction, even in the face of objections raised by committee members."

## THE INTRUSIVE ADVISOR

***Student:*** "I'd like to ask your opinion about a problem I may face. I have the same thesis advisor as Ed Sturdlee. Ed told me that he was embarrassed during the defense of his thesis yesterday when his advisor interrupted by answering questions the committee members had directed at Ed. If that happens to me, how should I handle it?"

***Friendly Faculty Member:*** "Advisors are always anxious that their students perform well in the oral exam. But an advisor who isn't confident in the student's ability to handle the questions may feel compelled to do the answering. Committee members may openly object to such intrusions—and rightfully so. But that may damage the meeting's social climate. Advisors who are wise will apologize to the committee, or at least back off and not intrude again. You, as the candidate, should just keep quiet. Any intervention on your part would simply do greater harm."

## INSISTING ON A DIFFERENT APPROACH

***Student:*** "My friend Jennifer was shocked in her oral exam when one of the committee members told her that she had used the wrong investigative method in her study. That started a big argument between the professor and Jennifer's major advisor about whether she should pass. She did pass, but just barely. How can I avoid getting into such a fix?"

***Advisor:*** "I've seen that happen. Sometimes it's the fault of a faculty member who forgot what was agreed on early in the dissertation process when the committee had first met to review the proposed study. But there are ways to protect yourself. First, be sure that the committee members are all present during the earlier meeting when an agreement is reached about an acceptable research approach. If any members aren't present, be sure to inform them about the agreement reached during the meeting. Do this politely and in written form, not just orally. Then, as you complete a draft of each chapter of the dissertation, provide a copy to every committee member and include an invitation for them to respond to the contents of the chapter. Some may not want to see your work chapter-by-chapter, but put it in their mailboxes anyway so you will later have evidence that they had a chance early in the game to register complaints or suggest improvements."

***Student:*** "But what if they're off campus?"

***Advisor:*** "Send them each chapter by mail. Include a self-addressed stamped envelope in which they can send a reply. In effect, you do everything you can to make sure all committee members have a chance to express their opinions prior to the final defense."

***Student:*** "But what if somebody at the defense still says I've done it wrong."

***Advisor:*** "Then it's your major advisor's responsibility to diplomatically remind the critic of the initial agreement about your research method. The other committee members will support that position."

## PROFESSORIAL DEBATES

***Student:*** "I understand that sometimes the members of the committee get into arguments with each other during the student's oral defense. What can a student do about that?"

***Advisor:*** "Indeed, during the exam session it's not unusual for faculty members to argue about some point brought up during the defense. The best thing for the student to do is keep quiet and not interfere. Let the committee members talk to each other as much as they like. The consequences of such discussions—or arguments—can be either good or bad. From your viewpoint as the student, debates are good if they use up 20 or 30 minutes of the three-hour exam time that otherwise would be dedicated to grilling you. But debates aren't helpful if they use up time you need for defending your work. And arguments are bad if they drive faculty members into an ill temper that affects their judgments of whether you, the candidate, should pass. That danger is particularly acute when an argument is between your major advisor and a vindictive colleague who vents his or her antagonism against your mentor by attacking your project. Finally, here's some advice I give students as they prepare for their defense: 'Answer committee members' questions precisely and concisely, and then STOP. The more you ramble on—which can be a natural tendency in such a stressful situation—the more likely you will expose issues that can harm your case.'"

## PROPER PROOFREADING

***Student:*** "Mike Carmichael said his oral exam was aborted before it even got started. He said some faculty members were prejudiced against him at the outset. I don't want that to happen to me. Since you were on the committee, could you explain what happened?"

***Advisor:*** "Remember the old adage, 'Haste makes waste'? Your friend Carmichael had multiple copies of his dissertation printed and placed in the committee members' mailboxes before his major professor had read the final version. As a result, the document was in pretty rough shape when we got it. What it needed was careful proofreading and correction before it was ever distributed. So, when the meeting opened, two of the members said they didn't want to waste their time dealing with such a flawed product. I agreed. If Carmichael couldn't even bother to get the mechanics of the dissertation straightened out, how could we trust the way he'd conducted the other phases of his project?

"Students sometimes feel that they need not pay attention to such mundane matters as spelling, grammar, and format, because they consider their basic ideas so valuable. They see themselves as so talented that they shouldn't be expected to waste their time on minor details. But faculty members, whose business is that of fostering responsible scholarship, don't see it that way. So, get your thesis in the best condition possible before it goes to the examining committee. And be sure your major advisor has plenty of time to inspect and correct your work prior to the defense."

FIFTEEN

# REACHING A WIDER AUDIENCE

*"I'd really like to publish my study someplace, maybe as a journal article or even on the World Wide Web. How should I go about it?"*

Graduate students often wish to have their research issued in a form that reaches a larger audience than does the typical thesis or dissertation. The purpose of this chapter is to identify eight potential publishing outlets for fulfilling that wish.

## A VARIETY OF PUBLISHING OPPORTUNITIES

The types of outlets reviewed in the following pages include conference presentations, academic journals, popular periodicals, books, chapters in books, taped and broadcast presentations, Internet publishing, and researcher-created print publications. The types are described in relation to nine variables—the length of the research report, the intended audience, the likely breadth of dissemination, the probability that the report will be accepted for publication, the time lapse before publication, the author's contribution, the publisher's contribution, the extent of author control over the publication's final form, and the extent of control wielded by the publisher.

## Conference Presentations

In many institutions, graduate students have opportunities to describe their research in seminars or colloquia attended by their peers and faculty members. However, they can reach a far larger audience when they present their findings at conferences of such academic and professional organizations as the American Educational Research Association, the Comparative and International Education Society, the American Psychological Association, and the like.

The presentation format at such events can be of various kinds—lectures, panels organized around themes, debates, question-answer sessions, poster displays, and open discussions. The poster presentation is a relatively recent innovation that consists of researchers being assigned positions in a room or hallway where each one displays key elements of her or his work and discusses the work with whatever interested individuals choose to stop by. The size of the audience reached by a presentation depends on several factors—the number of people attending the conference, the reputation of the presenter, the popularity of the topic being discussed, the time of day, and the number of parallel sessions going on at the same time so that the total audience is divided among multiple sessions. Because of such conditions, the number of people reached by a presentation can vary from more than a thousand to only two or three.

The length of time allotted to a speaker at a conference can vary from five minutes to an hour or so, depending on the eminence of the position the researcher enjoys in the field of interest and on the number of presentations the conference organizers have chosen to include. A speaker with a distinguished reputation or a breakthrough discovery will be assigned more time than will a graduate student or assistant professor who is reporting on a sound but hardly startling research effort. Fifteen minutes is a rather typical length of time allowed each presenter, thereby providing the opportunity to describe no more than the highlights of the research method and results.

The chance of having a research paper accepted for delivery at a conference is usually far greater than having it accepted for publication in a journal or as a chapter in a book. Conference planning committees, compared to journal and book editors, are typically more lenient in the standards they apply in judging submissions, and competition for having a paper accepted for a conference is usually less than for a journal. Frequently the opportunity to present a paper is limited to members of the organization that sponsors the conference.

There is usually little or no time lag between a researcher completing a research report and presenting it at a conference.

### Academic Journals

Authors of theses and dissertations frequently prepare a short version of their research report for submission to an academic journal. The world's academic journals number in the thousands. They can be issued monthly, bimonthly, quarterly, semiannually, or annually. The most common publication schedule is perhaps quarterly. Each journal accepts articles in a defined realm of interest that may be quite narrow. The journal's subject-matter focus can be

An academic discipline—*American Anthropologist, Comparative Education Review Journal of Cross Cultural Psychology, Journal of Economic Behavior and Organization, Social Forces*

A region—*Journal of Asian and African Studies, European Sociological Review, The Middle East Journal, Australian Journal of Language and Literacy, Georgia Historical Society*

A sociogeographic entity—*Education and Urban Society*

A professional specialization—*Journal of Correctional Education, Journal of the Association for the Severely Handicapped, The American Music Teacher*

An ethnic group—*American Indian Culture and Research Journal, Bulletin of Hispanic Studies, Journal of Black Studies, Journal of Japanese Studies*

A gender category—*Women's Studies Quarterly, Women's Rights Law Reporter*

A religious denomination—*Lutheran Theological Journal, Journal of Jewish Communal Services, Muslim Education Quarterly, U.S. Catholic*

The size and kind of a journal's reading audience are influenced by several factors—the publication's subject-matter focus, its reputation, its cost, how widely it's advertised, and whether it's issued by a professional society or association. Whenever a journal is a key publication of a professional group or scholarly society, everyone belonging to the society usually receives the journal as a right of membership. Thus, the larger the membership in the society, the larger the guaranteed reading audience. However, many other journals—not published by a society or not automatically distributed to a society's members—must depend solely on paid subscriptions for their distribution. Because subscription prices are frequently high, individuals often avoid buying the journals and depend, instead, on using copies in a college or university library. However, in recent years, as library funds have diminished, many libraries have eliminated subscriptions to journals that are seldom read or are especially expensive, so the reading audience for such publications has dwindled.

Journals can differ dramatically in the proportion of submitted articles they ultimately publish. The most prestigious and popular journals may accept as few as 15% or 20% of the papers they receive. In contrast, journals of substantially lower status or with a small potential audience may publish 80% or more of the submitted items. Journal editors usually maintain strong control over the form, topics, and scholarly quality of the articles they accept so that authors are obliged to abide strictly by journal editors' standards and preferences. Consequently, authors enjoy far less freedom and control over articles in journals than they do over conference presentations, researcher-produced publications, microfiche content, and—in many cases—book manuscripts.

The types of articles and their acceptable length can vary considerably from one journal to another. Some publications limit entries to ten printed pages or less. Others accept reports as long as 40 or 50 pages. Occasionally a lengthy work will be considered of such import that the editors will dedicate an entire issue of the journal to the report. Frequently the periodical's policy regarding length is described on the journal's inside cover (front or rear) in a notice to potential contributors. For example, a message in *Child Development* (the key publication of the Society for the Study of Child Development) informs readers that

> Empirical articles comprise the major portion of the journal. To be accepted, empirical articles must be judged as being high in scientific quality, contributing to the empirical base of child development, and having important theoretical, practical, or interdisciplinary implications. Reports of multiple studies, methods, or settings are encouraged, but single-study reports are also considered. Empirical articles will thus vary considerably in length (approximately 8 to 40 manuscript pages; text and graphics should be as concise as material permits. All modes of empirical research are welcome. (Notice to contributors, 2006).

The time lag between an author's submitting a paper to a journal and the paper's actually appearing in print can differ significantly from one journal to another. The time lapse can be affected by several conditions—the number of steps in the publishing process, the efficiency of the journal's personnel, the number of submissions the journal receives, the backlog of accepted papers, the frequency with which the journal is issued, and the number of pages in each issue of the journal.

An increasing number of journals provide a service that "enables authors to track their article—once it has been accepted—through the production process to publication online and in print" (Notice to contributors, 2006).

The publishing process for some journals is quite simple. A single editor takes responsibility for deciding which papers to publish, the editor makes few if any changes in the accepted manuscripts, the author submits a revised copy (if changes have been required), the author's typescript is photocopied instead of being newly set in type, the editor places the current issue's articles in a desired sequence, and that issue is printed.

However, for many journals, the publishing process is far more complex. If many articles are submitted during the same period of time, they may rest idly on some busy editor's desk until he or she gets to them. This is likely to occur when editors bear their editorial duties as a sideline, with their principal occupation being that of a college professor, therapist, business executive, government employee, or the like. After one or more editors in the journal's office briefly review a submitted paper, it's mailed to three or four evaluators—known as *referees, reviewers,* or *readers*—who are considered to be experts in the paper's subject matter. The referees are asked to evaluate the paper for the significance of its contribution to knowledge, the quality of its research, and its form of presentation. This procedure may take from one month to four or five months or more, depending on the efficiency and diligence of the referees. When the reviewers' judgments have all been received in the editorial office, the editors may find that the referees have disagreed about the quality of the paper. In this event, the paper may be sent to further reviewers for their opinions. Finally, when all reviews have been received, an editor—or group of editors—may decide to reject the submission, so they inform the author that the item has been judged unsuitable for the journal, and they may include the reviewers' comments about the piece (with the reviewers' names omitted from the page of comments). Frequently a paper will be accepted on the condition that specified improvements are made in its content or style. The author is informed of what needs to be done, so there is an additional time lapse while the author makes the changes and submits the revised document, which is once again inspected by one or more editors. If they decide the piece is now satisfactory, they schedule it for publication. But if further changes are required, the paper is returned to the author for additional work. After being deemed acceptable, the article is placed in line for publication. For a journal that is published quarterly, that publication date could be as early as six months from the time the final version has been approved or as late as three years after the final approval. Some journals inform potential contributors of the time lag to be expected.

Some journals don't accept unsolicited manuscripts but use only material from authors who have been invited to prepare articles on special themes.

Journals are not all alike in their policies regarding the costs that authors are expected to bear and the payments authors may receive. Most journals neither charge authors anything for publishing their articles nor pay authors for their work. However, some require that authors contribute to the expense of publication (usually a given amount per printed page), whereas others pay writers a nominal sum for articles. Authors usually receive two or three free copies of the issue of the journal in which their paper appears, and they may also be sent 25 or more offprints of their article.

### Popular Periodicals

The term *popular periodicals* in the present context refers to magazines, newspapers, and newsletters read by the general public. Contributions to periodicals may be submitted on an author's own initiative, at the suggestion of an author's literary agent, or at the invitation of the periodical's editors.

Compared with journal articles, versions of research studies published in the public press are usually briefer, contain few if any technical terms, limit statistics to percentages and averages, include illustrative examples familiar to a lay audience, and may suggest applications of the research results to everyday life. Authors of such works are often paid for their contributions, except in the case of letters to the editor of a magazine or newspaper.

Magazine editors usually maintain greater control over the focus and style of articles than do newspaper editors. The editing of material for a newspaper may be limited to simplifying complex sentences and shortening the piece to fit the available space.

A significant advantage of popular periodicals over the typical journal is that they reach far more readers. Whereas a journal may have only 1,000 or 1,500 subscribers, the Sunday edition of a major newspaper ends up in hundreds of thousands of homes.

### Books

For the purpose of the following discussion, books can be divided into two types—trade and academic. Trade books are intended for the general reading public and are available in regular bookstores and public libraries. Academic books are intended for such specialized audiences as students and faculty members in colleges and universities, teachers and administrators in elementary and secondary schools, physicians, social workers, therapists, engineers, industrialists, architects, lawyers, and the like. Academic books are found in the libraries of higher-education institutions, in college and university bookstores, and in academic publishers' catalogs.

Although most educational research is best suited for publication in academic books, a small proportion may appeal to the general public and thus qualify for the trade market. Some books can be successfully distributed through both general and specialized channels.

The procedure for offering manuscripts to publishers can be different for trade than for academic books. Particularly in the case of popular trade fiction, such as detective stories and romance novels, publishers are not likely to accept submissions directly from authors. It thus becomes necessary for an author to hire a literary agent to provide the initial screening of a manuscript. The agent first reviews the author's manuscript, estimates its potential, and advises the author about changes needed. Only then will the agent seek out a publisher who is willing to consider the manuscript. But in the case of academic publishing, an agent is unnecessary. Publishers of scholarly works are usually willing to receive submissions directly from authors. However, an author's manuscript may receive more serious and prompt attention if someone of respected stature in academia recommends the work to the editors.

Publishers can differ markedly in the amount of control they seek to wield over the content, structure, and format of the books they issue. For example, at the *least-control* end of the responsibility scale are publishers who conduct what are essentially *printing and distribution services.* In other words, they leave decisions about the subject-matter content, structure, and writing style entirely in the hands of authors. The responsibility of such publishing houses is thus limited to ensuring that the final printed book is free from typographical errors, bound attractively, and advertised to potential readers. In contrast, publishers at the *most-control* end of the scale conceive their responsibility to include verifying and—if judged necessary—changing the technical content of the work, revising the structure (altering the sequence of chapters, moving paragraphs, eliminating portions), altering the writing style (changing phrasing and vocabulary), determining the book's type font and format, binding the work, and marketing the finished product. Some publishers adjust their degree of control to the characteristics of the author and the submitted manuscript. The work of a prestigious, highly influential researcher is less likely to be altered than is that of an unknown neophyte, such as a recent MA or PhD graduate. A brilliantly crafted manuscript can pass through the editorial process unscathed, whereas a carelessly written document can be subjected to major editorial changes.

The monetary agreement between publisher and author can differ from one publishing house to another. The most common arrangement is for the publisher to pay nearly all production costs (except preparing illustrations) and to pay the author a royalty on each copy of the book that is sold. The amount of the royalty can be influenced by the size of the book's probable market, the reputation of the author, and the bargaining skill of the author or the author's agent. Here are examples of typical clauses regarding royalties as they appeared in the contracts offered to an author by two publishers of academic books.

> *First Publisher:* In the case of a regular clothbound edition of the book sold in the United States and its territories and dependencies, on the net price of the work (actual cash received), the author will receive a total royalty of 8% of the net price for all copies sold to 1,000 copies sold; 10% of the net price for all copies sold from 1,001 to 2,000 copies sold; and 12% of the net price for all copies sold in excess of 2,000 copies sold. One-half of the foregoing royalties will be paid on all sales made outside the United States and its dependencies and territories.

> *Second Publisher:* The publisher shall pay to the author in respect of its sales of the work a royalty calculated as follows: 10% of all income received on sales worldwide.

If a book appears to have the potential for greater sales, the publisher's royalty offer may be 12% on the first 1,000 or 1,500 copies sold and 15% on sales beyond that figure. But royalties higher than 15% are extremely rare for academic publications these days (though more common in the distant past), unless the author or agent can argue an unusually strong case.

For authors, publishing academic research is seldom a reasonable money-making venture. Only when a work is adopted widely as a textbook will it sell in the thousands. Rarely would a thesis or dissertation qualify as a text, so that a book based on a graduate student's research would be purchased chiefly by university libraries rather than by individual readers, making sales total no more than a few hundred copies over the life of the work. Hence, the most rational motives authors have for publishing research projects in book form are to gain prestige, to enjoy a sense of accomplishment, and to make a contribution to knowledge—but not to become rich.

The time lag between the initial submission of the manuscript and the eventual publication of the book can vary between eight or ten months and three or four years, with the average perhaps about 12 to 16 months. Among the conditions that affect this length of time are the number of manuscripts being reviewed by the publisher, the efficiency of editorial personnel at the publishing house, the quantity of revisions the author is required to make, how soon the author submits the revisions, delays in receiving permission to quote copyrighted passages from other books, and the backlog of edited manuscripts waiting to be printed.

## Chapters in Books

Short versions of theses or dissertations may be published in an edited book, with each summarized thesis or dissertation forming a separate chapter. The contributors to such collections receive the opportunity to have their chapter included in the collection by one of three means.

First, a person who is editing a volume on a particular topic selects the authors who will be asked to submit chapters for the volume. Such was the case with *Cultural Literacy and the Idea of General Education*—13 chapters (Westbury & Purves, 1988), *Curriculum Development in East Asia*—12 chapters (Marsh & Morris, 1991), and *Quality in Education*—38 chapters (Watson, Modgil, & Modgil, 1997).

Second, an editor selects a variety of already-published journal articles or excerpts from books to be reissued as chapters of a book. The result can be such volumes as *The Human Encounter: Readings in Education* (Stoff & Schwartzberg, 1969) and *Improving Instruction with Microcomputers* (Tashner, 1984).

Third, papers presented at a conference comprise a book's contents. Examples of volumes published from selected papers at three conferences of the Comparative and International Education Society's western region are *Human Rights and Education*—13 chapters (Tarrow, 1987), *Education's Role in National Development Plans*—12 chapters (Thomas, 1992), and *Education in the Urban Context*—12 chapters (Stromquist, 1994).

Editors of collections can vary considerably in the amount of control they seek to exert over the content and quality of contributors' chapters. Some editors publish the offerings without change, except for correcting spelling and grammar errors. Other editors return offerings to the authors with directions for substantial changes, or else an editor may choose to thoroughly rewrite submissions. Because the quality of chapters submitted for an edited volume frequently varies markedly from one author to another, an editor may accept certain manuscripts in their initial form while revising others in minor or major ways.

Authors usually receive a free copy of the volume in which their chapter appears but they are seldom paid for their work.

## Taped and Broadcast Presentations

At an increasing pace, reports of research projects recorded on audiotapes and videotapes are being broadcast over radio and television or presented directly to such on-site audiences as students in classrooms and participants attending professional conferences. In addition, the Internet and the World Wide Web are being adopted as media for disseminating research results.

Taped presentations can be produced by researchers themselves or by others, such as radio or television news reporters, talk-show personnel, and the like.

Researchers maintain the greatest control over the content and quality of tape-recorded reports when they create tapes themselves. Audiotapes are the simpler kind to produce, since they require a minimum of equipment, and program participants' comments can be recorded in nearly any quiet location. In contrast, videotapes require more elaborate equipment and proper visual settings in which to record program content. However, the extra bother that videotapes entail is compensated for by their ability to visually portray the episodes and people who are the objects of the research. Videotapes also permit the inclusion of information in cartoon, graph, map, or tabular form. Researcher-created tapes are more often used for classroom instruction and for conference presentations than for radio and television broadcasts, thereby enabling their creators to maintain greater control over the timing of their presentation. Unless the production of such tapes is financed by a research grant or an institution, the cost of the work must be borne by the investigators themselves.

Taped and live radio and television broadcasts produced by people other than researchers themselves are in the form of news spots, talk-show appearances, and special programs. A news spot is a brief segment within a half-hour or one-hour general program of current events, with the segment featuring a report of the principal conclusions of a project bearing on a topic of interest to the general public. A talk-show appearance consists of the researcher being interviewed during a half-hour program by the show's host. The program may include questions and comments by members of a studio audience or by listeners who phone in their opinions. Special programs are usually taped productions treating a research topic of public interest, with the program dedicated either to the work of a single scholar or to the findings of a variety of investigators who have studied that topic.

## Internet Publishing

The worldwide computer network consists of millions of websites or web *hosts* (information servers that connect to the network). As noted in Chapter 2, by 2007 there were 106 million hosts (half of them currently active) and over one billion *users* (consumers who are connected to the network). During 2006, 30.9 million sites were added to the total, surpassing the previous one-year record gain of 17.5 million sites in 2005. Thus, there were sites in over 140 nations from which Internet users could obtain information, simply by accessing the sources via a personal computer at home or in the office (Netcraft, 2006).

The rapid growth of the Internet and the subsequent World Wide Web has provided a new outlet for research reports, an outlet bound to expand at a fast pace in the near future as the amount of research continues to accelerate at the same time that traditional outlets (journals, printed books) have become so expensive to maintain that scholars face diminishing opportunities for getting their work into print and widely *disseminated.* There are numbers of ways to publish on the World Wide Web.

For newcomers to web publishing, a good place to start in understanding the vocabulary and elements of web pages is the website called *Learn the Net: Web Publishing* at the following World Wide Web address: www.learnthenet.com/english/section/webpubl.html.

The simplest way to disseminate a short version of your thesis or dissertation is by e-mail (electronic mail), which operates in much the same fashion as postal mail, except that messages are delivered over the computer network rather than by a mail carrier. An author, seated at a computer, transmits the research report either to (a) particular readers at their network addresses (with the names and e-mail addresses of people interested in the researcher's topic obtained from mailing lists available on the Internet) or to (b) one or more of the thousands of special interest groups found on the Internet, with appropriate interest groups identified and reached by means of such a web service as USENET (*users' network*). The service accepts information an author assigns to an electronic bulletin board intended for a particular type of audience. A thesis or dissertation abstract placed on the bulletin board or sent to a mailing list might reach millions of people. Each bulletin board or news-group has a name, and anyone interested in the topics under that name can visit the site.

A second publishing option involves transmitting your manuscript via the Internet to one of the hundreds of electronic journals and magazines that issue their products solely on the Internet, such as *Educational Policy Analysis Archives, Journal of American Indian Education, Current Research in Social Psychology, Post Modern Culture, Sociological Research Online, The International Electronic Journal for Leadership in Learning,* and *The World Wide Web Journal of Biology.*

With the costs of print publishing rising and the number of subscribers to many scholarly journals declining, traditional journals increasingly experience financial difficulties. Thus, a growing number are turning to electronic publishing as a solution to their money problems. University libraries are usually equipped to furnish an author the names of electronic periodicals suitable for publishing the particular thesis or dissertation—or a condensed version of it—that the author wants to distribute.

A third alternative is that of creating your own web page where you can post a report of your research. The task of devising a website can be performed rather easily by the use of such software packages as Dream Weaver, NetObjects Fusion, and Netscape Composer. The nature of such software is illustrated in the description of Netscape Composer posted on that product's website.

> Many of the pages you see when you browse the web were made by ordinary people like you. You don't have to be a computer whiz—you can use Netscape Composer, part of Netscape Communicator, to create, edit, and publish your own web pages.
>
> Composer helps you create and edit your own web pages and place (or "post") them on the web. Composer looks and acts like a word processing program, and is just as easy to use. Behind the scenes of each page on the web is code called HTML, which stands for Hypertext Markup Language. This name means that HTML is the computer language used for marking up documents with links in them. The code, called HTML source code, tells the web browser how a page should look and act.
>
> You don't need to know how to write HTML code to make a web page. Composer enables you to work in a WYSIWYG (what you see is what you get) environment—just like a word processor—and it automatically generates the HTML code you need to make your page do what you want it to do.
>
> The basic elements of a web page are text, pictures, and links. You can put all of these and more on your own pages, and then publish those pages on the web. (Building web pages, 2006)

A further available option is to have your thesis or dissertation published as an *e-book* (electronic book) that is posted on the Internet. Today there are publishing services which, for a fee, will issue your book to customers who purchase it in electronic form so it can be read on a customer's computer screen. Examples of such publishers whose websites can be found on the World Wide Web are *Online Originals, E-Book Time, iuniverse,* and *eBook Crossroads.*

Electronic publishing has a number of advantages over print media. First, it delivers the finished product to readers far more quickly than does print publishing. With books and journals, a year or two can elapse between the time a completed manuscript is submitted to editors and the time the work is finally in print. With electronic publishing, there is little or no wait between when the author puts the report on the network and it becomes available to readers. Furthermore, electronic publishing eliminates problems of distance. The World Wide Web now reaches virtually all parts of the world in which computers are available, so readers anywhere can receive the researcher's report as soon as it appears. Whereas traditional journals and books cannot be conveniently altered once they are in print, materials on the Web can be revised at any time—corrected, lengthened, updated. Publishing over the network also enables an author to receive rapid feedback from readers who send their comments to the author by e-mail. Documents placed on the Internet (with the World Wide Web as the *server* or intermediary) can include full color illustrations to accompany the text and motion pictures—features that are expensive in print media but are included at little cost on the Web. Finally, in Internet publishing, the author maintains complete control over the form of the report, since no editors are involved, except in the case of formal Internet journals and books that must pass through the editorial process before being issued on the Internet. However, a disadvantage of shortcutting the editorial process is that the author then lacks the professional aid with the writing style and the elimination of errors that editors usually provide.

### Researcher-Created Print Publications

The advent of the personal computer in the 1980s equipped researchers—at home or in the office—to produce high-quality printed reports of their studies. This movement is popularly referred to as *desktop publishing.* With no more than an up-to-date word-processing program, an author can create book or journal pages that appear to be professionally typeset. This means that the author, rather than the editors in a publishing house, maintains complete control over the format and quality of the final product. Furthermore, if a photocopy machine is available, the researcher can print quantities of the report.

However, there are several important disadvantages to self-published books and articles. A professional publishing facility provides copy editors and proofreaders who assume responsibility for ensuring that a manuscript's structure, grammar, syntax, and spelling are accurate. But in the case of researcher-produced publications, authors themselves must perform the laborious editing tasks and accept the blame for errors in the final product. And although authors can easily do the typesetting, few have the equipment and skill needed to bind a book or periodical proficiently. Thus, the task of binding must be contracted out to professionals, with the author paying the cost that would be borne by the publisher if the book or article were issued by a publishing house.

Then there is the problem of how to disseminate the finished work to a suitable audience. This is one of the most important functions of publishing firms. They typically operate a sophisticated marketing system, complete with specialists in writing advertising copy, providing lists of libraries and members of professional societies who are potential buyers, shipping books to booksellers, displaying books in booths at conferences, and delivering books and journals to customers. In the case of self-produced reports, authors are obliged to either market the reports themselves or contract out the distribution tasks to an organization that provides such service.

Whether books, audiotapes, videotapes, and other materials are issued by a publisher or by researchers themselves, authors can seek to enhance the dissemination of their works in several ways—presentations at conferences, announcements in newsletters and journals of professional societies, articles in newspapers and popular magazines, and appearances on radio and television talk shows. For authors who do not wish to spend the time and bother that such advertising efforts require, issuing their work through a professional publisher is likely a better method than desktop publishing for ensuring that their reports reach a wide audience.

## FURTHER GUIDES TO PUBLISHING

The following resources offer additional information about where and how to publish research studies.

Derricourt, R. M. (1996). *An author's guide to scholarly publishing.* Princeton, NJ: Princeton University Press.

Farber, J. (2006). *Millionaire's guide to e-book publishing.* Raleigh, NC: Lulu.

Glatthorn, A. (2002). *Publish or perish: Strategies for writing effectively for your profession and your school.* Thousand Oaks, CA: Corwin Press.

Henson, K. T. (1995). *The art of writing for publication.* Needham Heights, MA: Allyn & Bacon.

Moxley, J. M., & Taylor, T. (Eds.). (1997). *Writing and publishing for academic authors.* Lanham, MD: Rowman & Littlefield.

Thomas, R. M. (1998). *Conducting educational research—A comparative view* (Chapters 14 and 15). Westport, CT: Bergin & Garvey.

Zinsser, W. (2001). *On writing well: The classic guide to writing nonfiction.* New York: Collins.

## PLANNING CHECKLIST

If you hope to have your thesis or dissertation—or a brief version of it—disseminated in a form that reaches an audience beyond your supervising committee, you may wish to inspect the following summary of publishing outlets and place a check mark in front of each one that you regard as a feasible option.

Which one or more modes of disseminating your research report might you wish to use?

_____ 1. Conference presentation

(Name one or more conferences that would be suitable occasions for presenting the report.)

_____ 2. Academic journal article

(Name journals that would seem to be suitable outlets for the report.)

_____ 3. Article in a popular periodical

(Name magazines, newspapers, or newsletters that would seem to be suitable outlets for the study.)

_____ 4. Book

____ 4.1 Academic publication

____ 4.2 Trade publication

(Name firms that would seem to be suitable publishers for such a study.)

_____ 5. Chapter in someone else's book

(Suggest how the opportunity to publish the study as a chapter might be sought.)

_____ 6. Taped or broadcast presentation

____ 6.1 Audiotape—researcher produced

____ 6.2 Videotape—researcher produced

____ 6.3 Radio broadcast

____ 6.3.1 News spot

____ 6.3.2 Talk-show interview

____ 6.3.3 Special program

____ 6.4 Television broadcast

____ 6.4.1 News spot

____ 6.4.2 Talk-show interview

____ 6.4.3 Special program

*(Continued)*

(Continued)

_____ 7. Computer network entry—the Internet

_____ 8. Researcher-created publication

____ 8.1 Pamphlet

____ 8.2 Book

____ 8.3 Other (specify)________________________________

# APPENDIX: OUTLINE OF A DISSERTATION PROPOSAL

Title: *The Effects of Financial Stress in Higher Education*

Author: Robin Ganzert, University of North Carolina at Greensboro[1]

1. *Introduction*

   1.1 The financial function of an institution of higher education serves as a vital factor in the institution's long-term viability and success. The issue of financial stress in higher education is important for administrators to address, preferably in a proactive stance prior to crisis rather than as a reaction to a specific financial crisis. The importance and timeliness of this subject is apparent in reading almost any isssue of the CHRONICLE OF HIGHER EDUCATION.

2. *Statement of the Problem*

   2.1 The problem that will be addressed in this study is the determination of the patterns and processes used to address financial crisis in institutions of higher education. The study will explore the sources of financial stress, and the responses to financial stress during times of financial crisis.

3. *Definition of key terms*

   3.1 Financial stress is defined as an influence which disrupts or distresses the financial function in the institution's operations.

[1]The authors gratefully acknowledge Robin Ganzert's permission to publish her outline.

3.2 Environmental scanning is defined as the identification of environmental factors and the importance of those factors to the institution.

4. *Research Questions*

4.1 What are the major sources of current financial stress in institutions of higher education today?

4.2 What are the responses of the institutions to financial stress?

4.3 How are the core functions (academic, marketing and admissions) affected by the financial stress?

4.4 Where are the financial stresses evident (e.g., the endowment funds, operating funds or the plant funds)?

4.5 How is the response to the financial stress reflected in the annual budgeting parameters or guidelines?

4.6 What is the institutional strategic planning response to financial stress in higher education?

4.7 What are the patterns of information flow used to solve financial crisis situations?

4.8 What are the roles of the president, chief academic officer and chief financial officer in times of financial crisis at institutions?

4.9 How do the decision-making processes regarding financial crisis affect the culture of the institution?

5. *Study Methodology (Two Related Methods)*

5.1 Multiple case studies

5.1.1 Five sites

5.1.2 Interviews of Presidents, CAOs and CFOs

5.1.3 Focus on contemporary events, no control over behavioral events by researcher

5.2 Descriptive survey

5.2.1 Survey driven by case interviews

5.2.2 Stratified business officers

5.2.3 Piloted with regional senior finance experts

6. *Case Study Sites: Selection Criteria Matrix*

| *Institution* | *Type* | *Major Financial Stress Criteria* | *Unique Characteristic* |
|---|---|---|---|
| University A | Public, government supported | Deficit of $36 million | New rector addressing structural changes |
| University B | Public | Elimination of academic programs and majors | Faculty attack on university administration's autocratic style |
| University C | Private, religious | Elimination of staff positions | New president addresses revenue structure |
| University D | Private, non-denominational | Hiring freeze, small faculty pay increase | Faculty and students relate stress to increased technology support |
| University E | Public, historically Black institution | Continued problems with operating funds and deficits | Continued restructuring of administration |

7. *Review of Related Literature (Key Indicators or Headings)*
   7.1 Sources of financial stress
   7.2 Trends in response to financial stress
   7.3 Proactive strategies for response to financial stress
   7.4 The statesman role and the fiscal administrator
   7.5 An historical examination of financial stress in higher education
   7.6 Timeline of financial stress in higher education
   7.7 Implications of financial stress in higher education for the year 2000 and beyond
   7.8 The financial stressors in the modern curriculum

| Tests | Case Study Tactic | Phase of Research in Which Tactic Occurs |
|---|---|---|
| Construct validity | 1. Multiple sources of evidence with interviews, reports, memos, etc. at single institutions | Data collection |
| | 2. Chain of evidence with sources across institutions | Data collection |
| | 3. Key informants will review drafts | Composition of report |
| Internal validity | 1. Pattern matching within and across institutions | Data analysis |
| | 2. Explanation building | Data analysis |
| External validity | 1. Replication of questions with multiple cases | Research design |
| Reliability | 1. Case study protocol | Data collection |
| | 2. Case study protocol | Data collection |

8. *Tests of Research Design*

9. *Triangulation of Evidence*

   9.1 Public documents/reports (newspapers, financial statements)

   9.2 Internal documents

   9.3 Administrator interviews

10. *Case Study Protocol*

    10.1 Opening interview question: "What are your experiences with financial stress at your institution?"

10.2 Possible follow-up research questions:

"What is the major source of financial stress at your institution?"

"How did your institution respond to the financial stress?"

"How are the admissions and academic programs affected by the financial stress?"

"Where are the financial stresses evident at your institution (e.g., what fund)?"

"How is your institution's response to financial stress reflected in the annual budgeting parameters?"

"What is the strategic planning response to financial stress on your campus?"

"How does information flow during times of financial stress?"

"Any additional comments?"

10.3 Pilot case study at selected institution

11. *Survey*

11.1 Survey questions developed in interviews

11.2 Piloted by a panel of experts

11.3 Stratified sample of chief financial officers

12. *Conclusion*

12.1 The study will provide insights into the organizational decision-making processes in times of significant financial stress.

12.2 The study will provide insights into the planning for and response to financial stress, and the impact upon institutions of higher education.

# REFERENCES


Ball, S. (1985). Reactive effects in research and evaluation. In T. Husén & T. N. Postlethwaite (Eds.), *International encyclopedia of education: Research and studies* (1st ed., Vol. 7, p. 4200). Oxford: Pergamon.

Barker, R. G. (1951). *One boy's day: A specimen record of behavior.* New York: Harper.

Barker, R. G., & Gump, P. V. (1964). *Big school, small school.* Stanford, CA: Stanford University Press.

Barker, R. G., et al. (1970). The ecological environment: Student participation in non-class settings. In M. B. Miles & W. W. Charters, Jr. (Eds.), *Learning in social settings.* Boston: Allyn & Bacon.

Bem, S. L. (1987). Gender schema theory and the romantic tradition. In P. Shaver & C. Hendrick (Eds.), *Review of personality and social psychology* (Vol. 7). Newbury Park, CA: Sage.

Bennett, G. K., Seashore, H. G., & Wesman, A. G. (1952). *Differential aptitude tests: Manual* (2nd ed.). New York: Psychological Corporation.

Bloom, B. S. (Ed.). (1956). *Taxonomy of educational objectives: Cognitive domain* (Handbook I). New York: Longmans, Green.

Bogdan, R., & Knopp, S. (1992). *Qualitative research for education.* Boston: Allyn & Bacon.

Bozarth-Campbell, A. (1979). *The word's body.* Tuscaloosa: University of Ala-bama Press.

Bray, M. (Ed.). (1998). *Financing of education in Indonesia.* Hong Kong: Comparative Education Research Center.

Brubaker, D. L. (1994). *Creative curriculum leadership.* Thousand Oaks, CA: Corwin Press.

Brubaker, D. L., & Coble, L. D. (2007). *Staying on track.* Thousand Oaks, CA: Corwin Press.

Building web pages with Composer. (2006). *Netscape* Available online: http://wp.netscape .com/browsers/using/newusers/composer/

Cherry, M. (1998). Truth and consequences: Introduction. *Free Inquiry, 18*(4), 20.

*Chicago manual of style* (15th ed.). (2003). Chicago: University of Chicago Press.

Churchill, W. S. (1989). *Memories and adventures.* New York: Weidenfeld & Nicholson.

Conoley, J. C., & Impara, J. C. (Eds.). (1994). *Supplement to the eleventh mental measurements yearbook.* Lincoln, NE: University of Nebraska Press.

Conoley, J. C., & Impara, J. C. (Eds.). (1995). *Twelfth mental measurements yearbook.* Lincoln, NE: University of Nebraska Press.

Conoley, J. C., & Kramer, J. J. (Eds.). (1989). *Tenth mental measurements yearbook.* Lincoln, NE: University of Nebraska Press.

Conoley, J. C., & Kramer, J. J. (Eds.). (1992). *Eleventh mental measurements yearbook.* Lincoln, NE: University of Nebraska Press.

Cowan, P., & Cowan, R. (1987). *Mixed blessings.* New York: Doubleday.
Cremin, L. A. (1970). *American education: The colonial experience 1607–1783.* New York: Harper & Row.
Cremin, L. A. (1980). *American education: The national experience 1783–1876.* New York: Harper & Row.
Creswell, J. (1998). *Qualitative inquiry and research design.* Thousand Oaks, CA: Sage.
Denzin, N. K. (1989). *Interpretive biography.* Thousand Oaks, CA: Sage.
Denzin, N. K. (1997). *Interpretive ethnography.* Thousand Oaks, CA: Sage.
Denzin, N. K., & Lincoln, Y. (Eds.). (1994). *Handbook of qualitative research.* Thousand Oaks, CA: Sage.
Educational Testing Service. (1990). *The ETS test collection catalog: Vol. 4. Cognitive aptitude and intelligence tests.* Phoenix, AZ: Oryx Press.
*Encyclopaedia Britannica.* (2006). Chicago: Encyclopaedia Britannica.
*Encyclopedia of associations* (35th ed.). (1999). Detroit, MI: Gale Research.
Ethnography. (1994). In *Encyclopaedia Britannica.* Chicago: Encyclopaedia Britannica.
Eve, R. A. (1986). Children's interpersonal tactics in effecting cooperation by peers and adults. In P. A. Adler & P. Adler (Eds.), *Sociological studies of child development* (Vol. 1, pp. 187–208). Greenwich, CT: JAI Press.
Feinberg, W. (2006). *For goodness sake.* New York: Routledge.
Follman, J. (1984). Cornucopia of correlations. *American Psychologist, 39,* 701–702.
Franklin, B. (1951). *Autobiography.* New York: Heritage. (Original work published 1771–1788.)
Funderburg, L. (1994). *Black, white, other.* New York: Morrow.
Gadamar, H. G. (1975). *Truth and method.* London: Harvester Press.
Gardner, H. (1983). *Frames of mind.* New York: Basic Books.
Gardner, H. (1991). *The unschooled mind.* New York: Basic Books.
Gardner, H. (1993). *Frames of mind.* New York: Basic Books.
Gardner, J. I. (Ed.). (1986). *Mysteries of the ancient Americas.* Pleasantville, NY: Readers Digest Association.
Garfinkel, A. (1981). *Forms of explanation.* New Haven, CT: Yale University Press.
Glass, G. V., & Hopkins, K. D. (1984). *Statistical methods in education and psychology* (2nd ed.). Englewood Cliffs, NJ: Prentice Hall.
Glass, G. V., McGaw, B., & Smith, M. L. (1981). *Meta-analysis in social research.* Thousand Oaks, CA: Sage.
Glesne, C. (1999). *Becoming qualitative researchers.* New York: Longman.
Graduate School UNCG. (2007). *Electronic thesis and dissertation.* Retrieved March 9, 2007, from http://www.uncg.edu/grs/current/etdabout.html
Gretzky, W., & Reilly, R. (1990). *Gretzky: An autobiography.* New York: HarperCollins.
Habermas, J. (1972). *Communication and the evolution of society.* London: Heinemann.
Heermann, E. F., & Braskamp, L. A. (1970). *Readings in statistics for the behavioral sciences.* Englewood Cliffs, NJ: Prentice Hall.
Held, D. (1980). *Introduction to critical theory: Horkheimer to Habermas.* London: Hutchinson.
Hofstede, G. (1996). Gender stereotypes and partner preferences of Asian women in masculine and feminine cultures. *Journal of Cross-Cultural Psychology, 27*(5), 533–546.

Howell, D. (1997). *Statistical methods for psychology.* Belmont, CA: Duxbury.

Hoy, W. K., Tarter, C. J., & Witkoskie, L. (1992). Faculty trust in colleagues: Linking the school principal with school effectiveness. *Journal of Research and Development in Education, 26*(1), 38–45.

Hunter, J. E., Schmidt, F. L., & Jackson, G. B. (1982). *Meta-analysis: Cumulating research findings across studies.* Beverly Hills, CA: Sage.

Inhelder, B., & Piaget, J. (1964). *The early growth of logic in the child.* London: Routledge & Kegan Paul.

Jackson, M. (1996). *Things as they are: New directions in phenomenological psychology.* Bloomington, IN: Indiana University Press.

Johnston, D. K. (1988). Adolescents' solutions to dilemmas in fables: Two moral orientations—two problem solving strategies. In C. Gilligan, J. V. Ward, & J. M. Taylor (Eds.), *Mapping the moral domain: A contribution of women's thinking to psychological theory and education* (pp. 49–71). Cambridge, MA: Harvard University Press.

Jung, C. (1971). *Psychological types* (H. G. Baynes, Trans.). In *The collected works of C. G. Jung* (Vol. 6). Princeton, NJ: Princeton University Press. (Original work published 1921.)

Kapavalu, H. (1993). Dealing with the dark side in the ethnography of childhood: Child punishment in Tonga. *Oceania, 63*(4), 313–329.

Keith, A. B. (1925). *The religion and philosophy of the Vedas and Upanishads.* Cambridge, MA: Harvard University Press.

Kramer, J. J., & Conoley, J. C. (Eds.). (1990). *Supplement to the tenth mental measurements yearbook.* Lincoln, NE: University of Nebraska Press.

Krathwohl, D. R., Bloom, B. S., & Masia, B. B. (1964). *Taxonomy of educational objectives: Affective domain* (Handbook II). New York: McKay.

Macsporran, I. (1982). Hermeneutics: An alternative set of philosophical assumptions for comparative education? In R. Cowen & P. Stokes (Eds.), *Methodological issues in comparative education* (pp. 47–51). London: Association of Comparative Educationists.

Mannien, J., & Tuomela, R. (Eds.). (1976). *Essays on explanation and understanding.* Dordrech, Netherlands: D. Reidel.

Marsh, H. W., & Morris, P. (Eds.). (1991). *Curriculum development in East Asia.* London: Falmer.

Mazzeo, J. A. (1978). *Varieties of interpretation.* Notre Dame, IN: University of Notre Dame Press.

McGaw, B. (1985). Meta-analysis. In T. Husén & T. N. Postlethwaite (Eds.), *International encyclopedia of education: Research and studies* (1st ed., Vol. 6, pp. 3322–3330). Oxford: Pergamon.

Menchú, R., & Burgos-Debray, E. (1984). *I, Rigoberta Menchú: An Indian woman in Guatemala.* London: Verso.

Miles, M. B., & Weitzman, E. A. (1994). Appendix: Choosing computer programs for qualitative data analysis. In M. B. Miles & A. M. Huberman, *Qualitative data analysis* (2nd ed.). Thousand Oaks, CA: Sage.

Mitchell, J. V., Jr. (Ed.). (1985). *Ninth mental measurements yearbook.* Lincoln, NE: University of Nebraska Press.

*National Faculty Directory.* (Vols 1–2). (1999). Detroit, MI: Gale Research Co.

Netcraft. (2006, December). *December 2006 web server survey.* Retrieved March 9, 2007, from http://news.netcraft.com/archives/web_server_survey.html.

Notice to contributors. (2006, November/December). *Child Development, 7*(6), inside back cover.

Odman, P. J. (1985). Hermeneutics. In T. Husén & T. N. Postlethwaite (Eds.), *International encyclopedia of education: Research and studies* (1st ed.). Oxford: Pergamon.

Orwell, G. (1946). *Animal farm: A fairy story.* New York: New American Library.

Palafox, J. C., Prawda, J., & Velez, E. (1994). Primary school quality in Mexico. *Comparative Education Review, 38*(2), 167–180.

Palmer, R. E. (1969). *Hermeneutics: Interpretation theory in Scheiermacher, Dilthey, Heidegger, and Gadamer.* Evanston, IL: Northwestern University Press.

Parfit, M. (1998). Human migration. *National Geographic, 194*(4), 6–35.

Pfitzer, G. M. (1991). *Samuel Eliot Morison's historical world.* Boston: Northeastern University Press.

Piaget, J., & Inhelder, B. (1969). *The psychology of the child.* New York: Basic Books.

Pike, M. A., & Pike, T. (1994). *The Internet quickstart.* Indianapolis, IN: Que.

Postlethwaite, T. N., & Wiley, D. E. (1992). *The IEA study of science II: Science achievement in twenty-three countries.* Oxford: Pergamon.

*Publication manual of the American Psychological Association* (5th ed.). (2001). Washington, DC: American Psychological Association.

Ricoeur, P. (1976). *Interpretation theory.* Fort Worth, TX: Christian University Press.

Ross, K. N. (1985). Sampling. In T. Husén & T. N. Postlethwaite (Eds.), *International encyclopedia of education: Research and studies* (1st ed., Vol. 8, pp. 4370–4381). Oxford: Pergamon.

Rousseau, J.-J. (1773). *Emilius; or, A treatise on education.* Edinburgh: W. Coke.

Sapat, A. K. (1998). The political economy of state environmental policy innovations. *Dissertation Abstracts International,* 59(01), 308A. Ann Arbor, MI: UMI.

Schleicher, K. (Ed.). (1993). *Nationalism in education.* Frankfurt, Germany: Peter Lang.

Shavelson, R. (1996). *Statistical reasoning for the behavioral sciences.* Boston: Allyn & Bacon.

Shulman, L. S. (1992). Toward a pedagogy of cases. In J. H. Shulman (Ed.), *Case methods in teacher education* (pp. 1–30). New York: Teachers College Press.

Slavin, R. E. (1984). *Research methods in education.* Englewood Cliffs, NJ: Prentice Hall.

Spearritt, D. (1985). Factor analysis. In T. Husén & T. N. Postlethwaite (Eds.), *International encyclopedia of education: Research and studies* (1st ed., Vol. 4, pp. 1813–1824). Oxford: Pergamon.

Spickard, P. R. (1989). *Mixed blood.* Madison, WI: University of Wisconsin Press.

Stake, R. (1995). *The art of case study research.* Thousand Oaks, CA: Sage.

Steinem, G. (1992). *Revolution from within: A book of self-esteem.* Boston: Little, Brown.

Stoff, S., & Schwartzberg, H. (Eds.). (1969). *The human encounter: Readings in education.* New York: Harper & Row.

Stromquist, N. (Ed.). (1994). *Education in the urban context.* Westport, CT: Praeger.

Swift, J. (1980). *The annotated Gulliver's travels.* New York: C. N. Potter. (Original work published 1726.)

Tarrow, N. B. (Ed.). (1987). *Human rights and education.* Oxford, UK: Pergamon.

Tashner, J. H. (Ed.). (1984). *Improving instruction with microcomputers.* Phoenix, AZ: Oryx.

Thomas, R. M. (1985). Religious education. In T. Husén & T. N. Postlethwaite (Eds.), *International encyclopedia of education* (1st ed., Vol. 7, pp. 4275–4286). Oxford, UK: Pergamon.

Thomas, R. M. (1987). The advent of hermeneutics in educational parlance. *Perspectives in Education, 3*(1), 5–14.

Thomas, R. M. (1990). Into the future. In R. M. Thomas (Ed.), *International comparative education* (pp. 302–325). Oxford, UK: Pergamon.

Thomas, R. M. (Ed.). (1992). *Education's role in national development plans.* Westport, CT: Praeger.

Thomas, R. M. (1997). *Moral development theories: Secular and religious.* Westport, CT: Greenwood.

Thomas, R. M. (1998). *Conducting educational research: A comparative view.* Westport, CT: Bergin & Garvey.

Thomas, R. M. (1999). *Glimpses of England in pen sketch and verse.* Los Osos, CA: Encinas Imprint.

Thomas, R. M. (2003). *Blending qualitative and quantitative research in theses and dissertations.* Thousand Oaks, CA: Corwin Press.

Thomas, R. M. (2006). *Violence in America's schools.* Westport, CT: Praeger.

Thomas, R. M. (2007). *Manitou and God—North-American Indian religions and Christian culture.* Westport, CT: Praeger.

Thomas, R. M., & Diver-Stamnes, A. C. (1993). *What wrongdoers deserve.* Westport, CT: Greenwood.

Thurstone, L. L. (1938). *Primary mental abilities.* Chicago: University of Chicago Press.

von Wright, G. H. (1971). *Explanation and understanding.* Ithaca, NY: Cornell University Press.

Walberg, H. J., Zhang, G., & Daniel, V. C. (1994). Toward an empirical taxonomy of world education systems. In A. C. Tuijnman & T. N. Postlethwaite (Eds.), *Monitoring the standards of education* (pp. 79–99). Oxford: Pergamon.

Walford, G. (1993). Book review. *Comparative Education Review, 37*(1), 83–85.

Watson, K., Modgil, C., & Modgil, S. (Eds.). (1997). *Quality in education.* London: Cassell.

Weitzman, E. A., & Miles, M. B. (1994). *Computer programs for qualitative data analysis.* Thousand Oaks, CA: Sage.

Westbury, I., & Purves, A. C. (Eds.). (1988). *Cultural literacy and the idea of general education.* Chicago: National Association for the Study of Education.

Williams, C. L. (1981). *A modern "ship of fools": An account of one boy's journey through the mental health system.* Unpublished master's thesis, University of California Los Angeles School of Social Work, Los Angeles, CA.

Wolcott, H. F. (1988). Ethnographic research in education. In R. M. Jaeger (Ed.), *Complementary methods for research in education* (pp. 187–210). Washington, DC: American Educational Research Association.

# INDEX

The Corwin Press logo—a raven striding across an open book—represents the union of courage and learning. Corwin Press is committed to improving education for all learners by publishing books and other professional development resources for those serving the field of PreK–12 education. By providing practical, hands-on materials, Corwin Press continues to carry out the promise of its motto: **"Helping Educators Do Their Work Better."**